D0385563

BANKTOWN

BANKTOWN

The Rise and Struggles of Charlotte's Big Banks

Rick Rothacker

REMOVED FROM COLLECTION

423 4761

West Islip Public Library
3 Higbie Lane
West Islip New York 11795

JOHN F. BLAIR, PUBLISHER
Winston-Salem, North Carolina

JOHN F. BLAIR, PUBLISHER
1406 Plaza Drive
Winston-Salem, North Carolina 27103
www.blairpub.com

Copyright © 2010 by Rick Rothacker

All rights reserved, including the right to reproduce this book or portions thereof in any form whatsoever. For information address John F. Blair, Publisher, Subsidiary Rights Department, 1406 Plaza Drive, Winston-Salem, North Carolina 27103.

Manufactured in the United States of America

COVER IMAGE
Bank of America *(left)* and Wachovia *(right)* in Uptown Charlotte
BY LAYNE BAILEY
Courtesy of the *Charlotte Observer*

All other images courtesy of the *Charlotte Observer*

Library of Congress Cataloging-in-Publication Data

Rothacker, Rick.
 Banktown : the rise and struggles of Charlotte's big banks / Rick Rothacker.
   p. cm.
 Includes bibliographical references and index.
  ISBN 978-0-89587-381-1 (hardcover : alk. paper) 1. Banks and banking--North Carolina--Charlotte. 2. Financial crises--Northa Carolina--Charlotte. 3. Bank of America. 4. Wachovia Corporation. I. Title.
 HG2613.C35R68 2010
 332.109756'76--dc22
                              2010021720

DESIGN BY ANGELA HARWOOD

To Jen, Jack, and Will

Contents

Author's Note

Since the summer of 2001, I have covered the banking industry as a business reporter for the *Charlotte Observer*. This book is based on reporting conducted for the *Observer*, as well as new interviews and reporting. Some interview subjects agreed to speak on the record, while a number talked only on background, meaning the information they provided is not attributed to them. They cited the sensitive nature of the subject, lawsuits, and the potential impact on their careers. While I would have preferred on-the-record interviews, it was important to talk with these people to improve my understanding of the events surrounding Bank of America and Wachovia, especially over the past few years.

During the writing of this book, I also consulted court documents, depositions, securities filings, meeting minutes and notes, e-mails, and phone logs. I obtained some of these materials through Freedom of Information Act requests. As part of its investigation of Bank of America's Merrill Lynch & Company deal, the United States House Oversight and Government Reform Committee uncovered hundreds of pages of e-mails sent by Federal Reserve and Bank of America officials, as well as handwritten notes executives and officials took during key meetings. Merrill-related e-mails and meeting details referenced in the book largely came from these materials.

To write a book covering this historical breadth, I also found it necessary to consult books, newspaper articles, magazine pieces, and other sources. *Observer* coverage of the banks dating as far back as 1927 was an especially fruitful source. Particularly helpful books were *The Story of Nationsbank* by Howard E. Covington, Jr., and Marion A. Ellis; *McColl* by Ross Yockey; and *Too Big to Fail* by Andrew Ross Sorkin. *Frontline* interviews with Ken Lewis and John Thain were also insightful. The materials cited are compiled in the notes at the back of this book. The notes do not include stories I wrote or interviews I conducted. In some cases,

I talked to subjects about information that has also appeared in other publications. If I independently confirmed the information, I did not always include a note.

Some of the scenes depicted in the book are from events I covered for the *Observer* and witnessed firsthand. Others occurred outside the public eye and have been reconstructed through interviews with people familiar with what happened. I pieced together conversations by talking with people who were involved, who overheard what was said, or who were told about the exchanges. I have also re-created dialogue through accounts from other publications, depositions, and court documents. In some cases, the conversations may not be exactly as they occurred because of faded or jumbled memories or because they are amalgamations of multiple accounts. My intent was to represent the dialogue as accurately as possible.

SEQUENCE OF EVENTS

1804: North Carolina General Assembly approves charters for banks in Wilmington and New Bern.

1874: Commercial National Bank founded in Charlotte.

1879: Wachovia National Bank founded in what is now Winston-Salem.

1901: Southern States Trusts Company, later renamed American Trust, founded in Charlotte.

1908: Union National Bank founded in Charlotte.

1927: Charlotte branch of Federal Reserve Bank of Richmond opens.

1957: American Trust–Commercial National merger creates American Commercial.

1958: Union National–First National Bank and Trust merger creates First Union National Bank.

1960: American Commercial merges with Security National Bank to become North Carolina National Bank, or NCNB.

1977: John Medlin becomes CEO of Wachovia.

1983: Hugh McColl, Jr., becomes CEO of NCNB.

1984: Ed Crutchfield becomes CEO of First Union.

1985: Supreme Court upholds regional banking compacts.

1991: NCNB changes name to NationsBank after C&S/Sovran merger.

1994: Bud Baker becomes CEO of Wachovia.

1998: First Union buys the Money Store; NationsBank–BankAmerica merger creates Bank of America.

2000: Ken Thompson named First Union CEO.

2001: Ken Lewis named Bank of America CEO; First Union merges with Wachovia.

2006: Wachovia buys Golden West Financial.

Jan. 11, 2008: Bank of America announces deal to buy Countrywide Financial.

Apr. 14, 2008: Wachovia announces $393 million first-quarter loss, dividend cut, capital raising.

June 2, 2008: Wachovia announces Ken Thompson's retirement.

July 9, 2008: Bob Steel named Wachovia CEO.

Sept. 7, 2008: Treasury announces conservatorship for Freddie Mac, Fannie Mae.

Sept. 15, 2008: Bank of America announces deal to buy Merrill Lynch; Lehman Brothers files for bankruptcy; Bob Steel appears on *Mad Money*.

Sept. 21, 2008: Federal Reserve approves holding company status for Goldman Sachs and Morgan Stanley, both of which had considered mergers with Wachovia.

Sept. 29, 2008: FDIC announces Citigroup purchase of Wachovia banking subsidiaries; house votes down TARP.

Oct. 3, 2008: Wells Fargo agrees to buy Wachovia; Congress approves TARP.

Oct. 13, 2008: U.S. government injects $125 billion into nine major banks.

Dec. 5, 2008: Shareholders approve Bank of America's Merrill Lynch acquisition.

Dec. 17, 2008: Bank of America tells government it's considering escape clause in Merrill deal.

Dec. 31, 2008: Wells Fargo closes Wachovia deal.

Jan. 1, 2009: Bank of America closes Merrill deal.

Jan. 16, 2009: Bank of America discloses rescue package, Merrill's $15 billion fourth-quarter loss.

Jan. 22, 2009: John Thain leaves Bank of America.

Apr. 29, 2009: Ken Lewis loses his chairmanship.

June–July 2009: Ken Lewis, Ben Bernanke, Henry Paulson testify before House Oversight and Government Reform Committee.

Sept. 30, 2009: Ken Lewis announces he's retiring at year's end.

Dec. 16, 2009: Bank of America board picks Brian Moynihan as new CEO.

Feb. 4, 2010: SEC announces $150 million settlement with Bank of America; New York attorney general files civil charges against Bank of America, Ken Lewis, and Joe Price.

PROLOGUE

Bank of America Corporation chief executive Ken Lewis could not have chosen a more symbolic location for the official unveling of his biggest acquisition. During a frenzied weekend of negotiations, Charlotte-based Bank of America had forged a $50 billion deal to buy Merrill Lynch & Company. Now, on Monday September 15, 2008, the press was arriving at the auditorium of the bank's sparkling new Midtown Manhattan skyscraper, the second-tallest structure in the city, after the Empire State Building.

While Wall Street was burning, Bank of America was soaring to yet another audacious deal.

In 1969, Lewis, a Mississippi native who worked his way through Georgia State University, had taken a job as a credit analyst at a small Southern institution known as North Carolina National Bank. Like him, the Charlotte bank was aggressive and hard-nosed and couldn't care less about blue-blooded pedigrees.

Nearly four decades later, after dozens of swashbuckling deals, scrappy NCNB had turned itself into Bank of America, the nation's biggest consumer bank, with branches from coast to coast and operations around the world. Once the Merrill deal was complete, the bank would have about $2.3 trillion in assets.

On a different bleary-eyed Monday morning, Lewis or perhaps his predecessor, Hugh McColl, Jr., might have shown a bit more bluster after an adrenaline-fueled weekend of sealing a blockbuster deal. The bank that had gobbled up rivals from Georgia to Texas to California to Massachusetts, after all, was landing one of Wall Street's most iconic firms. But this news conference had a much more subdued feel. Perhaps it was the downward-pointing red triangles next to the stock prices trawling along the bottom of the TV screen. Perhaps it was the cataclysmic fear roaring through the financial system at a moment when Lehman Brothers Holdings, Inc., was bankrupt and Merrill's independence was at an end. Perhaps it was sheer exhaustion.

As shutters clicked, Lewis and Merrill CEO John Thain walked into the airy, wood-trimmed room, shook hands, and took their seats at a small table before an audience of reporters and TV cameras broadcasting the scene nationwide. Lewis didn't have any prepared remarks but briefly highlighted what he called a "strategic opportunity of a lifetime." Thain, also speaking off the cuff in a measured tone, said he was "excited about the prospects going forward." The former Goldman Sachs Group, Inc., banker had taken over at Merrill in 2007 with a "Mr. Fix-It" reputation after a successful tenure as CEO of the New York Stock Exchange. He took steps to clean up Merrill's toxic assets but was unable to keep the company independent—and preserve his own job.

As the questions rolled in, the CEOs acknowledged the quick pace of the talks, which had started Saturday as Thain fretted that his firm could be the next to fall after Lehman. Regulators hadn't forced Bank of America to buy Merrill, Lewis said, but they were happy to have it scratched off their to-do list. Since becoming CEO seven years earlier, Lewis had coveted Merrill Lynch, but the timing and circumstances had never been right. In the meantime, he had forged deals that expanded his bank into the Northeast and Chicago and made it number one in credit cards and mortgages. Now, Bank of America had finally seized Merrill's investment bank and its "crown jewel" brokerage firm with its "thundering herd" of stockbrokers serving middle- and upper-crust clients nationwide.

"I don't know if I'll ever get to do another acquisition during my career," Lewis said. "This is too important not to get right."

On the same turbulent day, the chief executive of Charlotte's other big bank was also in New York—and also about to go on national TV.

Unlike Ken Lewis, Wachovia CEO Bob Steel wasn't a company lifer ruddering the institution he had grown up with through the financial storm. The bank's board had coaxed Steel from a Treasury Department post in July 2008 to replace ousted CEO Ken Thompson. It made the change after a series of miscues and rising losses stemming from the ill-timed purchase of California mortgage specialist Golden West Financial Corporation at the height of the housing boom. Steel had a simple but daunting mission: Save Wachovia.

The bank carried the name of a storied, conservative institution once based in Winston-Salem, North Carolina, with roots to 1879. But underneath that veneer was another daring, some might say reckless, Charlotte bank. In 2001, First Union Corporation, the longtime rival to NCNB-turned–Bank of America, had bought Wachovia, taken its name, and resuscitated its own sullied reputation. But the Golden West deal, investment losses, and regulatory run-ins had shaken the company.

By the fall of 2008, Wachovia was emblematic of the critical wounds caused by the nation's housing collapse. Now, Steel was trying to heal his patient even as a pandemic swept through the hospital.

Steel, a former Goldman Sachs vice chairman who had overseen domestic finance at Treasury, was in New York on what was supposed to be a mini media tour, his visits with print and wire reporters capped by an appearance on Jim Cramer's *Mad Money* CNBC show. In light of the financial upheaval, the bank cancelled the early part, knowing reporters were too busy on this day for a meet-and-greet with Wachovia's new CEO. But CNBC had been hyping Steel's appearance for days, so Wachovia decided to go ahead with the appearance. Steel thought it would cause suspicion if he abruptly bowed out and didn't want to leave Cramer in the lurch. He flew up to New York for just the day.

By showtime, another bloody trading session had splattered Wall Street. Bank of America's shares had fallen 20 percent after the Merrill announcement, while Wachovia's had plunged by one-fourth. Earlier in the day on CNBC, star analyst Meredith Whitney had highlighted Wachovia's concentration of loans in California and Florida and cast doubt on the bank's estimate that housing prices were going to decline just 21 percent from the top of the market to the bottom. "I'm very curious . . . of their math there," she said. Amid this upheaval, Steel strode onto Cramer's cluttered Technicolor set in a suit and tie, his polished presence a contrast to the show's sweaty, jacketless stock-picker host. Cramer had been bashing Wachovia for months as its stock plummeted, but he lavished praise on his former Goldman Sachs colleague, calling him "the one guy I trust to turn this bank around."

After Steel gave an overview of how the nation's financial system had come to this dramatic point, Cramer homed in on the bank's "billions in bad mortgages." Steel, reiterating the plan he had laid out in July, said Wachovia was building capital by cutting costs and its dividend. The bank was also going to "focus like crazy" on the Golden West loans by trying to refinance borrowers into more traditional mortgages. Wachovia had "very exciting prospects when we get things right going forward," he said. Asked if he might sell the company, he gave an upbeat but couched response: "We have a great future as an independent company, but we're a public company, so we're going to do what's right for shareholders, I can promise you that."

Throughout their history, the banks that became Bank of America and Wachovia had followed remarkably similar paths. Now, their CEOs converged in New York on an infamous day for the financial industry their banks had helped create.

Both institutions grew up on Charlotte's main drag, Tryon Street, riding the growing wealth of a New South commercial center driven to outcompete bigger brothers in Atlanta and the North. They benefited from favorable laws that allowed banks in North Carolina to branch across the state. They gained stature in 1927 when the Federal Reserve planted a branch office in the city, confirmation that Charlotte was a budding financial center. And they blossomed under aggressive leaders like Bank of America's Hugh McColl, Jr., and First Union's Ed Crutchfield, who pushed regulatory envelopes, jockeyed for acquisitions, and pursued an eat-or-be-eaten vision for the financial services industry.

The final ingredient in creating the nation's number-two banking center, behind New York, came from looking across the street at each other's office buildings and, later, skyscrapers. "Why did Charlotte get huge banks and not Kansas City, and not St. Louis, and not Dallas, and not Atlanta, and, hell, not anybody except New York?" McColl asked in his distinctive South Carolina drawl during a March 2008 forum on the banks' rise. "We're talking about competition." Competition against each other, competition against Winston-Salem–based Wachovia when it was the state's biggest bank, and eventually competition against rivals around the country.

Miami-based banking consultant Ken Thomas compared the two to baseball's Yankees and Red Sox. "Never has there been a rivalry among big banks in America as intense as that between Bank of America and Wachovia," he said. Over time, some would question whether the clash was healthy or whether it spurred the banks to make moves based more on one-upmanship than shareholder interests, he said.

September 15, 2008, would prove a critical turning point for both banks. Just days later, as the financial tsunami rumbled inland, Wachovia scrambled to find a merger partner, falling into the arms of Citigroup, Inc., then Wells Fargo & Company. With that takeover, Charlotte would lose one of its banks and part of its identity. And in mid-December, Ken Lewis would be in Washington talking with regulators about possibly abandoning Merrill Lynch and its ballooning losses. The ensuing controversy over the deal would rattle the company and mar the final year of his tenure. His clashes with regulators, shareholders, and lawmakers would tarnish his company and his own reputation.

This is the story of how two Charlotte banks went from Southern institutions to national powerhouses to near wards of the state. How daring mergers created giant banks, then threatened their existence. It's the story of ambitious bankers like Hugh McColl, Ed Crutchfield, Ken Lewis, and Ken Thompson taking risks that sometimes paid off and sometimes didn't. They forged giant banks that created huge profits in good times while also helping to fuel a debt-burdened economy that unraveled when high-stakes bets made in Charlotte and around the world went awry. It's the story of two Charlotte banks that trumped competitors in city after city around the country, only to have their fate in the financial crisis decided largely by regulators, lawyers, and rivals in New York, Washington, and

San Francisco. It's a story dogged by what-ifs that still haunt the banks today.

The reverberations have been felt deeply in Charlotte, Winston-Salem, and other North Carolina cities. Employees have lost jobs by the thousands. Shareholders have lost billions. Charlotte has shed a bit of its pride and is now looking for a more diverse array of businesses to nurture its future. The banks may thrive once again. But at least in the case of Wachovia, it won't be as a stand-alone, homegrown institution. While Charlotte may continue to march forward as a revitalized banktown, it has lost part of its bravado, innocence, and once-unwavering momentum as it proceeds into a new era for the financial world.

Chapter 1

BANKTOWN BEGINNINGS

I n 1985, Charlotte's two big banks—North Carolina National Bank and First Union—were ready for a new era in United States banking to ignite. For decades, the nation's banks had been confined to operating in their home states or, in many cases, even smaller territories. But expansion-minded bankers were starting to chip away at the barriers. In 1982, NCNB had bought a small bank in Florida by seizing on a legal loophole. By 1985, state legislatures, after lobbying by financial executives, authorized "regional bank compacts." These agreements allowed banks within a region to cross state lines, while barring incursions from outsiders. A Supreme Court ruling on the legality of such pacts was due any day.

At that auspicious time, two ambitious, brash, and relatively young chief executives had just grabbed the reins at the Charlotte banks. Hugh McColl took over at NCNB in 1983 at age 48. Ed Crutchfield took charge at First Union in 1984 at age 42. They had been groomed by predecessors who bulked up their institutions by buying smaller banks across North Carolina, aided by the state's liberal branching laws. McColl and Crutchfield would compete vigorously for business and acquisitions in the coming years while cooperating on civic activities that elevated a small Southern city into the national consciousness.

For much of their history, the Charlotte banks had been overshadowed by Winston-Salem's Wachovia, one of the first banks to take advantage of the state's branching laws. In the 1970s, growth-hungry NCNB had moved ahead of Wachovia in total assets. By 1985, First Union was set to become number two once it completed an in-state merger with the state's fourth-biggest bank. Wachovia was led by CEO John Medlin, a former chief risk officer who embodied the institution's conservative ways.

On June 10, Ed Crutchfield was in his Charlotte office when a staffer handed him an update from a teletype machine: The Supreme Court had upheld the regional compacts. The banking industry's merger mania was about to begin.

Two hours later, Crutchfield was on the phone with Billy Walker, chief executive of a prized target: Atlantic Bancorp in Jacksonville, Florida. Only days after that, the First Union CEO was shaking hands on the outline of a deal. Sitting in the den at Walker's house in Ponte Vedra Beach, Crutchfield asked to use the phone. He wanted to get his lawyers and finance guys working on the agreement. Walker pointed him to a bedroom. Crutchfield sat on one of the twin beds and looked up to see Walker with a wicked grin on his face.

"You know who slept there last night?" Walker asked.

Crutchfield had no idea.

"Hugh McColl," Walker told him.

Crutchfield shook his head. Old Hugh was going to be hard to beat.

Unable to meet Atlantic's price, McColl had instead turned his attention to a Georgia bank, First Atlanta Corporation. His aggressive approach quickly turned off the bank's CEO. "I'm going to buy your bank," the blustery ex-marine told Tom Williams, the epitome of a Southern gentleman banker. So Williams called up his old friend John Medlin at Wachovia. They agreed their merged banks would be called First Wachovia and have dual headquarters in Atlanta and Winston-Salem. Medlin privately told a lieutenant that the name would change back to Wachovia someday.

On Tuesday, June 18, just eight days after the Supreme Court ruling, McColl was greeted by newspaper coverage of his rivals' coups. It was a miserable way to start his 50th birthday. In landing First Atlanta, Wachovia was poised to become the Southeast's biggest bank. First Union, after buying Atlantic, would become number two, pushing NCNB to number three.

McColl needed a drink, but he wouldn't be down for long. Cautious Wachovia wouldn't do another deal for six years, and the competition between NCNB and First Union was only getting started.

North Carolina was the last of the 13 original states to charter a privately owned bank. After a fierce debate among lawmakers, the North Carolina General Assembly in 1804 approved charters for the Bank of Cape Fear in Wilmington and the Bank of New Bern in the town then spelled Newbern.

The Bank of Cape Fear was allowed to open a branch in another growing population center, Fayetteville. This was the foundation for statewide branching, a capability that later allowed the Charlotte banks and Winston-Salem's Wachovia to expand across North Carolina, building up their size and expertise for later excursions outside the state. North Carolina would avoid the long and testy fights that other states experienced over branching.

In 1814, the general assembly gave a further stamp of approval to the concept, permitting directors of banks to establish branches or agencies at any locations they saw fit. The Bank of New Bern opened offices in Raleigh, Halifax, and Milton, while the Bank of Cape Fear expanded into Salem, Charlotte, and Hillsboro.

North Carolina banks survived the Civil War but not the aftermath. Hit by levies and losses on Confederate bonds and notes, every bank in the state ceased operations. To fill the void, a new wave of nationally chartered and state-chartered banks gradually rose. In the Moravian village of Salem, the Bank of Cape Fear branch did not reopen after the war, but the office's cashier, Israel Lash, began raising capital to start his own bank. He obtained a charter in 1866 for First National Bank of Salem and became its president.

When Lash died in the late 1870s, his cashier and nephew, William Lemly, closed the Salem bank and moved its safe and other furnishings "uptown" to Winston, Salem's growing sister city. Although it relocated only a few blocks away, the bank needed a new name and charter. On June 16, 1879, Wachovia National Bank opened for business with Wyatt Bowman as president and Lemly as cashier. One of its early customers was R. J. Reynolds, who had been expanding his tobacco company since 1875. The name Wachovia came from Moravian settlers who christened the land they bought in the North Carolina Piedmont after the Wachau Valley in Austria, the ancestral home of their benefactor, Count Nicholas Ludwig von Zinzendorf.

After the general assembly authorized the creation of trust companies, another Wachovia popped up in Winston in 1893—Wachovia Loan and Trust Company. The new Wachovia's president was Colonel Francis Fries. The local businessman with the honorary military title became an early pioneer of branch banking, opening Wachovia offices in Asheville, High Point, Salisbury, and Spencer in 1902 and 1903. In 1911, the two Wachovias merged, forming the Wachovia Bank and Trust Company, which boasted $4 million in deposits and total assets of $7 million.

Fries, president of the combined company, continued to add branches and build Wachovia's customer service reputation. After he died in 1931, his nephew Henry Fries Shaffner became chairman and Robert Hanes president. During the Great Depression, one of their jobs was to protect against runs on the bank's deposits. In troublesome branches, the heavyset Shaffner would sit in the lobby smoking a cigar, providing a reassuring presence for nervous depositors. Hanes, accompanied by guards, once took a suitcase full of cash to a Wachovia office and opened it on a lobby table to show customers the bank still had sufficient funds.

As it continued to expand, Wachovia entered Raleigh and arrived in Charlotte with the 1939 purchase of Charlotte National Bank. One of Hanes's goals was to beef up the bank's lending capacity, allowing Wachovia to compete with larger New York and Chicago banks plying North Carolina companies with loans.

He also encouraged lending officers to call on clients, a move once thought to be beneath the dignity of bankers.

While president, Hanes tackled public-service projects, a role that would be filled by many of the state's bankers. In 1945, he took a leave to spearhead implementation of the Marshall Plan in western Germany. Hanes and Wachovia chairman Archie Davis also worked with Governor Luther Hodges, Sr., to create Research Triangle Park, a future magnet for high-tech jobs. When Hanes retired in 1956, Wachovia was the clear banking giant of North Carolina and the Southeast, with $406 million in deposits and total assets of $522 million.

To the west of Winston-Salem, Charlotte was a longtime trading hub that made an early mark on the nation's financial scene when gold was discovered in nearby Cabarrus County in 1799. The United States Mint established a Charlotte branch in the 1830s. But the city didn't start to take off as a commercial center until the 1850s with the arrival of the railroads.

The improved transportation network turned a back-country farm town into a center for the textile industry and entrepreneurs who sold everything from textile equipment to the Coca-Cola and Pepsi drunk by mill workers. Other cotton production areas such as Charleston, South Carolina, suffered during the Civil War, allowing Charlotte to surface as a New South business center. The rise of local banks followed.

In 1874, with Charlotte's population now above 4,000, a group of prominent citizens organized Commercial National Bank with capital of $50,000. On its 25th anniversary in 1899, the bank issued financial statements that showed deposits had more than tripled to $745,683 from $215,705. "We take this opportunity of expressing our heartfelt thanks to all of those who have aided in building up this business either as stockholders, customers or those who have spoken good words for us," the statement, signed by president J. S. Spencer, read.

Another round of banks arrived after the turn of the 20th century. Southern States Trust Company opened in 1901 and was renamed American Trust Company in 1907. Stockholder minutes included a long list of activities the bank could engage in, from serving as an agent for selling stocks and bonds to warehousing cotton. American Trust would focus on serving as a correspondent bank, providing check clearing to smaller banks around the Carolinas and teaming with them on larger loans. "Our opportunity, in a growing commercial centre like Charlotte, is a broad one," founder Word Wood declared in a 1902 entry in the minutes. "If we live up to our opportunity, we have the power to develop a very large business. Our field is a promising one."

In 1908, H. M. Victor founded Union National Bank. Victor sold 1,000 shares of stock for $100 each and set up shop in a roll-top desk in the lobby of the Buford Hotel on Tryon Street. Cementing his reputation as a conservative banker, he long refused to make loans on the newly invented automobile. When he relented and made one on a Model T, he held the owner's keys and title until the loan was repaid.

The Charlotte region experienced a wave of growth as the cotton industry revived after World War I. Throughout the 1920s, mills headed south from New England in what became known as "the Second Cotton Mill Campaign." From 1916 to 1936, Charlotte's population more than doubled to about 91,000, and the city surpassed Winston-Salem in the 1930 census to become the state's most populous.

As early as 1915, the Charlotte Chamber of Commerce promoted the city's "Banking District" in brochures that highlighted the "skyscrapers" rising on South Tryon Street. A 1930s postcard labeled the growing financial canyon "the Wall Street of Charlotte." Image making was important to New South cities, but not everyone bought into Charlotte's bid for grandeur. In *The Mind of the South*, W. J. Cash smirked at the skyscrapers, saying the city "had little more use for them than a hog has for a morning coat."

Charlotte's reputation as a financial center took a major leap in February 1927 when the Federal Reserve Board in Washington approved the creation of a branch office in the city. The new office was an offshoot of the Federal Reserve Bank of Richmond and the first such location in the Carolinas. The Richmond Fed, covering the territory from Maryland to the Carolinas, was part of the larger central banking system founded in 1913. It processed checks for the region's banks, provided currency, and monitored local economies.

At least five cities—Charlotte and Greensboro in North Carolina and Columbia, Greenville, and Spartanburg in South Carolina—made cases to be the site, but Charlotte was helped by its central location in the Carolinas. The Fed branch opened December 1, 1927, inside the 20-story First National Bank Building. The structure had become the state's tallest office tower upon opening that same year on South Tryon Street, eclipsing the city's other skyscrapers and the 18-story R. J. Reynolds Building in Winston-Salem.

Behind the more than six-year push for the Fed branch was Word Wood, the founder and president of American Trust. After the Fed's decision, congratulatory telegrams inundated the banker. "Hot dog. Your splendid personal effort puts capstone on Charlotte as a great city," wrote one Greensboro supporter. Commercial National Bank of Raleigh sent regards: "We congratulate the Queen City on being made the banking center and hope it means much for all of us."

The news coverage that week quoted prominent bankers and businesspeople predicting the genesis of a banktown. "Charlotte will be placed in the class of the more important financial centers of the country," said W. H. Twitty, vice president of Charlotte National Bank. H. M. Victor, the Union National Bank founder, sent a telegram to D. R. Crissinger, chairman of the Federal Reserve Board: "Name convenient date when you can visit Charlotte to attend a banquet. Make us a talk and listen to us."

On January 19, 1928, more than 650 bankers and businessmen packed the dining room, lobby, and balcony of the Hotel Charlotte for a celebratory dinner. The guest of honor ended up being Treasury secretary Andrew Mellon, joined by a coterie of other top Washington officials. Former North Carolina governor Cameron Morrison served as toastmaster for the five-hour ceremony.

Speaking against the backdrop of a large United States flag, Mellon stressed the importance of an independent Fed, noting it was established under a Democratic president in 1913 but continued under Republicans. Mellon also explained how the Federal Reserve "had eliminated the danger of panics by providing an elastic credit system with a common reservoir."

His remarks came less than two years before the 1929 stock-market crash.

Unlike some Charlotte banks, American Trust, Commercial National, and Union National survived the Depression and emerged poised to grow when the nation's prosperity returned.

At American Trust, president Torrence Hemby, hired by Word Wood in 1906, began weighing his bank's next generation of leaders. In 1951, he hired a 42-year-old from Baltimore named Addison Reese as executive vice president. The tall, distinguished-looking Reese came to North Carolina with ideas of expanding the institution outside Charlotte. But he had to tread slowly with a board packed with prominent conservative Charlotte businessmen.

The first major merger in Charlotte banking history came six years later. It was a natural pairing of American Trust and Commercial National, next-door neighbors on South Tryon Street. The larger American Trust was primarily a correspondent bank, while Commercial National, the state's oldest bank, had a strong retail base, including the state's first drive-in branch, located in the Charlotte suburbs.

On November 29, 1957, the renamed American Commercial Bank debuted with about $250 million in total assets. The new bank became the state's second biggest, after Wachovia. Reese served as chief executive and president. Workers punched a hole in the walls separating the tall, skinny Commercial National building and the short, squat American Trust headquarters.

The hometown merger shook Union National president Carl McCraw, Sr., whose bank was on the other side of Tryon. He was now competing against an institution more than twice the size of his own. He called a meeting of his lieutenants and was soon contemplating a merger himself. In May 1958, Union National agreed to buy Asheville's First National Bank and Trust Company. The new bank, with $110 million in assets, would be called First Union National Bank.

As the merger rivalry heated up between the two Charlotte banks, so did the race to occupy the city's biggest buildings. After its start in the Buford Hotel, Union National moved to a location at the corner of Fourth and Tryon streets that had once housed Commercial National Bank. By 1955, Union National jumped to the nine-story Jefferson Standard Building at the corner of Third and Tryon. The bank dismantled the roll-top desk of honorary chairman H. M. Victor and reassembled it in the new building.

Meanwhile, Winston-Salem's Wachovia crashed Charlotte's homegrown rivalry with its own 16-story building on West Trade Street, the city's other main artery. But in 1958, Addison Reese trumped both Wachovia and First Union by announcing the construction of an 18-story building that would replace the aging, side-by-side American Trust and Commercial National buildings. Reese was keeping his bank at a historic location. A plaque in the sidewalk stated that Confederate president Jefferson Davis was standing at the spot when he was informed of Abraham Lincoln's death on April 18, 1865. In an odd historical confluence, Reese's great-grandfather had owned Ford's Theatre in Washington, the site of Lincoln's assassination.

Though the Charlotte banks competed fiercely with each other, their bankers agreed on one thing: They despised Wachovia.

Reese in particular had his sights on overtaking the Winston-Salem giant, which was politically connected and held about 20 percent of the state's deposits. Wachovia was the envy of banks in North Carolina and around the country. A Wachovia loan was not only a source of funding but a stamp of approval for any venture. A taunting sign painted on a building on Fourth Street in Charlotte read, "Wachovia Bank & Trust, the largest bank between Philadelphia and Dallas."

Reese renewed his assault on Wachovia in 1960 by inking a merger with Security National Bank in Greensboro. The combined institution had dual headquarters in Greensboro and Charlotte and about $500 million in assets, behind only Wachovia's $658 million. Its new name: North Carolina National Bank, or NCNB.

In his pursuit of Wachovia, Reese emphasized the importance of injecting new talent into the bank, launching a training program for college graduates. One of the early recruits was Hugh McColl, who joined the bank in 1959. One who got away was Ed Crutchfield, who chose First Union. Reese also made another key hire, luring Tom Storrs from his post leading the Charlotte Fed branch. Reese installed Storrs as head of Greensboro operations, giving him an insider in the company's other headquarters.

While NCNB expanded, Union National's Carl McCraw also scoured the state for deals, snapping up small banks to build his branch network. First Union made a big score in 1964 when it bought a Raleigh mortgage firm, Cameron-Brown Company. Both NCNB and Wachovia had been interested, but president

Cliff Cameron preferred First Union. "I felt like if there was going to be any possible opportunity of me going higher in the organization instead of just going in and managing the mortgage company, it had to be a small company," Cameron said later of his choice.

Cameron, 44, was from Meridian, Mississippi, the son of a railroad man and a devout Baptist mother. After graduating from Louisiana State University with an engineering degree, he commanded a mortar battalion in World War II that rendezvoused with the Russians on the Elbe River. In 1949, tired of the refinery job he landed after the war, he teamed up with a friend in Raleigh, James Poyner, who was interested in launching a mortgage company. That firm grew into a top-10 United States mortgage lender with offices around the country.

Initially, Cameron was an executive vice president of the bank and head of the mortgage company. But two years later, he took charge after a power shift that displaced McCraw. By May 1968, First Union was a leader in pioneering a new way for banks to expand into non-banking businesses. First Union National Bancorp became the first "one-bank holding company" in the state and the second registered in the nation. The rules allowed for expansion into everything from computer services to insurance. Congress soon began looking at ways to rein in these entities, while Cameron led a national lobbying effort that worked to soften the blow. The end result was that the Federal Reserve began regulating the holding companies.

Meanwhile, with Reese's tenure as CEO nearing an end, the push was on at NCNB to best Wachovia. The big moment arrived in the spring of 1972, when both banks released first-quarter earnings. With $2.9 billion in assets, Reese's bank was now the biggest in the Southeast. It was a slim margin, but NCNB had surpassed Wachovia's $2.7 billion in assets.

In Winston-Salem, Wachovia in 1974 named a president who would carry on the bank's conservative ways.

John Medlin, Jr., a Benson, North Carolina, native, had joined the bank in 1959 out of the navy, where he was a paymaster aboard a submarine support ship. He learned leadership lessons from Chester Nimitz, Jr., son of the renowned World War II admiral. "Knowledge is supreme," Nimitz preached.

Medlin had no aspirations of becoming a banker, but he had a wife and child and needed a job. "I came to Wachovia. I liked what I saw, was offered a job, and accepted without looking around," he said in a later interview. After training, he became a loan administration officer. By 1970, he was head of the department, an area now called risk management.

The bank's culture, referred to as "the Wachovia Way," was reflected in the principles and philosophies passed on to employees, including the importance of risk management, Medlin said. "Our mantra was soundness, profitability and growth in that order of priority," he said. "We practiced progressive and some-times aggressive business strategies within sound financial principles."

Imparting those values to new employees was part of Medlin's routine. He talked with every group of college graduates that came into the bank. He didn't sugarcoat the importance of honesty and integrity. "If you violate the banking laws, we will have to report you to the FBI," he told them. "You'll be tried and probably go to jail. If you violate our code of conduct, you will be subject to dismissal."

He favored formal dress for employees. "If you want to be a senior VP, wear a suit and tie," he told an executive who wanted to start a Casual Friday policy.

Though NCNB had passed Wachovia in size and First Union was also on the move, Medlin said he wasn't bothered by the chase. "One analyst said NCNB had an inferiority complex," he noted. "We never felt that pressure. We had self-confidence. It was part of our Moravian heritage. We did not have a go-go, keep up with the Joneses worldview. Being in Winston-Salem you didn't look across the street and see someone building a bigger building."

NCNB gained a new leader the same year Medlin became president of Wa-chovia. Tom Storrs, the former Greensboro executive, succeeded Reese as CEO on January 1, 1974. Storrs had worked as a runner at the Federal Reserve Bank of Richmond in high school, served in the navy during World War II, and become head of the Charlotte Fed branch before joining NCNB in 1960. As CEO, he continued to promote the aggressive, youth-oriented culture pioneered by Reese while also placing an emphasis on examining data before making decisions. "It wasn't a disaster to be wrong," Storrs said in a later interview. "It was a disaster to make a decision that wasn't properly based."

Storrs and Medlin took charge just as a brutal national recession was building.

NCNB was in particular danger because it funded itself largely with bor-rowed money, instead of more stable retail deposits. During the Fourth of July holiday in 1974, the bank discovered it would be $40 million short of the money it needed. Scrambling to save itself, the bank tapped its London office for help in securing the necessary funds. The bank came dangerously close to insolvency.

At First Union, Cliff Cameron got his first case of bleeding ulcers in the 1970s. The overheated real-estate market in the Southeast meant banks faced ris-ing defaults and a rash of foreclosures on unwanted properties. In one instance, First Union wound up owning a Disney World hotel in Florida. Cameron sold it to the Hyatt chain, but only after he agreed to build a convention center at the hotel. "Those were tough days," he said. "Tough nights."

At Wachovia, Medlin, who became CEO in 1977, watched his bank's shares fall from $44 in the spring of 1973 to $10 in the fall of 1974. But he said the bank remained in good shape. "First Union and NCNB," he said, "were much more stressed."

. . .

In 1979, Austin Adams, an executive at North Wilkesboro–based Northwestern Financial Corporation, attended a cocktail party hosted by NCNB at Charlotte's Raintree Country Club. He heard Hugh McColl in a loud conversation from across the room and went to check out the commotion.

Locked in a heated debate, McColl gestured with his finger to make a point. "There's going to be a $20 billion bank in the Southeast, and it will be us," McColl declared.

Is this guy crazy? Adams thought.

Interstate banking had largely been quashed by the McFadden Act of 1927. One of its provisions limited the expansion of federally regulated banks to the restrictions placed on state banks. If state banks couldn't expand beyond their city, county, or state limits, then national banks in the same areas couldn't breach those barriers either.

NCNB, now the nation's 24th-biggest bank with more than $6 billion in assets, wanted to escape state boundaries for a multitude of reasons. Expansion would enable it to build a bigger stable of deposits, fend off competition from brokerage houses and other new rivals, and make bigger loans to its corporate customers. Florida was one of the most alluring states, thanks to its rich trove of deposits and booming population. Another target was Georgia, home to the South's most prominent city, Atlanta.

"We realized that if we didn't leave North Carolina, we would never amount to anything, that we would not be important," said McColl, who credited Tom Storrs for the push to expand across state lines. "The reason was North Carolina was the 11th-largest state in the union, so ergo you could never be better off than the state's growth would be. Even though we were growing rapidly we could never catch up with New York or somebody like that who already had the benefit of hundreds of years of being a money center. So we realized that if we were going to be successful we had to get bigger. So that then set us on the path of trying to get interstate banking."

Although Walter Wriston's Citicorp had aided NCNB when its funding dried up in 1974, McColl retained an animosity against Northern bankers, who cherry-picked prime corporate clients across the South and represented a region that had battered the South's capital base in the Civil War.

"After the War, the South was really a hugely defeated nation that was depleted of capital," McColl said. "And unlike Germany and Japan after the Second World War there was no Marshall Plan for the South. None. So we had to pull ourselves up by our own bootstraps, as I see it. And that drove me my entire career. It's no doubt that when we passed Wachovia we transferred our aggressive enmity to the New Yorkers."

NCNB, of course, wasn't the only bank itching to break free of state boundaries. Northern banks such as Citicorp were also looking to enter new geographies and businesses. The Southern banks that didn't expand might become takeover fodder for these giants. At First Union, Cliff Cameron was building his bank in North Carolina while also cultivating potential takeover possibilities in Florida, anticipating the arrival of interstate banking. The personable CEO brought along promising lieutenant Ed Crutchfield to bankers' conventions, laying the ground-work for future courtships.

NCNB struck a major blow for interstate banking after its general counsel, Paul Polking, discovered a loophole that appeared to allow it to buy a Florida bank because it already owned a trust company in the state. The NCNB team, led by Storrs and McColl, needed a test-case acquisition. In 1981, NCNB forged a deal to buy tiny, struggling First National Bank of Lake City. The Federal Reserve signed off on the purchase. In January 1982, NCNB became a two-state bank.

The next step was the creation of regional banking compacts. For North Carolina banks, these arrangements were critical because they allowed them to bulk up their size without fear of competition from much larger Northern banks. When the Supreme Court upheld the pacts in June 1985, the table was set for the new leaders at NCNB and First Union.

Chapter 2

Rivalry Personified

Born the son and grandson of bankers in 1935, Hugh McColl, Jr., grew up in the cotton country of Bennettsville, South Carolina, southeast of Charlotte. Driven to succeed at a young age, he once proudly brought home a report card showing him second in his class. His grandmother Gabrielle McColl patted him on the hand and said, "You'll do better next time, son."

After getting a business degree from the University of North Carolina at Chapel Hill, he served as an officer in the Marine Corps from 1957 to 1959. When his unit set sail for a mission in Lebanon and its orders changed mid-trip, McColl spent much of the tour raking in poker pots. Upon leaving the service, he thought he might return home to run the family businesses, but his father told him succinctly, "We're getting along fine without you. You better go up to the American Trust Co. and get yourself a job."

The bank, by then known as American Commercial, had aided McColl's father's bank during the Depression. Addison Reese agreed to hire McColl into its training program. Part of the new wave of college graduates permeating the institution, McColl wasn't greeted warmly in the fall of 1959. "I didn't ask for you. I don't want you. I don't like college boys. And I don't like you," an operations executive named Benny Shaw, who would later become a close friend, said to McColl.

McColl spent his early days traveling dusty South Carolina roads to meet with small banks and businesses. It was tiring work, but it helped him nurture a growing network of friends and business colleagues. Just shy of five-foot-seven, with a Cheshire-cat grin, he had an outsized personality brimming with good ol' boy charm, common-sense smarts, and the kind of self-confidence needed to make snap decisions betting the bank's money. One of his early contacts was former pro football star Jerry Richardson, who had started a Hardee's restaurant franchise.

As a young executive, McColl was known for his confident attitude and his knack for needling competitors and critics. When NCNB passed Wachovia in assets, he was fond of saying the Winston-Salem bank had become the biggest between Mocksville and Kernersville, small cities on either side of the bank's hometown. As CEO, he would preside over thousands of job cuts but would be revered by many of his workers. He walked the floors of the bank's headquarters and grabbed beers to celebrate deals. McColl and other NCNB executives posed wearing army helmets in front of a Florida flag to commemorate their invasion of the state. "He's a very aggressive guy and a very fair guy, somebody who loves to win," general counsel Paul Polking later said.

When he became CEO in 1983, McColl took over an institution with $12 billion in assets, about 7,600 employees, and operations in two states. While not denying his aggressive streak or reservoir of confidence, he contended those traits had been engrained in the NCNB culture much earlier. He recalled a 1977 visit to Addison Reese at Charlotte's Mercy Hospital, where the retired CEO was dying of cancer. McColl told him about problems at Northwestern Financial, which was the subject of FBI and IRS investigations. McColl said NCNB was talking to the bank's customers, trying to lure away business.

Reese reached out and patted McColl's hand. "Show them no mercy," he said. "We won't," McColl replied.

In 1941, E. E. Crutchfield was an FBI agent chasing Canadian bootleggers in Dearborn, Michigan, when his first child was about to arrive. In a rush, he called for a police escort, and his son, Ed Crutchfield, Jr., was delivered safely at Henry Ford Hospital.

After World War II, the family returned to its North Carolina roots in the small town of Albemarle, east of Charlotte. A rebellious child, Ed Crutchfield had stern taskmasters to keep him in check: His father became a district attorney, his paternal grandfather was a Baptist preacher, and his maternal grandfather was a judge. Crutchfield's English-teacher mother, Katherine, gently steered him toward banking, bringing him by an Albemarle branch on a hot July day. He liked the cold touch of the marble floor on his bare feet, though he didn't care for the look of the caged teller windows. "There are other jobs in the bank beside those," his mother told him. Later, Crutchfield began reading the stock pages in the *Observer* and invested $100 of his own money when he was around age 16. In his high-school years, his mother encouraged him to study business at the University of Pennsylvania's prestigious Wharton School.

At Albemarle High, the broad-shouldered, six-foot-two Crutchfield played offensive and defensive tackle on a football squad named the state's top team by sportswriters. At Davidson College, he continued to play the sport while also participating in the Reserve Officers' Training Corps. A second lieutenant when he graduated in 1963, he received a deferment from active duty to attend graduate school at Wharton. When he finished in 1965, he reported to the naval depot in Philadelphia, only to have a doctor diagnose a back problem from his football-playing days. "We don't want any part of you in the army," the doctor said. Crutchfield drove to Charlotte and had back surgery two days later.

Although he had job offers from banks in New York, Crutchfield wanted to stay in Charlotte. He interviewed at NCNB but gauged the competition and decided he had better chances of moving up at the smaller First Union. "I wanted to run something even if it was a service station," Crutchfield said. "I took a flier and went with the smaller bank." Wharton later sent out a survey of its recent graduates, and Crutchfield's $7,200 salary was dead last.

About a year after joining the company, Crutchfield bumped into Cliff Cameron, who had recently sold his mortgage company to First Union. Chatting in a hallway in the bank's headquarters at Third and Tryon streets, Cameron asked him what he did, and Crutchfield offered to show him his municipal bond–trading operation. "It was the same skills as in mortgage banking," Crutchfield said. "We hit it off."

Restless a few years later in 1969, Crutchfield landed a job offer from an insurance company. His boss told him he should talk to Cameron first. On his way to the meeting, Crutchfield stuffed two sealed letters into his pockets—one accepting the job, one declining it. Cameron said he had a new position for Crutchfield as head of human resources, making him one of the top 10 executives in the company at age 28. "You've got a deal," Crutchfield said. He dropped one of the letters in the mail chute, momentarily panicking that he had released the wrong one.

In 1973, Crutchfield got another job offer. This time, Charlotte businessman C. D. "Dick" Spangler wanted him to run the Bank of North Carolina, a struggling institution Spangler's father had been instrumental in founding in the eastern part of the state in 1951. Crutchfield knew Spangler from his early days in Charlotte. Many of the city's young professionals, including Spangler, Crutchfield, and McColl, had lived in the same Selwyn Village apartment complex at various times. Sunday entertainment featured backyard touch football games that got rougher as the day went on. Spangler's job offer would make Crutchfield a CEO, give him a raise, and hand him a big chunk of stock.

He went to Cameron again. "So you're trading down, are you?" his boss said coyly. "That's a lot smaller bank. Why not sit tight for a while?"

About two months later, Crutchfield was named president of First Union's banking unit. At age 32, he was the youngest president of a major bank in the country. By 1984, he was CEO of the whole company. Cameron handed over his chairman's title to Crutchfield in 1985 but stayed on the board until 1991.

"He sort of grew up with me," Cameron later said of Crutchfield. "He was a strong, smart, talented individual who seemed to be there at the right time when we had a problem."

Taking over at First Union, Crutchfield saw overcapacity in the banking system and economies of scale that could be seized by cutting costs at acquired banks. As new technology ranging from ATMs to satellite uplinks proliferated in the industry, it became easier for banks to expand their territory nationwide. But the cost of maintaining state-of-the-art systems also drove many banks, unable to afford the necessary investment in new technology, into mergers.

In 1984, Crutchfield told his board at First Union that it had two choices: Sell the bank or seek an aggressive acquisition strategy. "I think you as a director have to make a choice," Crutchfield recalled telling them. "If you're not on an acquisition path, you're going to be playing defense. Unanimously, they said, 'Go get it.' That's all I needed to hear."

Knowing his bank needed to bulk up further, Crutchfield approached the new chief executive at Northwestern Financial, Ben Craig, who was reviving the bank after the IRS and FBI investigations. First Union was the state's number-three bank by assets, and Northwestern was number four. "We're not big enough to get there," Crutchfield said. "You aren't either. Together we might be."

After an initial rejection, First Union announced in March 1985 that it was buying Northwestern. Boasting about $10 billion in combined assets, First Union became the state's second-biggest bank, eclipsing Wachovia's $8.7 billion in assets. Nationally, First Union was set to break into the top 30 banks. It was now ready to duel with NCNB for acquisitions around the Southeast and later the country.

In 1988, Hugh McColl's bank pursued a target in a state outside the banking compact: Texas.

As the Lone Star State's oil economy sputtered, NCNB bid for First Republic-Bank Corporation. Because the Dallas bank was near collapse, NCNB was allowed to make a leap outside the compact if the Federal Deposit Insurance Corporation arranged the deal. Helped by a ruling that would give the bank an estimated $700 million in tax savings, NCNB outdueled San Francisco's Wells Fargo and New York's Citicorp for the score. Once the acquisition was completed, NCNB nearly doubled in size to $55 billion in assets, making it the nation's 10th-biggest bank.

Back in Charlotte, the deal was a blow to Ed Crutchfield, who was not the type to be easily rattled. When the stock market crashed in October 1987, First Union executives found him trading bonds on a terminal on the bank's executive floor, coolly betting hundreds of millions of the bank's dollars in the middle of a massive market meltdown. On the Monday after the NCNB announcement,

Crutchfield began his regular staff meeting on a sober note. "Guys, we're a good bank on our way to being a great bank," he said. "But after the deal NCNB did, we're going to be No. 2."

After winning First Republic, McColl sent a number of top executives including Ken Lewis to Texas. At the top of the chain of command at NCNB Texas National Bank was Buddy Kemp, a trusted McColl lieutenant who had been with the company since 1967. The Davidson College and Harvard Business School graduate had helped McColl work out bad loans in the 1970s, revived retail banking for the company, and run all of its North Carolina operations.

In McColl's mind, Kemp was in line to be his successor. "Buddy had it all," he said later. "He had a great personality. People liked him. He could be warm and as friendly as anybody. He was intellectually tough."

McColl wanted to retire at age 60, which meant that in 1988 he had about seven more years to groom his replacement. But soon after taking over in Texas, Kemp was diagnosed with a brain tumor. He died in November 1990. Kemp's passing was "a tremendous loss to our company," McColl said. "When Buddy died it was impossible for me to retire. We didn't have a successor in place."

At the end of 1991, McColl renamed his company NationsBank after buying C&S/Sovran Corporation, which was based in Atlanta and Norfolk, Virginia. C&S/Sovran was led by a CEO who had rejected NCNB's advances two years earlier. With the purchase, McColl, the ex-marine, began a practice of handing out crystal replica hand grenades as field medals to key lieutenants.

Meanwhile, at First Union, Crutchfield continued to win his share of deals, rising to number two in Florida by snapping up Florida National Banks, Inc., in Jacksonville and winning an FDIC-assisted bidding contest for Southeast Banking Corporation in Miami.

In sharp contrast to the barrage of deals pursued by NCNB and First Union, Winston-Salem's Wachovia had gone quiet since snatching First Atlanta away from McColl in 1985. But in 1991, John Medlin wooed South Carolina National Corporation in Columbia. Wachovia, which had dropped the "First" from its name, now had retail branches in three southeastern states.

On January 1, 1994, John Medlin handed his CEO title to Bud Baker, a former chief credit officer who had risen to president. Medlin would stay on as chairman. Baker inherited the desk of Francis Fries, the Wachovia president from 1893 to 1931. Ever since then, the antique had been passed down by each Wachovia leader to the next generation. Baker opened up one of the drawers to find a prank note written by Medlin: "Don't screw it up.—Col. Fries."

The back-and-forth acquisitions fueled the suspicion among some that McColl and Crutchfield were engaged in an expensive game of one-upmanship. The rivalry extended to the banks' buildings as well. In 1988, Crutchfield opened a new 42-story headquarters in Charlotte. McColl responded with plans for a 60-story tower at the center of Uptown.

Both men denied glancing across town before making their next moves. When it came to building his new tower, McColl said he was motivated not by his rival but instead by his desire to build something "meaningful"—a skyscraper rather than a mere tall building. In the end, famed architect Cesar Pelli crafted a tower that telescoped into a crown-like peak, a fitting summit for the Queen City.

While the two banks often clashed on deals, they continued to cooperate on hometown civic initiatives, just like their predecessors. If competition reared its head, it was usually a positive for the city because it meant the two banks were vying to raise money for various charitable causes.

The cooperation also contained an element of self-interest. Both banks knew they had to recruit talented employees to a little-known city in the South. "People in London and New York didn't want to live in a small town," Crutchfield said. "They wanted pro sports, a symphony, good schools."

Over the years, Crutchfield and McColl would become part of what was known as "The Group"—select business leaders who met to discuss ways to improve Charlotte. Other key members included Duke Power CEO Bill Lee and *Observer* publisher Rolfe Neill. One task the bankers thrived at, not surprisingly, was raising money. For example, Crutchfield chaired a campaign that raised about $60 million for Johnson C. Smith University in 1998. The kickoff event was held in the dining room at McColl's bank.

Both banks supported the arrival of major-league sports in Charlotte, starting with the Hornets NBA team in 1987, a development that gave the city more national attention. McColl played a critical role in helping his old friend and customer Jerry Richardson land a Charlotte NFL franchise in 1993. He aided with financing and in pitching the bid to the league. Later, under Ken Lewis, Bank of America would secure the naming rights for the Panthers' stadium.

McColl became best known for revitalizing North Tryon Street and other neighborhoods in the center city, called "Uptown" in the local vernacular. He was determined to bring people back to the once-empty area by making it a 24-hour hub of housing, shops, and entertainment. As McColl championed other projects, his name ended up attached to the business school at Queens University of Charlotte and a visual arts center.

Under Crutchfield, First Union's campus expanded on the south side of Uptown. He made education a primary focus of his company's civic involvement, crediting that push to his schoolteacher mother. One of the bank's initiatives was to give workers paid time off to volunteer in schools. "I'm proud of what you do at the bank," Crutchfield's mother once told him, "but I won't be proud of you if you don't do something for education."

· · ·

By the mid-1990s, the southeastern banking compact had done its job. The merger frenzy unleashed in 1985 produced two Charlotte banks capable of competing with money-center institutions in New York. Now, they were ready for the next phase of interstate banking, which would extend beyond the Southeast to the rest of the country.

In the fall of 1994, banking industry lobbying paid off when President Bill Clinton signed the Riegle-Neal Interstate Banking and Branching Efficiency Act. McColl got part of the credit for the bill after cultivating a relationship with Clinton. The new law allowed banks to enter any state in the nation, not just regional pockets. They could also better merge their existing operations, allowing customers to tap a NationsBank or First Union account at branches around the country. One brake on the industry's growth was a provision that prohibited any bank from gaining more than 10 percent of United States deposits through an acquisition.

Once the new law was in place, Crutchfield, who earned the nickname "Fast Eddie" for his rapid-fire deals, took his bank to the Northeast by agreeing to buy New Jersey's First Fidelity Bancorp in 1995 and Philadelphia's CoreStates Financial Corporation in 1997. After nabbing Signet Banking Corporation for $3.3 billion in 1997, he bragged about the technique he used to win over the Virginia bank's management: "I just kept stacking billion-dollar bills on the table." McColl also made major moves, landing St. Louis–based Boatmen's Bancshares, Inc., in 1996 and jumping to number one in Florida in 1997 by nabbing Barnett Banks, Inc.

Geographic expansion wasn't the only new frontier for the Charlotte banks.

Both First Union and NationsBank built capital markets operations in the 1990s as the industry gradually eroded Depression-era restrictions preventing commercial banks from dabbling in Wall Street–style services such as underwriting stocks and bonds. As they entered these businesses, banks had both profits and survival in mind. Wall Street firms were eating into their corporate-lending business by helping big companies raise money through securities offerings and other methods. And brokerage houses were nabbing retail customers by enticing them with investment options that offered an alternative to checking and savings accounts.

In the fall of 1992, First Union executives were on the 40th floor of the bank's headquarters giving presentations on how they could expand the group that would become the bank's capital markets unit. Crutchfield brought the executives over to the window and pointed to a peregrine falcon swooping around the building's upper reaches. Then he showed them the eviscerated pigeons the falcon had deposited on the ledge outside the conference room window.

"You see those carcasses," Crutchfield said. "If we don't figure this out, that's going to be us in less than five years."

As 1997 came to a close, Charlotte claimed a heady title fueled by the NationsBank and First Union buying binge—it was the nation's number-two banking city by assets, behind only New York. With the Barnett, Signet, and CoreStates deals, the Queen City jumped ahead of San Francisco by a margin of $488.9 billion in assets to $415.3 billion.

Not everyone cheered the rapid expansion. Ever-changing bank names befuddled customers. Cities across the country lost jobs and bank headquarters. Community groups feared less lending to minorities and low- and moderate-income borrowers. And analysts complained about the high price of the deals.

One of the industry's biggest foes was Boston-based Neighborhood Assistance Corporation of America. The group's leader, Bruce Marks, was a self-described "bank terrorist" who targeted First Union as the "invisible bank in working people's neighborhoods." In 1995, while Marks was in Charlotte to spar over Crutchfield's First Fidelity deal, McColl sat down with the NACA leader in what was initially a rocky meeting. Marks told McColl that bankers were evil and out for a profit. The NationsBank CEO retorted that nonprofits wanted handouts without accountability. But weeks later, McColl committed $500 million to NACA's affordable-housing program. The banker and the bank terrorist would become unlikely allies over the years.

McColl and Crutchfield also feuded with bank analyst Tom Brown, who criticized their deals as destructive to shareholder value. Crutchfield jawed with the analyst at an investors' conference after First Union's $17 billion CoreStates deal. McColl took offense when the analyst sent a letter to about 40 bank leaders quoting Warren Buffett's disdain for mergers: "The sad fact is that most major acquisitions display an egregious imbalance. They are a bonanza for the shareholders of the acquirees; they increase the income and status of the acquirers' management; and they are a honey pot for the investment bankers and other professionals of both sides. But, alas, they usually reduce the wealth of the acquirers' shareholders, often to a substantial degree."

In the spring of 1998, Crutchfield was fly-fishing in New Zealand when he got a heads-up about a prospective deal. His lieutenants had lined up the purchase of a consumer finance company called the Money Store, Inc.

The firm was perhaps best known for late-night commercials featuring retired athletes like New York Yankee Phil Rizzuto and Baltimore Oriole Jim Palmer. Its primary product was higher-rate home-equity loans peddled to customers with spotty credit histories.

Crutchfield said he asked some questions but didn't have much involvement in the deal. At a price of $2.1 billion, it was a relatively small purchase for a bank that had just spent more than eight times that amount on CoreStates.

In the March 4, 1998, press release announcing the deal, First Union said the acquisition, which created the nation's biggest home-equity lender, would allow the bank to "provide credit to homeowners who may not otherwise qualify for bank credit." the Money Store's so-called subprime loans carried a higher risk of default for the bank but also paid higher interest rates.

The bank's press release also highlighted First Union's ability to securitize the loans through its capital markets unit. Securitization is the process of packaging assets like mortgages into investment products for outside investors such as pension funds. The process would play a major role in the next decade's mortgage market meltdown. The bank had been bundling home-equity loans into securities since 1994, freeing up "additional capital to be reinvested in First Union's communities," it said.

Just a few months earlier, in October 1997, First Union and investment bank Bear Stearns Companies had announced what author William Cohan called the first-ever securitization of subprime loans—the packaging of $385 million in Community Reinvestment Act loans. In a news release, the bank called them "affordable mortgages" and said they were targeted to low- and moderate-income borrowers and neighborhoods.

Other banks including NationsBank had checked out the Money Store but taken a pass.

First Union chief information officer Austin Adams, who had joined the bank in the 1985 Northwestern deal, got a bad feeling about the purchase when he ran into a counterpart at Wells Fargo. The San Francisco bank had taken a look at the Money Store and decided against it. "It's a big black hole and there is nothing there," the executive told Adams. The Wells official didn't see a way to make the deal profitable in his lifetime. First Union, however, said in its press release that it expected the deal to add to earnings right away.

Chapter 3

THE NEXT GENERATION

By late 1997, NationsBank had a sweeping name but still stretched only as far west as New Mexico. Though big in Florida and Texas, it needed to be in California to be a true national player.

Hugh McColl had rejected a proposed BankAmerica merger in 1995 because NationsBank would have been the subordinate player. But the Barnett deal in Florida brought a significant turn of events: NationsBank was now bigger than BankAmerica in market value, assets, and profits. NationsBank considered pursuing Wells Fargo, but strategy executive Greg Curl thought that purchase would be too expensive. The former Boatmen's executive laid out charts in McColl's conference room and showed him why the bank's target should be BankAmerica or New York's Citicorp. Soon, NationsBank zeroed in on BankAmerica, which had become a West Coast giant thanks to acquisitions and California's branching laws.

NationsBank CFO Jim Hance and his BankAmerica counterpart, Mike O'Neill, kicked off the talks in late February 1998 and began working through some of the key issues. The headquarters remained a sticking point. BankAmerica had earlier suggested Chicago as a central location. It wasn't wedded to San Francisco but didn't want Charlotte. Chicago didn't make any sense to McColl because neither bank had much of a presence there. He proposed Dallas as a possibility, but BankAmerica didn't like that either.

One Saturday morning, Hance stopped by McColl's home in the upscale Eastover neighborhood to give him an update on the talks. When it came to the headquarters, BankAmerica didn't want to be perceived as a Southern company, Hance said.

"Tough! That's who we are," McColl barked.

McColl stepped up the wooing on April 1 when he met with new BankAmerica CEO David Coulter in San Francisco. By the end of the day, the deal was coming together. McColl and Coulter had started agreeing on top people for the combined company. McColl did not rule out changing the NationsBank name.

The next day, both Coulter and McColl were scheduled to attend a bankers' meeting in Phoenix. They agreed to rendezvous at a different hotel, but McColl got delayed by, of all people, Ed Crutchfield. They bumped into each other as McColl was trying to slip out of the conference. The flustered McColl dodged the conversation by saying he had left something in his car.

Across town at the Ritz-Carlton over burgers and drinks, McColl and Coulter dug into what deal makers call "social issues"—headquarters, names, and top jobs. Hance and O'Neill had already worked out the financials. For one, the purchase would be considered a merger of equals. BankAmerica shareholders wouldn't receive a premium for doing the deal but would become investors in a much bigger company with greater earnings potential.

Coulter accepted Charlotte as the corporate headquarters. San Francisco would be the home of wholesale banking. The holding company's name would be BankAmerica Corporation, but the final brand was to be determined. The bigger NationsBank would have 11 directors to nine for BankAmerica. Hance and Ken Lewis would lose their board seats, a change that didn't sit well with either of them. Back in 1997, McColl had set up a competition between the two executives to see who would succeed him. Now, it looked like both had lost their shots.

Before the two CEOs left Room 940, they dictated a "Memorandum of Understanding" to McColl's longtime secretary, Pat Hinson. The document listed the six executives—including Lewis and Hance—who would stay with the bank. McColl would be CEO, and Coulter would serve as president. In addition, it was the "present intention of the boards for Mr. Coulter to succeed Mr. McColl."

On April 13, Easter Monday, McColl and Coulter announced their $66.6 billion coast-to-coast blockbuster. At age 62, and after almost 15 years as CEO, the former American Commercial trainee had transformed a small North Carolina bank into a national behemoth. The CEOs debuted the deal at New York's Waldorf Astoria, the same hotel where Citicorp had announced its $80 billion combination with Travelers Group, Inc., a week earlier. McColl donned a San Francisco 49ers hat for the occasion, while Coulter pulled on a Carolina Panthers cap.

The new bank would have $570 billion in assets, hold 8 percent of the country's total deposits, and boast corporate relationships with 85 percent of Fortune 500 companies. It expected to shed $2 billion in annual expenses, partly by cutting 5,000 to 8,000 jobs. The combined company had about 180,000 employees, including NationsBank's 9,700 in Charlotte. "Together, we will be America's bank—at home and around the world," McColl said, adding that he and Coulter believed "bigger is, indeed, better."

Though Wall Street loved the deal, it got a rockier reception from shell-shocked San Francisco and from community groups. In BankAmerica's hometown, many resented losing their headquarters to a little-known Southern city. Some politicians and pundits worried about the acceptance of gay employees and the loss of arts and charitable funding.

"Why should the headquarters of the new B of A move from San Francisco, home of the 49ers, haute cuisine and culture, to Charlotte, home to the Panthers expansion team, stock car racing and pork slathered in barbecue sauce?" a *San Francisco Chronicle* article said. "The Bank of America merger is so frightening on so many levels that it's hard to grasp," *Chronicle* columnist Ken Garcia added. "The new twin cities: San Francisco/Charlotte. What a concept: pickled pigs' feet—the San Francisco treat."

NationsBank countered with a pledge to lend and invest $350 billion over 10 years to help low- and moderate-income neighborhoods and small businesses nationwide. McColl declared his goal for the new company was to be the "best community development bank in the country."

After winning Federal Reserve and shareholder approval, NationsBank and BankAmerica officially merged on September 30, 1998. That same day in a nationally broadcast TV commercial, the bank revealed its new name: Bank of America.

The Bank of America moniker had been around for decades, compared to just seven for NationsBank. It also tested better with customers. But McColl said he later regretted the switch because it preserved part of the BankAmerica culture he wanted to transform. In particular, he disliked what he saw as the BankAmerica tendency to endlessly debate issues without ever making a decision. Inaction was the antithesis of the NationsBank way of doing business.

"If you've got a culture that you wished to change you shouldn't leave any vestige of the old culture in existence," McColl said. "You must destroy the culture in its entirety. My marketing people disagreed with me. Everybody who knows anything about advertising disagreed with me that the Bank of America name was the best bank name you could have. Intellectually, I know it's the best name. But in the context of retaining the NCNB culture it worked against it."

While Bank of America's brand won out, it became clear early on that the deal wasn't really a merger of equals. NationsBank took charge at the combined company. NationsBank's Gene Taylor was named head of the company's Western region, and Ken Lewis headed the combined retail bank. Although Coulter was the heir apparent to McColl, analysts were already betting he wouldn't survive NationsBank's warlike culture.

On October 14, the merger's problems went from cultural to financial. When the bank reported its first quarterly results as a combined company, executives revealed a $372 million loss from a relationship with hedge fund D. E. Shaw & Company. The New York investment firm had employed complex computer-driven investing methods that went awry when Russia defaulted on its debt, roiling world markets that summer. BankAmerica had forged ties with D. E. Shaw, and now the loss was blotting the results of the combined company.

Wall Street investors were furious that the San Francisco bank had made such a big investment in a risky hedge fund. Shares of the combined bank plunged 11 percent on the news.

Shareholders and lawmakers criticized the timing of the revelation, which came after the deal had closed. Lawsuits later alleged the bank intentionally withheld information about the loss, a claim denied by Bank of America.

David Coulter, now president of the combined company, had presided over the D. E. Shaw relationship. He met with McColl confidant Hootie Johnson, known as the CEO's hatchet man. Just 20 days after the merger closed, Coulter announced his resignation, effective October 30. He would leave with a severance package that gave him $5 million a year for life, plus medical benefits and 300,000 shares of stock. Upon Coulter's departure, McColl agreed to stay past his scheduled retirement in June 2000, when he would turn 65. He now would remain chairman and chief executive until June 2002 or longer.

Litigation related to the D. E. Shaw blowup would take years to resolve. In July 2001, the bank reached a settlement in which the Securities and Exchange Commission found that BankAmerica had violated securities law but didn't assess any monetary penalties. In February 2002, the bank announced a settlement resolving all class-action lawsuits, agreeing to pay $333.2 million to former NationsBank shareholders and $156.8 million to former BankAmerica shareholders. The bank did not admit wrongdoing in the cases.

Problems were also emerging with one of First Union's acquisitions.

In September 1998, an internal "risk diagnostic" report on the Money Store delivered a harsh assessment of the company First Union had purchased months earlier. "Significant issues have been identified relating to fair lending and consumer compliance practices at TMS," stated the report, which was developed by First Union's internal audit department and outside auditors at KPMG. "While we noted weaknesses in several areas of the business, the most common element missing in the Money Store is a solid risk management process."

The bank's third-quarter earnings release in October 1998 didn't mention any problems with the Money Store. But in November, mortgage head Jim Maynor acknowledged trouble in the securitization market in an *Observer* interview. After market turmoil that summer, investors were no longer interested in buying risky subprime-backed securities. That meant subprime lenders were filing for bankruptcy, laying off employees, and closing offices.

Overall, though, First Union was performing well. Executives had even begun mulling the construction of a new building that would top Bank of America's

60-story headquarters. First Union's buildings were running out of room. Crutch-field thought the bank could handle a building of 80 to 90 stories. It selected an architecture firm. Renderings depicted what an *Observer* architectural critic later called a "rocket ship of a building touching the sky at 84 stories." The structure was slated to displace the 12-story tower that had been the bank's new home back in the 1950s.

As the year closed, First Union was completing an ambitious overhaul of its branch network in a project dubbed "Future Bank." The branches would be filled with colorful signs and greeters who steered customers to phone banks, ATMs, or tellers, if needed. The goal was to deploy more salespeople pitching loans, mutual funds, and other products. Branches were becoming stores, not just transaction centers.

On January 14, 1999, the bank reported record operating earnings for 1998 of $3.7 billion, up 27 percent from 1997. But less than two weeks later, it released stunning news: It was back-pedaling on 1999 profit estimates because of a sof-tening economy, spending on investments, and a change in accounting practices related to the Money Store. Four months later, First Union issued another profit warning, citing problems with the CoreStates acquisition and the Future Bank makeover.

The CoreStates takeover had sparked a huge backlash in Philadelphia, espe-cially after account glitches hit customers during system conversions. Since the deal closed in April 1998, First Union had shed 400,000 of CoreStates' 2 million customers. Even the renaming of the CoreStates Center, the arena home of the Flyers and 76ers, earned derision. In Philadelphia, the First Union Center quickly became known as the "FU Center." First Union's Future Bank initiative was also irritating customers who wanted to talk to tellers in person, not on the phone.

The projected drop in earnings shattered the bank's credibility with investors and spurred speculation that First Union could be an acquisition target. Since the first profit warning, the bank's stock had fallen nearly 20 percent. "They did too much too fast," Tom McCandless of CIBC World Markets commented at the time. "What it boils down to is that somebody didn't have accountability for the numbers. . . . Nothing more, nothing less."

In July, First Union shook up its management ranks. President John Georgius was retiring at year's end. Ken Thompson, 48, head of the bank's growing capital markets unit, would succeed him, becoming Crutchfield's heir apparent. Geor-gius had been a key player in the bank's growth but also an architect of the Future Bank initiative. Now, he was widely seen as taking the fall for the bank's problems.

George Kennedy Thompson grew up in the textile and tobacco town of Rocky Mount in eastern North Carolina. While the community missed out on the prosperity that had reached the state's bigger cities, it served as a surprising cradle for prominent businesspeople and politicians, including future JPMorgan Chase & Company CEO William Harrison and future North Carolina governor Mike Easley.

Thompson described Rocky Mount in the 1950s and 1960s as reminiscent of *Leave It to Beaver*. His father, Maynard Thompson, a manager in a textile mill, coached his youth sports teams while his teacher mother, Stacy Kennedy Thompson, ran the house. The short, stocky Thompson was one of the town's best athletes.

"I grew up in a family where my parents were very involved," he told the *Observer*. "I had two brothers. The three boys were the center of attention. Our parents' lives revolved around us. I felt loved and cared for and challenged. My parents were big on making sure we had big goals and that we worked hard, so I've got a lot of traditional values."

Sports played a big role in Thompson's school years. "I played baseball, basketball and football in high school, played tennis in the summers," he said. "I guess I've got all those values that say work hard and you'll get rewarded. Follow the golden rule; treat people like you want to be treated. Be honest."

Thompson was about seven years younger than William Harrison, the future JPMorgan CEO, but he was a good friend of Harrison's sister. "I first remember Ken Thompson because we had a basketball goal behind our house where all the kids would come on weekends to play," Harrison told the *Observer*. "Ken was a great athlete, and he'd come down and play even as a young guy. He was an outstanding student, athlete, leader in high school in Rocky Mount." On the field, Thompson could be intense, chewing out football players who didn't give their all, teammate Mike Easley later recalled.

Thompson won an Optimist Club speech contest at age 12 and later earned a prestigious Morehead Scholarship to the University of North Carolina, arriving on campus in 1969. Although he was chairman of a group that helped integrate Rocky Mount's high school, he stayed out of the counterculture revolution sweeping American universities. After graduating from Chapel Hill, he went home to help care for his mother, who soon died of cancer. Having no career plans in place, he pursued an MBA at Wake Forest University's business school, where his people skills and problem solving stood out among his classmates.

After Wake Forest, he landed an interview with First Union in Charlotte and in 1976 began a career in banking. He started out in the national division and two years later was sent to New York. The smart, gregarious Thompson was quickly noticed by top leaders. In the early 1990s, Crutchfield put him on a list of five possible successors and started rotating him through high-profile assignments such as president of Florida operations and co-director of capital markets. As he climbed in the company, a survey of First Union's top 30 leaders ranked Thompson number one in three categories: Integrity, leadership, and teamwork.

Thompson later recalled a key moment in his career when Crutchfield tapped him for a major post back at headquarters. Thompson and his wife, Kathylee, had just settled in Atlanta, where they bought an old home to remodel. "I was sound asleep, phone rang and it was Ed," Thompson remembered. "He said, 'I want you to come back to Charlotte and be head of human resources.' I had a lot of time with him in that 18 months where I could hear him talk about his philosophy and watch how he dealt with people around the company and it gave him a chance to know me better as well. I would say that was a turning point in my career."

When he was named president, it became clear Thompson was in line to succeed Crutchfield. But his ascension came faster than expected. In March 2000, Crutchfield stopped by Thompson's office and gave him jarring news: He had a curable form of lymphoma.

"Are you ready to run the bank?" Crutchfield asked an emotional Thompson.

"Yes, I am," Thompson replied. "But I didn't want to do it this way."

"I didn't want to do it this way either," the 58-year-old Crutchfield said.

Thompson officially took over as CEO at the April shareholders meeting. Crutchfield, who was staying on as chairman, wore a black-and-green First Union cap to hide hair loss caused by chemotherapy. Directors and top managers also donned hats in a show of support.

With Crutchfield in cancer treatment but still serving as chairman, Thompson launched a full-scale review of the company's strategy, calling in outside advisers from investment bank Credit Suisse First Boston, consulting firm McKinsey & Company, and investment bank Merrill Lynch.

Credit Suisse's bankers came to a radical conclusion: Unless a bank was in the top three in originating a type of loan, it broke even or lost money. That was because the lender could not get the necessary economies of scale to make enough profit in a competitive business. First Union had an enviable branch network but wasn't making enough money from its lending operations.

To tackle the Money Store problem, Thompson assigned one of his top lieutenants, David Carroll, also a Rocky Mount native, to a project First Union executives started calling the "search for the bottom." The examination turned up poor controls, lax accounting, and shriveling revenue. The initial due diligence team missed key red flags.

In June 2000, Thompson announced a bold restructuring of the company. First Union was shuttering most of the Money Store, slashing jobs, selling its mortgage-servicing business to Wells Fargo, and looking for a buyer for its credit card unit. The price tag: A net $2.8 billion after-tax charge against earnings.

In making the moves, Thompson was declaring one of his mentor's acquisitions a failure. Selling the mortgage operation also hit the legacy of Crutchfield's predecessor, Cliff Cameron, who had sold his mortgage company to First Union.

Plans for a new skyscraper also had been scrapped. "We're simply taking the organization that Ed built over 15 years through a lot of acquisitions and we're sort of chipping away the rough edges and the barnacles off it," Thompson said.

The bank announced that chief financial officer Bob Atwood and chief credit officer Mal Murray were leaving, signaling a further transition in leadership. Both executives had played major roles in the bank's big deals. Thompson said their retirements were long planned. Later in the year, he hired Bob Kelly as his new CFO, handing the former Toronto Dominion Bank executive the key task of rebuilding the bank's relationship with analysts burned by missed earnings forecasts.

With his cancer in remission, Crutchfield announced in October that he was cutting his final ties to the bank and officially stepping down as chairman in March 2001. He insisted he wasn't being forced out by disease or directors. It was time to make a clean break and let Thompson run the company.

As CEO of First Union, Crutchfield had rolled up more than 80 banks since 1984. The bank had grown from $7 billion in assets to $258 billion from Florida to Connecticut. He had fulfilled a vision of expanding operations geographically, as well as into new capital markets businesses.

His retirement agreement entitled him to a payment of $1.8 million per year for the rest of his life, plus use of First Union's aircraft for up to 120 hours per year for 10 years. (He gave up the aircraft perk a year or two later.) He owned about 1.25 million First Union shares in early 2001, according to a securities filing. In 1997, the board had awarded him a special grant of about 300,000 restricted shares worth $15 million at the time, vesting over six years.

At a meeting for senior leaders held in October at the Charlotte Convention Center, Crutchfield gave a farewell address. The bank, after some tough decisions, now had a "near-perfect" business model, but he acknowledged challenges ahead. In his choice of a successor, he gave himself an "A++," praising Thompson's character, personal courage to make tough decisions, and competitive nature. "Other leaders in the industry will be attracted to him," Crutchfield said. "I think that's very critical to this company's future."

In his remarks, Thompson called Crutchfield a "personal hero for us all," adding, "Few people in American business history have ever created such a clear and compelling vision and then been able to execute on it."

In an interview in late 2009, Crutchfield acknowledged problems with the Money Store and CoreStates acquisitions. But he placed those deals within a broader strategy to build a bank that would be a survivor in a consolidating industry.

"When you set out on a strategy to make a lot of acquisitions, you have to go down the road 10 to 15 years, know where you're trying to go," he said. "Not all are going to be 10s. Nobody is perfect. People would criticize me terribly. 'You paid too much.' They don't put it in context. They don't realize the whole is a lot greater than the pieces."

He said of CoreStates, "It wasn't a badly made deal. It was a badly integrated deal. No excuses."

The Money Store was a casualty of bad timing. "The business was cresting," he said. "The market went to pot. It wasn't as well run as we hoped it would be."

Crutchfield departed First Union with the company in a major rebuilding campaign. But he said his team had worked hard to carry out a successful vision. "I'm very proud of what we did," he said.

In January 2001, McColl confirmed that he would leave Bank of America soon after his old rival Crutchfield retired. Since taking over in 1983, McColl, 65, had built Bank of America from a $12 billion, two-state bank into a $642 billion, 21-state giant. But he, too, was departing a company struggling to digest a major deal.

In his retirement, McColl, under a consulting contract, would receive an office and 150 hours of corporate jet time per year for at least five years. At the end of 2001, he owned about 2.8 million Bank of America shares, according to a securities filing. In 1999, the bank's board had awarded him 600,000 restricted shares, worth $44.7 million at the time.

Ken Lewis, now president and chief operating officer, would take over at the April shareholder meeting. For years, he had been the man who made McColl's bold deals work. Now, he would get his chance to run the entire company.

Despite initial plans for McColl to stay longer, analysts had expected the move. Some even welcomed Lewis's focus on improving operations at a company cobbled together through years of deals. Longtime nemesis Tom Brown, now running his own hedge fund, even purchased stock in Bank of America, as well as First Union.

Kenneth Lewis was born in Meridian, Mississippi—the same birthplace as Cliff Cameron—because his hometown of Walnut Grove didn't have a hospital. His father, Vernon Kenneth Lewis, joined the army to escape work in the local sawmills. The family lived briefly in Germany before settling in the military town of Columbus, Georgia. Two bully brothers once ganged up on young Ken Lewis when the family was living in Germany. His mother, Byrdine, came out and told them they had to fight her son one at a time. He won both fights.

Lewis's parents divorced when he was young, after which his mother worked double shifts as a nurse as she raised him and his sister. Lewis suffered a serious back injury in a Pop Warner All-Star game, cutting short a budding football and baseball career. He worked odd jobs, peddling Christmas cards door to door, delivering the newspaper *Grit*, and selling shoes as a senior in high school. Small commissions on each pair of shoes taught Lewis the importance of high-volume sales. He put himself through Georgia State and graduated into a booming job market in 1969. He preferred NCNB over General Electric and Shell Oil, as well as banks that included First Union and Wachovia.

"There was something about NCNB that seemed to relate to my own personality," he told the *Observer*. "That they weren't bluebloods like at the time Wachovia was. There was a spirit of 'We don't care who your family was or where you went to school, but how you perform.' I thought that was the best environment for me."

At NCNB, Lewis started out as a credit analyst and landed in McColl's national division. In 1977, he took over the international division in New York even though he didn't know anything about the business. He studied at New York University at night, struggled to get a mortgage loan on his $30,000 salary, and fought off feelings of isolation. He began running to take his mind off the tension.

Lewis's big break came when Buddy Kemp pegged him to run Florida operations. McColl sent for Lewis to give him the news. "When can you go?" McColl asked.

"When you're finished talking to me," replied Lewis, never known as a loquacious conversationalist.

By the early 1990s, he was the favorite to succeed McColl. When McColl named Lewis president in 1993, NationsBank employees were already calling him "Little Hugh." After years working in other cities, Lewis returned to Charlotte for the post. He made news when he and his wife, Donna, bought the Morrocroft mansion, which had long been in the family of former North Carolina governor Cameron Morrison, for just under $1.1 million. Though his clear path to the top was slowed by the competition with Hance and then the BankAmerica deal, Lewis was back in the president's job by January 1999.

Especially in contrast to the gregarious McColl, Lewis had an aloof, even cold personality. If McColl walked into a room of 30 people, he would talk with all of them. Lewis would settle in with one or two. As he moved up through the company, his advisers placed him in situations where he could thrive. Whereas McColl could lead an all-day off-site meeting, Lewis would pop in for quick appearances with small groups. One of his early allies was personnel executive Steele Alphin, who worked with Lewis in Florida. To polish his speaking skills, Lewis would record himself and share the tapes with Alphin for his critiques. They also golfed together as Lewis worked on a way to ease relationships with board members and business peers. Even as he became a key lieutenant for McColl, Lewis fretted over the inevitable comparisons with his boss, said a former bank executive. "Things Hugh did well weren't his thing," the executive said.

By the time the April 2001 annual meeting arrived, Bank of America's shares had slumped more than one-fourth since the NationsBank–BankAmerica deal was announced. But the tone of McColl's final meeting was one of celebration for a CEO whose defiant personality had become emblematic of the company he helped create. In his farewell speech, McColl acknowledged that the merger's fallout had caused "great pain and suffering, mainly to our shareholders, but to the management and associates as well." But, he added, "we pushed on to the finish line and the last merger . . . has, in fact, given us a framework from which we will be successful."

At the meeting, McColl formally handed the company over to Lewis. "I'm going to join the ranks of shareholders who'll be looking for dividend increases and [earnings per share] gains," he said. "I know you'll give them to us. I have great confidence in you and your team." After a video tribute, a cart was wheeled out carrying McColl's retirement gift—a football-sized crystal hand grenade.

Following the meeting, a crowd of employees spilled into Founders Hall, the mall attached to the headquarters building constructed during McColl's tenure. Wearing a black shirt, jeans, cowboy hat, and boots, he came down the stairs, fists raised high, as the song "Stay" by Maurice Williams blasted from huge speakers.

In an interview afterward, McColl said he had no regrets about a career full of buying banks. "We're glad about all of it," he said. "Even the bad parts. [It's] part of living."

Two titans who constructed their banks through daring acquisitions had left the scene. Now, their replacements were expected to be the caretakers who stitched together far-flung operations.

Chapter 4

THE NEW WACHOVIA

Since taking over as CEO in 1994, Bud Baker had maintained the conservative tradition that earned Wachovia nicknames like "the Tiffany bank," while also pushing into new territory. Under Baker, the Winston-Salem bank entered Florida and Virginia, started selling mutual funds and investment banking services, and laid out a strategy to create a wealth management unit with a national scope.

By 2000, his predecessor, John Medlin, had stepped down from the board. Wachovia was fully in the hands of an unlikely banker often described as a Renaissance man for his wide range of interests. The former marine captain enjoyed trout fishing, opted for a pickup truck while touring his farm north of Winston-Salem, and juggled half a dozen books at a time.

Leslie "Bud" Baker, Jr., grew up in Lovettsville, Virginia, a tiny town near the Maryland border. His mother died when he was 12. His father was a longtime railroad man. When Baker was young, he worked odd jobs from painting houses to digging graves. At the University of Richmond, he majored in English and initially planned to be a teacher. But in 1964, he entered the marines and went to Vietnam. While in the service, he took his business school admission test in a Quonset hut at the end of a runway in Danang.

After graduating from the University of Virginia in 1969, Baker went to work at Wachovia as a commercial banking trainee in the loan administration office. At the time, the bank had $1.8 billion in assets, compared with $68.8 billion by 2000. As CEO, Baker had to contend with critics who said the bank was too conservative and made its acquisitions after rivals had already passed it by. "I think wanting to be the biggest is a perfectly legitimate goal. But that's not what we're about," Baker said in May 2000.

By June of that year, the conservative Wachovia ran into problems of its own. The bank said it would take a special $200 million charge to protect against losses and nonperforming loans. And in August, it revealed it was cutting 1,800 jobs—or 8.5 percent of its work force—to reduce costs and boost earnings.

Like Ken Thompson at First Union, Baker began evaluating his bank's strategy. Among the conclusions: The bank needed more mutual funds as an alternative place for customers to deposit their money, it required a bigger branch footprint to spread out costs, and it needed a stronger investment banking business as Wall Street firms increasingly poached bread-and-butter corporate customers. Baker also wondered if the bank had the management talent it needed.

Increasingly, a merger with another big bank looked like the best option. Baker mulled potential partners ranging from Pennsylvania's PNC Financial to New England's Citizens Financial Group to Atlanta's SunTrust Banks, Inc. In 2000, he was also approached by John Allison, CEO of Winston-Salem's BB&T Corporation, which had become a sizable North Carolina bank after a 1995 merger. The two companies could cut overlapping operations in Winston-Salem and build on varying strengths in small business and corporate lending, Allison thought. Baker declined the invitation.

The Wachovia CEO "was interested in creating a bigger institution than the Wachovia/BB&T merger would create," Allison said later, "and also thought Wachovia was more sophisticated than BB&T, as BB&T had grown from a small farm bank in a relatively short timeframe."

SunTrust had long been considered the most likely match for Wachovia, pairing two venerable Southern institutions that had followed a more conservative growth path than Charlotte's rival banks. The potential pairing was called the "Coke-and-smoke" merger because of SunTrust's ties to Coca-Cola and Wachovia's connections to R. J. Reynolds. Back in 1997, Wachovia and SunTrust had performed due diligence on each other but couldn't work out their differences.

As Baker pondered possible matches, longtime advisers at investment bank Credit Suisse First Boston suggested the Wachovia CEO also talk to First Union. Credit Suisse knew both companies well and thought the CEOs' personalities would be a fit. The deal also offered cost cutting from trimming overlapping work forces and branch networks. In the final years of his tenure, Ed Crutchfield had talked informally with Baker, but the theoretical musings of two avid fly fishermen hadn't progressed beyond that.

Starting in September 2000, Thompson and Baker had several preliminary conversations about a possible combination. They agreed that a merger-of-equals approach would be best. Advance scouts from both sides began discussing the possible pricing of a deal and the timing for due diligence. But before the talks entered the next stage, the two CEOs pulled the plug, contending they preferred to focus on their cost-cutting initiatives.

In early November, Baker met in Atlanta with SunTrust counterpart Phil Humann. By the following month, they sketched the outline of a merger of equals.

The combined company would be called Wachovia but be based in Atlanta. Baker would be CEO for the first two years. Humann would take over after that. On Saturday, December 9, the two banks signed a confidentiality agreement, and the CEOs' lieutenants and advisers met to discuss credit and financial due diligence issues.

SunTrust executives later said the negotiations were on track for an announcement on Monday, December 18. But doubts were emerging on the Wachovia side. For one, SunTrust had dismissed a request to use a type of accounting in the merger that would allow Wachovia to sell off its credit card unit. Wachovia executives also became worried about SunTrust's earnings prospects and about strategy disagreements. SunTrust later contended the banks had a dispute over how the wealth management business would be organized but said it was willing to shift to Wachovia's approach.

On December 14, Baker called off the discussions and informed his board.

Ken Thompson found himself in what would normally be enemy territory on a Sunday morning in early 2001. Dressed in khakis and a casual shirt, he was sitting at the oval conference table on the 27th floor of Baker's Winston-Salem headquarters. It was Thompson's first visit to Baker's office. The Wachovia CEO gave him a tour of his paintings by Carolinas artists.

After the four-hour meeting, Thompson drove home to Charlotte. He was consumed by, but also nervous over, the "compelling" idea of a merger. Doing such a deal would impact thousands of employees. Baker was also excited but worried about the fallout for Winston-Salem.

As the talks moved into the spring, secrecy increased. For one meeting, Thompson chose a Comfort Inn in Salisbury, located off I-85 between Charlotte and Winston-Salem. Baker's black BMW and Thompson's black Lexus stood out in a parking lot mostly empty except for construction workers' trucks. During one break, Thompson asked a First Union employee assisting with the meeting what he thought about changing the bank's name to Wachovia. The employee didn't think it was a problem: First Union was a pretty generic name, but Wachovia was distinctive.

The banks' boards began considering the deal as Easter weekend approached. Board members including Duane Ackerman, the CEO of regional phone company BellSouth Corporation, pushed for a higher price. At Wachovia's request, First Union agreed to increase the exchange ratio to two shares of First Union stock for each Wachovia share, up from 1.9 First Union shares. Wachovia also would pay a special dividend of 48 cents per share before the deal closed. The extra amount was designed to equalize the dividend for Wachovia shareholders who would see a small dilution to their current payout.

In return, First Union wanted a "poison pill" measure that would allow it to buy 19.9 percent of Wachovia's shares if another suitor made a play for Wachovia. At the board meeting, Wachovia's advisers discussed the possibility that SunTrust might make a hostile offer, but they didn't think the Atlanta bank could offer a bid that would top First Union's by enough and still be worthwhile for SunTrust.

On Saturday, April 14, SunTrust CEO Humann called Baker to say he had heard rumors of a First Union deal with Wachovia. He'd gotten a tip from an investment banker on Good Friday. SunTrust was still interested in talking, Humann said. Baker said he was aware of rumors on message boards and chat rooms.

While shaving before work Monday morning, Humann received confirmation of the news he expected: Wachovia and First Union had agreed to a $13.4 billion merger to create the nation's number-four bank, totaling $324 billion in assets. The headquarters would be in Charlotte; the name would be Wachovia. The timing echoed the Easter Monday unveiling three years earlier of the NationsBank–BankAmerica blockbuster.

The bank chiefs selected the New York Palace hotel for the announcement. Nearly a year earlier, Thompson had arrived at the same location to disclose First Union's dramatic overhaul. "This is a different kind of merger," Thompson told investors. "It's a superior transaction to others in the industry—certainly to other deals we have done in my own company."

In what executives unofficially called "the new Wachovia," the banks planned to eliminate $890 million in annual expenses, largely by cutting 7,000 jobs from a combined work force of 90,000. Baker, 58, would serve as chairman; Thompson, 50, would become president and CEO. Among the next 12 top executives, seven would be from First Union and five from Wachovia. The board would be split, nine directors from each side.

First Union was paying $63.84 per share, a 6 percent premium over Wachovia's previous closing price. Baker made it clear he didn't consider the deal a sale, deflecting criticism that he sold the bank cheaply. His company could have remained independent, Baker insisted. "There's absolutely no force whatsoever that would compel us to sell the company or do something like this," he said.

Hugh McColl later advised Thompson not to call the deal a merger of equals, having learned his lesson with the BankAmerica union. "You are acquiring them," McColl said. "You are not having a merger of equals. It's something you wish you hadn't said but you say it. A merger of equals means you got it cheaply. It makes people feel better."

John Medlin, who had left the Wachovia board in 2000, said he was supportive of the deal because his successor, Baker, backed it. The longtime Wachovia leader also knew Thompson from the Wake Forest University Board of Trustees. The First Union CEO was "very sensible and down to earth," said Medlin, whose hometown of Benson was just down I-95 from Thompson's native Rocky Mount. Thompson "seemed to be our kind of person," he said.

Medlin, however, gave Thompson a not-so-subtle reminder that CEOs needed to keep their egos in check as they ran their institutions. After the merger announcement, he sent Thompson a crass cartoon that showed McColl and Crutchfield boasting about the size of their bank towers. Nathan Tothrow, a former Wachovia employee and former cartoonist for the *Charlotte Observer*'s Gaston section, had drawn the cartoon, although it never appeared in the paper. Tothrow showed it to a former boss, and it ended up in Medlin's hands. "Put this in your desk and look at it once in a while," read Medlin's note to Thompson.

On Sunday, May 13, Merrill Lynch investment banker Greg Fleming got an urgent call from Ken Thompson, the client he was advising in the First Union–Wachovia deal. Thompson had heard that SunTrust was considering an unsolicited bid for the Winston-Salem bank.

"They're going to jump the deal," Thompson said.

"What's the price?" asked Fleming, who ran Merrill's global financial institutions investment banking group. He had previously worked with Thompson on First Union's restructuring plan.

Thompson thought SunTrust's offer was at least $70. First Union's bid started at $63.84 and fluctuated with every trading day. Fleming noted the big difference between $70 and $75. If the offer was $70, he thought Wachovia and First Union had a chance to hold off the bid.

Inside SunTrust, executives and directors had debated extensively over whether or not to make a contentious bid, John Spiegel, the bank's CFO at the time, later said. In the end, they decided it was too good of a combination to take a pass. The banks "were so closely aligned it made all the sense in the world," he said.

On Monday, May 14, SunTrust declared it was offering a total of $14.7 billion for Wachovia, about $70 per share. It would also increase its dividend to make it equivalent to Wachovia's. SunTrust's bid was more lucrative, although the offers narrowed as SunTrust's shares sank and First Union's rose.

The combined company's headquarters would be in Atlanta. SunTrust said it would cut $500 million in annual expenses, likely meaning fewer job losses. It didn't have a Carolinas presence and so had less overlap to trim.

First Union issued a statement reiterating its commitment to the deal but didn't say if it would up its offer. Wachovia didn't reject the SunTrust bid outright, saying its board would meet in the "near future" on the proposal.

Although SunTrust was making a rare hostile bid for a bank, CEO Humann didn't consider his offer unfriendly. "This is not a hand grenade–throwing exercise," he said. "This is not someone completely unfamiliar coming in from the outside. The hostile offer came April 16," when First Union had also made its bid.

SunTrust said it planned a court challenge to the provision allowing First

Union to buy 19.9 percent of Wachovia's stock. But to encourage First Union to go away, SunTrust said it was prepared to pay a $400 million "breakup" fee.

Within days, Thompson and Humann were dueling in newspaper ads and at investor conferences. In a full-page ad, Humann claimed his deal was the "superior transaction" for North Carolina, claiming SunTrust would cut fewer employees and be a better partner with the state's communities. At an investor conference, Thompson suggested SunTrust would gut "the entire headquarters function" of Wachovia and hurt the Carolinas. "I suggest to you that the SunTrust proposal is about getting bigger, not better," he said.

To combat personal criticism, Wachovia's Baker gave up half a million dollars in extra annual retirement pay that could have resulted from the deal. Under his current contract, Baker, who was about to turn 59, was to receive $1.5 million a year in supplemental retirement benefits. The merger agreement with First Union, however, would have given him $2 million a year.

On May 22, Wachovia's directors met for five hours in the 27th-floor boardroom of the Winston-Salem bank's headquarters. Earlier that day, First Union had sweetened the deal by offering shareholders two dividend options worth the $2.40 per year that Wachovia currently paid. By a 14–1 vote, the board rejected SunTrust's offer and stood by the First Union agreement. The directors contended the SunTrust offer would mean slower growth for the company and a more difficult integration. Morris Offit, a director who had sold his wealth management firm to Wachovia and was a major shareholder, backed SunTrust's bid.

"Our board's view is the First Union transaction is overwhelmingly positive for our shareholders, customers and the communities we serve," Baker said after the meeting. Thompson called the move "great news for us and even better news for Wachovia shareholders."

The dispute soon headed to court. SunTrust was protesting the breakup fee, while Wachovia and First Union accused SunTrust of infringing on their deal. Both sides prepared to send ballots to Wachovia shareholders, creating a rare bank merger proxy fight. Wachovia wanted shareholders to vote for the deal. SunTrust wanted them to vote against it, keeping alive the hope of a SunTrust–Wachovia combination.

By late May, SunTrust decided not to increase its bid, leaving it to the vying CEOs to crisscross the country like politicians, meeting with large and small investors to pitch the competing deals. The banks' stock prices were key to the deal, leading Thompson to frequently check the terminal in his office for the latest numbers. SunTrust's deal was a little less than 4 percent higher than First Union's. Humann acknowledged that a spread of 6 to 7 percent would make the decision easier for shareholders.

"We constantly debated about whether to sweeten the pot and what would the reaction of First Union be," Spiegel, the SunTrust CFO, said.

· · ·

As the battle moved into summer, the barbs began to fly, an unusual occurrence, at least in public, for the supposedly genteel world of Southern banking. In one of the sharper ripostes, SunTrust sent a letter to the Federal Reserve alleging First Union used aggressive accounting to inflate its earnings in 2000. One Sunday morning over coffee at Starbucks, First Union CFO Bob Kelly mapped out one of his bank's ads, which listed six things that First Union didn't expect to be covered in SunTrust's second-quarter earnings report. One of the items: "We believe SunTrust's earnings momentum has 'hit the wall.' "

The First Union team held morning and afternoon conference calls Monday through Friday, plus a weekend session, to plot strategy. Merrill's Greg Fleming contracted Lyme disease that summer but initially didn't realize it. He attributed his exhaustion to the marathon work in the proxy fight. The finish line was the August 3 Wachovia shareholders meeting, at which investors would decide whether to accept or reject First Union's offer.

Another key adviser was Rodgin Cohen, a top national banking lawyer with the New York firm of Sullivan & Cromwell, who had been advising First Union on deals since the early 1980s. On one Friday-afternoon conference call in June, Cohen proposed lobbying for a change to North Carolina law that would make it more difficult for SunTrust to call a special shareholder meeting if the First Union deal was voted down. Such a meeting could be used to add new directors favorable to SunTrust's bid. Cohen said he thought the bill could be approved the following week. Fleming put the call on mute and turned to Eric Heaton, another Merrill banker working on the deal.

"Is he serious?" Fleming asked, skeptical the legislature could move that fast.

"He sounds like it," Heaton responded.

The Wachovia team, including advisers at Credit Suisse First Boston, wasn't particularly fond of the idea, considering the proposal a distraction that might irritate undecided shareholders. But by the end of the next week, the law passed. "Both corporations involved in this merger are North Carolina corporations, this is a North Carolina legislature and in its wisdom, we want to look at what is best for North Carolina," said State Senator Fletcher Hartsell, a Republican from Cabarrus County.

Ahead of the Friday, August 3, showdown, the First Union–Wachovia pairing gained momentum as an influential proxy advisory firm backed First Union's bid. Wachovia and First Union executives expected a close win, although Thompson worried about a "doomsday scenario" in which a large institutional shareholder reversed course. SunTrust executives knew their bank was the dark horse but weren't sure of the outcome until the night before, after a few big investors shared their votes.

Wachovia's annual shareholders' meetings were typically staid affairs. Usually, fewer than 100 people showed up. But for this gathering at Winston-Salem's Benton Convention Center, shareholders flew and drove in from around the country.

Before the meeting, shareholders, many of them retirees, recalled the memories of ancestors from whom they had inherited their Wachovia stock. Legendary leaders such as Colonel Francis Fries and Robert Hanes were also mentioned. A few shareholders said they wished Wachovia directors had negotiated a higher price for the bank, or that SunTrust's pursuit had sparked a bidding war. First Union's bid was now worth $14.5 billion and SunTrust's $15.4 billion.

Security was tight. Some attendees stood along the back wall of the packed meeting room. Wachovia employees watched by video feed. Baker, flanked by enormous video screens, opened the meeting by welcoming shareholders to what he called "a historic event."

During the meeting, some opponents lamented First Union's customer service woes. "They are of a big-bank mentality," Strother Smith, a shareholder from Abingdon, Virginia, said of First Union. "I think we ought to have Wachovia stay Wachovia."

John Medlin rose to endorse the deal. The merger with First Union was "consistent with the long expansion of Wachovia," he said. Attendees clapped longer for Medlin than for any other speaker.

The proxy contest ended at 11:27 A.M. when Baker closed the shareholder voting and announced the deal's victory, based on a preliminary ballot count. Upon his words, the room crammed with nearly 1,000 shareholders erupted in long, loud applause. "Occasionally in a lifetime, there's a chance to do something bold, imaginative and exciting," Baker told the audience.

After the meeting, SunTrust vice chairman Ted Hoepner, who was in the audience, officially gave up the fight. Fleming was home in New York recuperating from his Lyme disease. He received an e-mail from Merrill colleague Eric Heaton: "SunTrust concedes."

The First Union–Wachovia team believed the two banks had outworked and outmaneuvered SunTrust during the summer-long spat. First Union and Wachovia executives logged countless plane flights to meet with investors around the country and in Europe. In the post-vote celebration, the bank printed up mock concert tour T-shirts that highlighted the cities visited and distributed them to key players as mementos. The fight against a common enemy helped the two companies come together, both sides felt.

First Union's offer may also have been helped by stock purchases made during the proxy fight. In 2004, Wachovia agreed to pay $37 million to settle allegations that it did not properly disclose purchases made in connection to the merger. In its complaint, the SEC said Wachovia should have released more information about its purchase of $555 million in First Union stock between May 2, 2001, and June 28, 2001. The stock purchases likely propped up First Union's share price, which made its bid more attractive to Wachovia shareholders voting on the merger, the SEC said. In the settlement, Wachovia neither admitted nor denied wrongdoing.

First Union's victory cemented Charlotte's status as a key banking center and eliminated a chance for Atlanta to raise its profile. The vote eased concerns that First Union could become a takeover target itself and was a high-profile accomplishment for a new CEO. The union became official on September 1, 2001. First Union traded in its "FTU" ticker symbol for Wachovia's "WB" and appointed the combined board's members. Offit, who had favored the SunTrust combination, wasn't among them.

Not much else changed. To avoid the glitches of the CoreStates deal, branches and signs would be switched over during a three-year period. Baker even called to get tips from Wells Fargo CEO Dick Kovacevich, who had meticulously integrated his Minnesota-based Norwest Bank Corporation into Wells starting in 1998. The First Union name, dating to 1958, would be gradually erased along the East Coast. A bank famous for its quick changeovers was learning to take it slow.

Chapter 5

EXPANDING EMPIRES

Ten days after the Wachovia deal closed, the September 11 terrorist attacks rocked the nation. Both Charlotte banks had employees in the World Trade Center towers in New York. Most escaped, but five from Wachovia and three from Bank of America perished. Ken Thompson was in New York on September 11 and ended up riding back to Charlotte in a hastily hired limousine.

In the wake of the attacks, Federal Reserve vice chairman Roger Ferguson, Jr., was on the phone with Bank of America and Wachovia, checking to see if they could open the next day and making sure they could cope with the delay in check processing caused by the grounding of the nation's air fleet. "The fact that we did not have to declare a banking holiday, that banks around the country opened, even in New York on September 12, was a force that helped to stabilize the macro-economics and allowed folks to focus on the specific repairs that had to be done," Ferguson said later.

Ken Lewis, CEO for less than six months, appeared on CNBC and ABC News three times after September 11, emphasizing that his bank was "open for business" and that it wouldn't desert New York City. He planned to continue expanding in the city and to build a high-rise building "over the next several years," he told Peter Jennings of ABC News. "New York City was the financial capital of the world the first part of this week, it is the financial capital of the world now and it will continue to be," Lewis said.

The way the attacks buffeted the economy tested both banks' new CEOs.

After taking over a company that had spent decades jumping from acquisition to acquisition, Ken Lewis turned inward at Bank of America, focusing on improving operations, boosting flagging customer satisfaction scores, and expanding through internal growth. Hugh McColl had assembled a giant bank with the potential to become a massive moneymaking machine. It was the new CEO's job to make it purr.

In his first significant move, Lewis decided in August 2001 to abandon two risky businesses: Auto leasing and subprime mortgage lending. The decision came with the hefty price tag of a $1.25 billion after-tax charge against third-quarter earnings. "The bottom line was these businesses are too volatile and don't produce attractive returns," Lewis said.

By late 2002, Bank of America hadn't birthed a major acquisition in more than four years, a surprisingly barren span for the deal-hungry company. Lewis snapped the streak in December with a rare foray outside the United States. Bank of America waded into international waters by agreeing to pay $1.6 billion in cash for a 24.9 percent stake in Mexico's third-largest bank, Grupo Financiero Santander Serfin. The idea was to partner with a local bank that could provide insights on serving the growing Latino market in the United States.

In the spring and summer of 2003, Lewis and CFO Jim Hance began work on another deal, striking up conversations with British bank Barclays PLC. The banks held meetings in New York, London, and Miami and were close to fleshing out the first major cross-Atlantic merger. The headquarters of the holding company would be in Charlotte, but United Kingdom operations would be headquartered in London. At the time, European banks were making excursions onto American soil, and Bank of America knew it was getting close to the 10 percent deposit cap in the United States.

But as the deal was coming together, Hance heard that FleetBoston Financial Corporation, New England's biggest bank, might be looking to sell and that Citigroup was the leading candidate. He went to see Fleet president Gene McQuade, whom he knew well because both executives had Cape Cod summer places. Hance made his pitch. "If you're really thinking of doing a deal you should think about us as opposed to Citi or whoever," Hance told McQuade. "We're easier to deal with. We're flexible on price. It could be a better answer for you than to be swallowed into Citi or something." Bank of America told Barclays it was heading in a different direction.

Another interested Fleet suitor was Wachovia, but Thompson wasn't willing to pay the premium Fleet was looking for, especially after stressing his commitment to affordable deals.

Heading into the fall, the talks between Bank of America and Fleet would play out over a dinner meeting in Cape Cod and at clandestine sessions in New York corporate apartments. As the discussions progressed, Hance and McQuade brought in their bosses, Lewis and Fleet CEO Chad Gifford.

As Lewis moved toward his first big deal, his campaign to create one of the world's most admired companies sustained a major setback. New York attorney general Eliot Spitzer shook up the normally mundane world of mutual funds in September 2003 when he reached a $40 million settlement with a New Jersey hedge fund for allegedly making illegal trades with major fund families, including Bank of America's Nations Funds. For Bank of America, it was a potentially embarrassing allegation for a company that had avoided Spitzer's investigation of biased Wall Street research. Earlier in the year, the bank had launched an advertising campaign with the tag line, "Higher Standards."

The mutual fund scandal didn't stop Lewis from sealing his first major deal. On Monday, October 27, 2003, Bank of America announced it was paying $47 billion for FleetBoston. It was the third-biggest bank deal as of that time, behind BankAmerica–NationsBank and Travelers-Citicorp. The union would create the nation's number-two bank. The combined bank's $933 billion in assets would bump it ahead of JPMorgan Chase but still leave it behind Citigroup.

The consumer-banking behemoth, which would keep Bank of America's name and headquarters, would have 5,660 branches and 16,500 ATMs. The 21-state franchise that stopped at Maryland would now add eight more states in New England and the mid-Atlantic region. Already in competition with Wachovia in six southeastern states, Bank of America would go head to head in four more along the East Coast: New York, Pennsylvania, New Jersey, and Connecticut.

"We are now truly the Bank of America," Lewis said at the New York announcement.

Lewis would become CEO of the new company; Fleet CEO Chad Gifford would stay on as chairman. Bank of America expected to trim $1.1 billion in annual expenses but didn't give details on possible job cuts. While the CEOs were all smiles, Wall Street was wary of the deal. Bank of America was paying a huge 43 percent premium for the franchise. Its stock plunged more than 10 percent to $73.57.

In the combined company, Gene McQuade was slated to become president and Fleet's Brian Moynihan head of wealth and investment management, while Rich DeMartini, who headed the unit that included Bank of America's mutual funds, quietly retired. The board would have 12 members from Bank of America and seven from Fleet. In the merger negotiations, Bank of America had agreed to base wealth management and other businesses in Boston and pledged to keep the same level of employment and charitable giving in New England.

As Bank of America expanded over the years, it had established major outposts in cities such as St. Louis and Dallas. Now, it was migrating north with a major anchor in Boston and an expanded presence in New York. Fleet came with sponsorship ties to the Boston Red Sox and the New York Yankees and even a giant electronic billboard in Times Square.

This was just the beginning of Bank of America's Big Apple ambitions. Not long after the Fleet deal, Lewis, not known for wandering from his 58th-floor perch in the bank's headquarters, popped his head into a staff meeting under way in a large 57th-floor conference center nicknamed "the War Room." The executives in the meeting looked up quizzically at their boss. In his grip was a rendering of the bank's planned skyscraper in New York, the tower Lewis had alluded to after the September 11 attacks. "I have to show this to you," he said. The crystalline Midtown Manhattan tower, to be known as "the Bank of America Tower at One Bryant Park," would become the city's second-tallest structure, after the Empire State Building. The total cost: $1 billion.

The Fleet purchase became official on April 1, 2004, making Bank of America the nation's second-biggest bank—until a pending JPMorgan Chase–Bank One merger. Before the deal closed, Bank of America and Fleet resolved the probe of both companies' mutual fund operations. The two banks would cough up $675 million in fines, restitution, and reduced fees in settlements with Spitzer and the SEC. They neither admitted nor denied wrongdoing.

Less than a week later, Lewis was in New York to mark the purchase on the floor of the New York Stock Exchange, where he got a tour from John Thain, the exchange's CEO. The mood inside Bank of America, however, was much less celebratory. For the first time, the bank detailed the acquisition's toll on employees. It planned to eliminate 12,500 jobs, or about 7 percent of the combined company's work force of more than 180,000 employees. Later in the year, Bank of America said it planned to eliminate an additional 4,500 jobs nationwide.

When the cuts began hitting New England later in the year, the bank faced a backlash from local politicians, who questioned its pledge to preserve employment in the region. Bank of America moved to quell the storm by announcing plans to base more wealth and investment management executives in Boston. The unit's leader, Brian Moynihan, was now among a slimmer group of top Fleet executives after early departures by Gene McQuade and others. At the end of 2004, Chad Gifford announced he would step down as chairman but remain on the board.

At Wachovia, Ken Thompson proceeded with the careful First Union integration, which even included the blending of the banks' green and blue colors in the new logo. The company was merging operations in phases up the East Coast. In the Northeast, ads featured a pronunciation guide for the bank's funny-sounding name: *Wa-ko-vee-ah.*

The Wachovia CEO also made major strides in reviving a customer service reputation sullied by First Union's troubled CoreStates acquisition. Dropping the First Union name was a good first step, but the bank also ramped up customer surveys, implemented new compensation schemes, and instituted high-level service reviews. In 2002, Wachovia climbed to the top of the American Customer Satisfaction Index rankings for big banks, a spot it would hold for years to come.

During the integration, Bud Baker took the merger-of-equals concept seriously, looking out for the job security of former Wachovia executives. First Union had agreed to keep the Carolinas and wealth management headquarters in Winston-Salem and to maintain 3,000 to 3,300 jobs in the city. Still, that meant the loss of up to 1,300 jobs and the corporate headquarters. BB&T, continuing to expand under CEO John Allison, became Winston-Salem's biggest bank after the merger.

As the process progressed, it was clear that First Union executives had the upper hand in running the company. The operating committee that reported to Thompson and Baker was split eight from First Union (including the addition of community affairs executive Mac Everett) and five from Wachovia. Of the next 105 positions, 70 came from First Union. Of another 27 regional executives, 16 were from First Union.

By February 2003, Baker decided to retire. Under the merger agreement, he was slated to stay until 2004, but he had said he might leave sooner if the company was running smoothly. When he first plotted the merger back in 2001, Baker had penned a white paper that laid out a newly designed company formed of the best parts of First Union and Wachovia. He thought the new company was capable of double-digit earnings growth over a five- or six-year period. He expected the bank to focus on organic growth, rather than acquisitions, although he wasn't totally opposed to deals. He even pondered a pairing someday with Wells Fargo, a long-touted marriage of East and West coast stalwarts.

"I believe this will set the standard by which other combinations will be judged," Baker said in a statement as he handed his chairman's title to Thompson. The Colonel Fries desk went to Stan Kelly, a Wachovia executive who now ran wealth management for the combined company.

Sometime after the Wachovia merger, probably in 2002, Ed Crutchfield had encouraged Ken Thompson in one of their occasional phone calls to keep looking for more acquisitions.

"I urged him to do more deals," Crutchfield said. "I didn't think we had seen the full development of interstate banking. It wasn't in the context of a specific deal. You have to continue to grow. If that means more deals, it means more deals. I felt you either grow or you die."

In February 2003, Thompson reached a joint venture agreement with Prudential Securities that married Wachovia's brokerage business with Prudential's without paying a premium. While he was continuing his mentor's acquisitive legacy, it was another example of Thompson's search for shareholder-friendly deals that didn't dilute the stock of existing shareholders. The combined firm would have about 12,000 brokers, compared to about 14,000 at number-one Merrill Lynch.

In another conservative approach to expansion, Wachovia in February 2004 said it would enter Texas by building about 250 new branches, instead of snaring an existing bank. But Thompson would soon explore a way to speed up the bank's Lone Star State expedition. Starting in late 2003, he began talking to Wallace

Malone, Jr., CEO of Alabama-based SouthTrust Corporation. Malone's bank had a major presence in the Southeast, plus a growing toehold in Texas. In December, Thompson flew to Birmingham for a face-to-face meeting.

Malone was a legend in Southern banking, having built his family's bank in Dothan, Alabama, into a major regional player. In the process, Birmingham became the second-biggest banking center in the South, after Charlotte, serving as the home to four major regional banks. SouthTrust bragged that it was the first major non–North Carolina bank holding company to establish a presence in the Tar Heel State. At age 67, Malone was starting to consider retirement and wasn't sure he had a capable successor inside the bank. The talks broke off for a while, but in June 2004 Thompson agreed to pay $14.3 billion, a 20 percent premium, for SouthTrust. Malone would join the bank as vice chairman.

With the deal, Wachovia became the largest bank in deposits in the Southeast, leapfrogging Bank of America in an eight-state territory. It would slash 4,300 jobs in both franchises, Birmingham ultimately suffering the brunt of the cuts.

When Thompson became CEO of First Union in 2000, Hugh McColl, still leading Bank of America at the time, had visited him in his office. He reminded the rival bank leader of his place in the city's power structure. "You can be a great leader in this city, and I hope you will," McColl said.

In the following years, Thompson had emerged as the heir apparent to McColl in Charlotte, the business leader who was as comfortable emceeing a Habitat for Humanity homebuilding event as running a shareholder meeting. He landed a Wachovia-sponsored PGA Tour stop at Charlotte's Quail Hollow Club and promoted civic causes ranging from minority-owned businesses to arts projects.

In 2005, when Queens University of Charlotte was celebrating the 25th anniversary of its McColl School of Business, Thompson was the moderator of an "Evening with Hugh McColl." During the program, the younger Wachovia CEO acted mostly like an attentive student, picking the brain of one of the nation's best-known bankers. McColl praised the efforts of Thompson, Ken Lewis, and Duke Energy CEO Paul Anderson in becoming the next generation of community leaders. "We had good role models growing up," Thompson said.

While Bank of America remained a civic mainstay in Charlotte, Ken Lewis became known for dispatching lieutenants such as Jim Hance and Cathy Bessant to represent the company in various causes. He was focused on running a major bank.

Like their predecessors, the CEOs continued to work together on civic projects in Charlotte. In their most visible effort, Thompson and Lewis in 2002 brought a $100 million proposal to the Charlotte City Council that jump-started the building of a new center-city arena that later became the home of the Charlotte Bobcats NBA team.

The bank leaders also continued to transform the city's skyline. In April 2005, Wachovia said it would expand a planned project on South Tryon Street to include condominiums and museums. A bank tower on the site would eventually grow to 48 stories and be set to become Wachovia's new headquarters.

A couple of months later, Bank of America said it was building a 150-room Ritz-Carlton hotel across the street from its headquarters, a project that would later include a companion 32-story bank tower. Lewis and Marc Oken, the bank's new CFO after Hance retired, had discussed the Ritz idea on a flight home from New York. Oken spent the next few months making the bank's case to the luxury hotel chain. "The list of cities in the world that rate a Ritz-Carlton hotel is a short one," Lewis said at a Founders Hall announcement for employees and dignitaries.

In the 1950s, the two banks' buildings had straddled South Tryon Street. But in later decades, Bank of America migrated to the north side of Uptown, while Wachovia clung to the south. In Bank of America territory, dark-suited, nametag-wearing "associates" dominated. A few blocks to the south, more casually dressed Wachovia employees populated the bank's campus. Neither bank planted retail locations in each other's turf until Wachovia opened a glitzy ATM across the street from Bank of America's headquarters in 2006. Bank of America followed with a branch on Wachovia's side of town.

While the banks were mostly polite to each other in public, they couldn't resist occasional jabs. At Bank of America's 2005 annual shareholder meeting, Oken noted that the company's consumer bank had bigger revenues and profits than all of Wachovia. In 2007, when Wachovia was celebrating its sixth straight year as the number-one bank in the American Customer Satisfaction Index, general bank head Ben Jenkins urged an employee gathering to elicit a cheer that would resound up Tryon Street. "They know we are celebrating," Jenkins said. "They hate it."

In 2005, China's burgeoning middle class was an increasing draw for United States companies looking for new markets for expansion. Bank of America, which already had a small presence in China, had begun talking to government officials a year earlier about ways to get bigger. By June, it was negotiating an investment stake in Beijing-based China Construction Bank, one of the country's four big banks.

Ken Lewis flew over for the closing discussions with CCB chairman Guo Shuqing. The Charlotte bank initially agreed to spend $3 billion for a 9 percent stake in the bank, giving Bank of America a partner to help it pitch credit cards and other products to the country's 1.3 billion people. As in Mexico, Lewis's international strategy was to team with premier banks in growing countries.

Wachovia CEO Ken Thompson was also looking for deals. A month earlier, he had signaled interest in getting back into the credit card business. As part of its 2000 restructuring, First Union had sold its $5.5 billion credit card portfolio to MBNA Corporation, based in Wilmington, Delaware. A return to the business would bring more consumer loans and a bigger foothold in electronic payments.

A couple of weeks later, MBNA, now struggling, contacted Wachovia, looking to negotiate exclusively with the Charlotte bank. On June 16 and 17, Wachovia and MBNA executives met with investment bankers in Manhattan. After the talks ended, MBNA executives left the city by helicopter. Their chopper plunged into the East River, and CEO Bruce Hammonds and five others barely escaped. At the time, the company was mum about why executives were in New York.

The near-tragedy didn't slow the talks. Some executives inside Wachovia thought Thompson was edging toward a deal. One opponent was Wallace Malone, the former SouthTrust CEO. In a meeting in June, he laid out his concerns, including Wachovia's lack of current experience in the business and the fact that the deal would make credit cards a huge piece of the overall company.

MBNA was looking for a price of about $27 per share but was willing to go a little lower for Wachovia, which had developed a reputation as a skilled acquirer. MBNA's investment bankers, from the Swiss bank UBS, knew Thompson was holding a board meeting on June 21 and expected him to come back with a reasonable offer. The next day, Thompson instead proposed paying about $17 per share, shocking MBNA and its advisers. Thompson clearly had experienced a change of heart.

"We're pretty sure we can get something pretty quickly from your neighbors across the street," one of the UBS advisers said to Thompson. By Thursday, June 23, Ken Lewis and MBNA CEO Hammonds were dining at the Wilmington Club in Delaware. The merger was announced a week later, on Thursday, June 30.

Bank of America was betting once again on the American consumer, agreeing to pay $35 billion to become the nation's biggest credit card company, with $143 billion in balances. The price, $27.50 per share in stock and cash, was about a 30 percent premium over the previous day's closing price. Bank of America planned to eliminate 6,000 jobs.

Losing MNBA appeared to be a case of Wachovia's getting outfoxed by its crosstown rival. But to Thompson's defenders, it was a sign of his deal-making restraint. MBNA was certainly an easier meal to digest for the much bigger Bank of America. As a consolation prize, Wachovia was in line to receive a $100 million payment from Bank of America. As part of its agreement with Wachovia, MBNA was required to pay that sum if it ever sold itself to Wachovia's main rival. By November, with the MBNA deal expected to close January 1, 2006, Wachovia announced that it was cutting ties with the Delaware company and that it planned to launch its own credit card business. The $100 million would serve as seed money.

A few weeks after losing MBNA to Bank of America, Thompson told analysts he would continue doing deals, but only at the right price. "We are in a consolidating industry, and we will participate," he said. "I think we've proved beyond a shadow of a doubt that we will be very disciplined."

Chapter 6

WACHOVIA HEADS WEST

I n January 2006, Ken Thompson took the stage before hundreds of his peers. He was one of the keynote speakers at the North Carolina Bankers Association's economic forecast luncheon, held each January in the Triangle area. Amid the clinking of silverware and the buzz of lunch-table conversation, the event gave bankers from large and small institutions a chance to shake off their collective holiday hangover, network among friends, and gear up for the coming year.

Despite losing out on MBNA, Thompson strode to the podium after an impressive five-plus-year run as CEO. Wachovia was poised for another year of record profits, after making $6.6 billion in 2005. And it continued to lead the way in customer service. At a year-end gala, the *American Banker* newspaper had named Thompson its "Banker of the Year," citing his leadership in reviving the institution he took over in 2000. In particular, the industry publication praised the bank's "creativity and caution" in mergers and acquisitions. Still, throughout the industry, storm clouds were gathering. In particular, analysts increasingly worried that a white-hot housing market had to eventually fizzle, dousing the nation's economic growth.

In his remarks, Thompson acknowledged these worries but remained upbeat. Growth would slow just a bit in 2006 but continue at a healthy pace, he said. The housing market was likely to slow at some point, but he wasn't seeing it in Wachovia's business yet. As to the question of whether or not the nation faced a housing bubble, he said, "There are pockets around the country where we indeed are experiencing a bubble but happily in most places and particularly in North Carolina that is not the case."

One aspect of the housing market, however, did give him pause: The nation's growing wave of toxic home loans. In particular, Thompson warned of so-called option adjustable-rate mortgages, or option ARMs. With these loans, homeowners could end up owing more at the end of the month than the beginning, which could be a "tough situation" for customers and lenders particularly if home prices should fall.

"I have literally been amazed at the terms offered by some mortgage lenders, thankfully not at Wachovia and thankfully not so much in North Carolina," Thompson told the group.

The admonition wasn't a new one. Thompson had pointed out his bank's refusal to do the loans during an investor conference the previous fall. "We continue to be conservative in our underwriting standards here," he said at the Lehman Brothers Financial Services Conference in September 2005, adding, "We don't do option ARMs."

Thompson's stance was also in line with the growing concerns of federal regulators.

In a December 2005 speech to the Consumer Federation of America, new comptroller of the currency John Dugan warned about potential problems with option ARMs. These loans, the regulator of national banks reminded the audience, offered a variety of payment options, including a minimum payment that did not always cover the interest and fees due, resulting in an increase to the principal borrowers owed. This phenomenon was known in the industry as "negative amortization," or "neg am," a practice that Dugan said raised "significant safety and soundness and consumer protection concerns."

In addition to negative amortization, Dugan also worried about "payment shock." In a typical option ARM, borrowers could make low monthly payments for five years. But then in the sixth year, they had to start paying the full amount of interest each month and begin paying down the increased principal over the remaining 25 years of the mortgage. Their payments could jump by 50 percent or more. Later in December, the Office of the Comptroller of the Currency and other federal regulators issued proposed guidance for banks on nontraditional mortgage products that urged the institutions to maintain "prudent lending practices" that included sound loan terms and underwriting standards.

While other mortgage lenders pushed the envelope in a heated housing market, Thompson, echoing Dugan and other regulators, seemingly fired off a warning flare for the crowd of Tar Heel bankers.

Early in 2006, Thompson's executive suite lost two of its most vocal members.

First, former SouthTrust CEO Wallace Malone announced he was retiring at age 69. In the SouthTrust deal, Thompson had handed Malone a board seat and a vice chairman's role, although the Wachovia CEO made it clear he was in charge of the combined company. Still, the management team was losing an experienced leader who wasn't afraid to speak his mind and whose opinion carried weight because he was one of the company's biggest individual shareholders. The departure mostly generated attention because Malone was eligible for severance and other benefits that could total more than $134 million, under employment contracts forged at SouthTrust.

In a bigger upheaval, Bob Kelly, the CFO who had helped Thompson bring more transparency to First Union's books and regain the trust of investors, left at the end of January for the top job at Pittsburgh-based Mellon Financial Corporation. The native Canadian reportedly had been passed over for the top spot at Toronto Dominion Bank before coming to First Union in 2000. Becoming a CEO was a long-term-goal. Kelly, at 51, was close in age to Thompson and wasn't likely in line to become CEO at Wachovia.

Thompson and Kelly weren't always of the same mind when it came to strategy and outlook. Kelly was skeptical about mergers and acquisitions, feeling they often created no shareholder value or even destroyed it. He was also increasingly worried about the housing market, especially on the West Coast. Although he exhibited restraint as CEO, Thompson had grown up in Ed Crutchfield's deal-making machine. He had sounded positive notes about housing earlier that month at the bankers' conference. With Kelly's departure, Thompson was losing a confident executive who figured speaking his mind was part of a CFO's job.

His replacement was Tom Wurtz, who had joined the bank in 1994 and become treasurer five years later. Wurtz, more reserved than Kelly, was respected for his intellect. "Tom is one of the most astute financial professionals I have ever known," Thompson said in announcing the change. "I am confident that Tom's direction and guidance will ensure strategic continuity and sustained financial discipline."

In 2005, banks made big profits in a roaring housing market. Average home prices increased nearly 13 percent, climbing at a near-record pace. In California, they were up more than 117 percent over five years. But late in the year, loan delinquencies and foreclosures edged up. Economists warned of the possible risks of a slowing housing boom but didn't make apocalyptic predictions.

Thompson had shown discipline in passing on major deals like Fleet and MBNA, but investors still expected another big one, a fear that weighed on Wachovia's stock price. After passing up MBNA in June 2005, the CEO had laid out plans to launch the bank's own credit card unit, build 200 new branches in California, and hire 700 mortgage loan officers. The moves lacked the panache of a major deal but showed an appetite for riskier loans and westward expansion.

In September 2005, Wachovia announced back-to-back acquisitions of California niche lenders, snapping up Irvine-based Westcorp, a national auto finance company, for nearly $4 billion and San Diego–based AmNet Mortgage, Inc., for $83 million. Westcorp came with 19 branches in Southern California, making it Wachovia's first retail banking toehold on the West Coast. With both deals, Wachovia gained subprime loans made to borrowers with weak credit in return for higher interest rates.

Referring to Westcorp in a conference call with analysts, Wachovia general bank president Ben Jenkins said the purchase provided "a good opportunity to re-enter the nonprime lending market in a conservative and measured way." Thompson, in another call, emphasized the bank's "tremendous due diligence" in examining Westcorp's books for bad loans, a problem that had plagued the Money Store. "This is an entirely different ball game," Thompson said.

The bank's mortgage officials had suggested passing on the AmNet purchase, former executives said. But Wachovia's corporate and investment banking executives liked the company as a source of mortgages that could be packaged into securities. Thompson sided with the corporate and investment bank, the capital markets business he once presided over.

Wachovia's plan to wade cautiously into California and the mortgage business took a dramatic turn in late April.

At a charitable function on the evening of April 27, Sullivan & Cromwell attorney Rodge Cohen bumped into a Lehman Brothers investment banker working for Golden West Financial, an Oakland-based savings and loan that was considering a sale. Golden West had more than 100 branches in California and a major residential mortgage operation. Its primary product was option ARMs, the same category of loans Thompson had cautioned against at the North Carolina bankers' luncheon.

The next day, Lehman Brothers called Thompson to gauge his interest. Thompson then called the company's husband-and-wife co-CEOs, Herb and Marion Sandler, to say he was familiar with Golden West and interested in a possible deal. The two sides began outlining a transaction. A few days later, Thompson and new CFO Wurtz were on a plane for California.

In more than four decades at the helm of Golden West, the Sandlers had turned a savings and loan with a few locations into a top-20 mortgage lender with 285 branches. Herb Sandler and Marion Osher, both children of Jewish immigrant families, were making their way on Wall Street when their paths first crossed. He was a lawyer, and she was a bank analyst. They met through a mutual friend while staying in the Hamptons and were married in 1961.

The marriage soon became a business partnership. Marion studied promising savings and loans in California. Herb had clients in the state. They drove west in a Chevy convertible and bought the Oakland thrift that would become Golden West in 1963. Starting in 1981, the lender's core product became a type of adjustable-rate mortgage later known as the option ARM. The loans helped the company match the cost of its funds with the interest rates it charged customers. The Sandlers insisted that they made the loans the right way, touting features designed to protect consumers from payment shock.

Through economic ups and downs, the tall, sarcastic lawyer and the short, quiet analyst gained a reputation for running one of the nation's most successful financial institutions. The pair became known for creating a mom-and-pop culture that eschewed layoffs in a notoriously cyclical business. They focused relentlessly on curbing expenses and consistently produced double-digit annual profit growth. Herb was the face to Wall Street, while Marion oversaw the numbers. Famous for knitting at meetings, she kept a hand in many of the company's details, even helping design new bank branches.

During most of the company's history, its option ARMs had produced virtually no losses, even in major downturns. In a 2002 interview with *Fortune* magazine, Herb Sandler said that home loans were "the safest type of loans." He listed the products his company avoided: "No commercial loans, subprime, or loans for high-end homes in Silicon Valley." While the thrift made some acquisitions over the years, the pair avoided purchases that diluted earnings. Sandler kept words of wisdom from Warren Buffett in his wallet: "If a CEO is enthused about a particularly foolish acquisition, both his internal staff and his outside advisors will come up with whatever projections are needed to justify his stance. Only in fairy tales are emperors told they are naked."

But an aging leadership team and a dependency on just one type of mortgage led Golden West to explore its alternatives.

On Tuesday, May 2, 2006, Thompson and Wurtz met over sandwiches with the Sandlers and other Golden West executives at a downtown San Francisco hotel. Herb Sandler, in his mid-70s, said he and his team had investigated Wachovia and heard good things about Thompson and how he handled mergers. Thompson and Wurtz seemed to know a lot about the company's business already. It may have helped that Wurtz had previously worked for the Office of Thrift Supervision, which regulated Golden West. At the agency, the Sandlers' company was seen as a model lender.

Thompson soon grew comfortable with Golden West's nontraditional loans. Its option ARMs, known as "Pick-A-Payment" loans, gave customers four monthly payment options. Choosing the minimum payment, which didn't always cover all of the interest owed, could cause the loan balance to grow instead of shrink. But Golden West's loans included consumer safeguards such as a cap on how much the minimum payment could increase each year. Compared to its competitors' products, the loans also gave customers more time before the payment potentially recast—10 years, versus five or less. Unlike lenders that packaged their subprime and prime loans into mortgage-backed securities for investors, Golden West kept the loans in its own portfolio, a major incentive to make good mortgages.

In a letter to regulators in March 2006, Sandler had distinguished his company's approach from practices he said competitors were increasingly employing. He urged scrutiny of loans made with introductory teaser interest rates as low as 1 percent. He also raised alarms about the packaging of option ARMs into securities. "Our concern is that foolish lenders who eventually stumble under the weight of their missteps will bring down innocent borrowers with them and leave the rest of us to clean up the mess, as we have done before," Sandler wrote.

The meeting at the San Francisco hotel went well. The Wachovia contingent was impressed that Golden West executives weren't seeking "golden parachute" exit packages. The Sandlers, in fact, would ultimately negotiate an extra $50 million severance pool for non-senior executives. The meeting concluded with a deal well under way. Both sides moved into investigating each other's operations.

Thompson was back in Charlotte the next day, Wednesday, May 3, to play golf with PGA Tour star Vijay Singh in the Wachovia Championship pro-am event. In the coming days, he would juggle high-stakes deal making with his tournament-hosting duties. After playing with Singh, he even took time for a quick interview with *Observer* golf writer Ron Green, Jr. Thompson praised the officials who organized the tournament and discussed his favorite moments playing the Quail Hollow course.

"I'm a 10-handicapper so I'm an average golfer," Thompson said. "Two years ago in the pro-am I had three birdies on the front nine. That was a real thrill for me. Now, the back nine, I sort of came back to my handicap."

Would Thompson ever want to trade being a bank CEO for a spot on the PGA Tour? Green asked.

"Just standing on the first hole at a pro-am with everybody watching makes me realize I'm never going to quit my day job and try to be a golfer," Thompson said. "The pressure they're under is amazing to me."

During the rest of the week, Wachovia executives including chief risk officer Don Truslow and general bank head Ben Jenkins conducted due diligence on Golden West. Teams visited Golden West sites in California and Texas.

Top Wachovia mortgage executives were notified the purchase was in the works but weren't drawn deeply into the process or put in a position to recommend for or against the deal. That contrasted with earlier acquisitions investigated by the bank. Only a few months earlier, for example, mortgage executives had helped vet a possible investment in mortgage and auto lender GMAC and recommended against the move. Thompson didn't do the deal. Another top official who wasn't a player was David Carroll, who had helped with the Money Store and become a leader of the bank's merger integrations. A lawsuit would later allege that Carroll urged more due diligence but was told to stay out of it. Some technology executives who had helped check out past purchases also weren't clued in. "From everything I saw it was very different," one former executive said of Golden West. "It was a done deal. Make it work."

Wachovia reviewed Golden West's loan portfolio, but how deeply is unclear. Its executives were impressed with Golden West's low loan losses during a major California downturn in the early 1990s, when housing prices fell 20 percent and unemployment hit 10 percent. Thompson and other executives also took comfort in the relatively small size of Golden West's loans, which averaged around $338,000 in California. That stemmed from a strategy of avoiding the potentially more volatile high end of the housing market.

Had CFO Bob Kelly still been around, he was the person most likely to push back against Thompson over a large acquisition, former colleagues later believed. Some suspected he would have tried to stop the deal. In an August 2006 interview, Thompson discussed the importance of the CFO position. Asked if he had any weaknesses, he said he needed a "really good CFO, and I've got one, because I'm not a numbers guy."

Since the 2001 First Union–Wachovia merger, the dynamics of Thompson's operating committee—the top tier of management—had changed. When the team first came together in the wake of difficult times for both banks, executives were willing to discuss thorny issues. But over the years, the operating committee grew by adding executives who didn't report directly to Thompson. With more people at the table and the company performing well, debate ebbed, some former executives said. Some felt the team operated in segmented fashion, its leaders worrying only about their own businesses and not questioning the actions of others.

One area where Thompson made it clear he was in charge was mergers and acquisitions, some executives said. During the Golden West negotiations, he wasn't a pushover, pressing for a lower price at least once during the talks. Wachovia executives weren't particularly leery of a blowup in the loan portfolio. Instead, they focused on the company's future earnings projections and the expense of transforming savings-and-loan branches into full-fledged banking centers.

In a meeting in his Charlotte office, Thompson asked Tom Wurtz if he would do the deal at the original premium they had contemplated. When the Wachovia CFO said no, Thompson asked why not.

"I don't think it's worth it," Wurtz said.

Thompson agreed, realizing he would have to go back to the Sandlers. "I'm not looking forward to this call," he said.

In further talks on Friday and Saturday, the two sides agreed on a price equal to $81.07 per Golden West share in cash and stock. That was equal to a 15 percent premium over the Golden West closing price on Friday, May 5.

The Wachovia board met on the morning of Sunday, May 7. Thompson and his team made a final presentation to the board, including an assessment of credit quality and risk management. Providing the necessary fairness opinion, investment bankers from Merrill Lynch said the price of the deal was fair financially to Wachovia, based on assumptions as of that day, the standard caveat in such opinions.

The directors, who met at least three times during the due diligence period, had an extensive discussion, recalled former director Robert Brown, a public relations specialist in High Point, North Carolina. "The fact of the matter," he told the *Observer*, "is that when the discussion took place—go back and check the fact book—Golden West had one of the lowest loan default rates in the country." In addition to Golden West's mortgage operations, a "major consideration for us was that they had a lot of branches in California and the West," he added.

The directors unanimously approved the acquisition. The Golden West negotiations, from first contact to board approval, had taken 11 days, the due diligence covering no more than six days.

Normally, CEOs in the throes of deal making mask their activities carefully, meeting with their counterparts at clandestine locations for the initial wooing and finalizing the details cloistered away in law firm conference rooms, corporate war rooms, or even their own homes. But Thompson still had the Wachovia Championship to worry about.

Having debuted in 2003 as the bank was smoothly melding Wachovia and First Union operations, the tournament was a symbol of the company's ability to pull off big events. The tour stop was an instant hit among fickle pros, who enjoyed first-class perks such as Mercedes courtesy cars. The bank entertained thousands of clients at the event each year, providing them with catered meals and drinks in air-conditioned "chalets" as golfers like Phil Mickelson, Tiger Woods, and Sergio Garcia attacked one of the country's top courses. On Sunday afternoon while waiting for Golden West's board to make its decision, Thompson needed to make an appearance at Quail Hollow Club—along with 35,000 other golf fans.

Most years, the tournament's attendees—country-club linksters and blue-collar trunk slammers alike—couldn't keep enough sunscreen on hand to ward off burns as they shuffled between holes. But the 2006 event was drenched by rain. On Sunday, as the players raced to beat intensifying showers, Trevor Immelman held the lead but was fighting off Jim Furyk, who was charging on the back nine. The showdown would come down to the grueling 18th hole, the kicker to a brutal finishing run known as "the Green Mile."

As the golfers prepared for their final clash, CBS sent the TV coverage down to the 18th green for the obligatory interview with the sponsoring company's CEO. Wearing his garish blue Wachovia Championship blazer, Thompson didn't let on to the huge deal in the works, although word had started to leak out that afternoon. He appeared fresh and upbeat despite a draining week.

Interviewer Peter Kostis said the rain-jacketed crowd had stepped up despite the weather.

"Isn't it incredible, Peter?" Thompson said. "We've got the best golf fans in the world right here in the Carolinas, and they have proven it again this weekend."

Kostis noted the possibility of a playoff ahead.

"We may be here awhile, and that'll be fun. I hope we are," the CEO replied, smiling and giving a glance into the camera.

Back in the booth, announcer Jim Nantz praised Thompson and "his whole distinguished team" for another great tournament week.

Indeed, a one-hole playoff was needed to determine a winner. Furyk prevailed with a fist-pumping flourish. Thompson shook the winner's hand a little after six that evening and walked off the green smiling. As the rain picked up, he briefly waited alone outside the Quail Hollow clubhouse for a car to take him to the airport.

The Golden West board meeting started Sunday afternoon. Some participants were in New York and some back in Oakland. Wachovia's executives and advisers hadn't heard anything by the time they boarded flights for New York, raising anxiety that the deal could get derailed. In the meeting, Golden West executives debated the sale extensively but eventually gave their unanimous approval. The Wachovia team got the welcome news after landing. The banks issued a news release that evening.

The Golden West purchase would increase Wachovia's assets to about $669 billion from about $542 billion, bolstering the bank's rank as the nation's fourth-largest. The total cost of the deal was $25.5 billion, the biggest ever for First Union or Wachovia.

"For four decades, Golden West has taken industry-wide challenges in stride and maintained a singular focus as a risk-averse residential mortgage portfolio lender," Thompson said in a statement. "The result is an astonishing 25-year track record of 17 percent compound growth in earnings per share and virtually no credit losses realized even in the toughest year in its history."

When Wachovia mortgage executives heard the deal was official, they were less effusive. They privately hoped Golden West would not be Thompson's Money Store.

On Monday morning, at the analyst presentation held at a New York hotel, Thompson bubbled with even more praise for his merger partner. "We are thrilled," he told the audience. "The only way I can describe it is Golden West is a crown jewel."

Golden West extended Wachovia's retail presence into high-growth West Coast markets and created a mortgage lender with size and complementary products, the bank's presentations said. While Golden West, which also operated under the World Savings name, was primarily an adjustable-rate mortgage lender, Wachovia offered more fixed-rate loans. The deal was also significant for Thompson because the company regained the mortgage-servicing business he had sold in First Union's 2000 restructuring.

He introduced the Sandlers as "icons" of the industry but accidentally flip-flopped the number of years they had been in business. "Ken just made me nervous because he does not seem to be too good with the numbers," Herb Sandler joked. "He says it is 34. He inverted it. It is 43. You are forgiven, Ken."

Eschewing the typical "puffery" he had seen at such events before, Sandler said he would speak from the heart, listing all his company's accomplishments over the years. "So the question before the house is, Why in God's name are we selling, and why are we selling to Wachovia?" he asked. The short answer was that Golden West was a one-product company that someday would need a full array of services for its customers.

"We are competitive," Sandler said. "We must win. We don't take second to anybody. We have to find a partner who fills what we missed, and we found a partner that was a perfect cultural fit."

He also slipped in a dig at option ARM critics. "I read all these stories about the option ARM . . . and nobody knows what they are talking about," he said. "They all discovered it two years ago. We have been doing it for a quarter-century. We know the loan better than anybody."

As the presentation continued, Thompson said Wachovia had been impressed when executives visited Golden West and studied the thrift's process. "Here is my promise to you," he said. "Like the Hippocratic oath, we will do nothing to screw up that model."

Thompson praised Golden West's underwriting and pointed to the size of its loans as another comfort. The focus on small-sized mortgages "gives you incredible confidence" partly because they would get hit less than larger ones "in a difficult environment," he said. "You would have to have huge unemployment and a huge downdraft in home values before the portfolio gets hit in a big way."

Despite the CEOs' enthusiasm, analysts were skeptical. Could Wachovia successfully convert Golden West's branches? Could the thrift's employees handle selling a variety of products? Were the Sandlers cashing out at the top? Would the option ARMs' performance start to show cracks?

"I was listening to the brilliant Bloomberg today and MSNBC today, and I heard all the brilliant comments that were called in," Sandler said. "Well, they were worried about the option ARM. 'We are going to have a real-estate crisis. They are selling at the high.' I mean, that is a bunch of garbage."

Another questioner wondered if Sandler was worried that Wachovia would do more big deals.

"If I was worried about that, I'm not worried anymore," he said. "These guys are tough sons of bitches. And they hew to their financial model, and they are willing to let a deal break if it doesn't meet the financial model."

Acknowledging the sensitivity of his next comment, he added, "This deal could not have been made eight years ago under Crutchfield because I could not trust his desire to grow and grow and add," he said. "You have to do it right."

Wall Street wasn't convinced. In the first day of trading, Wachovia shares sagged nearly 7 percent to $55.42.

"Our concern is how . . . you put together these very diverse companies," said analyst Gary Townsend of Friedman Billings Ramsey. "It's not easy, although it sounds that way listening to Ken and Herb."

"I am surprised and a bit disappointed," said Nancy Bush of NAB Research in New Jersey. "The Street is looking for them to be out of the deal business."

Later in the week, two Wachovia executives came under fire in the media for the timing of stock sales they had made in late April, right around when talks started with Golden West. Wachovia said that, at the time of their transactions, general bank head Jenkins and investor relations head Alice Lehman were unaware the bank had been contacted about the potential acquisition.

As the bank's shares slipped further that week, Tom Wurtz held an unusual follow-up conference call with analysts on Friday. "The stock price reaction was not anything like I anticipated," Wurtz admitted. He said the bank held the call not to change investors' minds but to clear up what he said were misperceptions about the deal. For example, he said most of Golden West's branches were in prime locations and in good condition, although some would need ATMs and drive-throughs added.

One analyst asked about Golden West's average loan size, wondering if the small size implied its customers were less credit worthy.

Wurtz said that wasn't necessarily true. He pointed to the small loans as a sign of Golden West's lending discipline.

Another question was whether or not the Sandlers sold at the top of the market.

"They have said very specifically that that is not the motivation for their sale . . . and I believe them," Wurtz said.

By the end of the day, the bank's shares dipped 27 cents to $54.67, putting them down about 8 percent for the week.

Soon after the announcement, Thompson stopped by comptroller John Dugan's office in Washington to brief him on the deal. The OCC didn't have a role in approving the acquisition. That task fell to the Federal Reserve Board. Thompson was merely reaching out to a regulator who had expressed concerns about option ARMs.

Golden West was different, Thompson told Dugan, a lawyer and longtime player in financial regulation. Golden West was the most experienced lender in the field, had the best underwriting, and had survived past crises. That's why Wachovia could do the deal.

Dugan expressed concerns about option ARMs and the potential for interest rate shock. But he had no reason to believe Wachovia was wrong about the quality of Golden West's lending. By then, the subprime mortgage market was starting to show cracks, but option ARMs were holding up.

· · ·

Shortly after the acquisition's announcement, more than two dozen executives from both companies gathered at Wachovia's Uptown headquarters complex for a get-to-know-you session.

Sitting in was Jim Judd, a top Golden West executive who had long piloted the lender's mortgage machine with a no-nonsense, even combative management style. Now in his late 60s, he would soon be charged with leading the combined mortgage unit, even though his company was the one being bought. That meant some of Wachovia's executives were likely to lose their jobs.

As a Wachovia mortgage executive explained the bank's customer satisfaction surveys, Judd questioned how the data was used. The Wachovia executive said the surveys helped gauge employee performance and calculate incentive pay. Judd dismissed the effort as stupid.

Wachovia executives were shocked by the remark, which seemed to disparage the company's ingrained focus on customer service. The gruff Judd, however, may have been reacting to the bank's complex compensation structure. The summit, at which Thompson made an appearance, marked the beginning of a culture clash that would embroil the combined mortgage unit.

At Wachovia, mortgage executives didn't see their Golden West counterparts as true mortgage bankers skilled in making a variety of loans and packaging them into securities for investors. Instead, they viewed them as slick salesmen who knew how to pitch only one product. They found Golden West executives cocky because their company's loans had higher profit margins. The Charlotte bank, however, saw mortgages as just one of many products—from checking accounts to mutual funds—that the company wanted to pitch customers.

The cultural differences became clear to some Wachovia executives at a one-day training session in Delray Beach, Florida. At a Golden West facility there, one of the company's executives explained how Pick-A-Payment loans were the answer to seemingly every borrower's needs. "We'd call it drinking the Kool-Aid," said one former Wachovia executive.

As the companies planned the integration, some found it difficult to get information about Golden West's operations. Wachovia executives also struggled to understand how Golden West's loans performed so well. "Don't poke the bear," was the admonition about crossing Jim Judd.

Meanwhile, Golden West was frustrated by Wachovia's polite, deliberative culture. At Golden West, executives prided themselves on walking out of boring meetings and grilling each other before making decisions. They were bewildered by Wachovia's complex management structure and bemoaned the mind-numbing conference calls in which scores of people dialed in and no decisions were made. The PowerPoint presentations seemed endless—and pointless. Perhaps most importantly, Wachovia's mortgage business wasn't very profitable, and compensation schemes were geared to benchmarks other than overall company earnings.

At Golden West headquarters in Oakland during a regular visit, Herb Sandler met with Thompson and outlined his concerns, ranging from management structure to employee incentive pay. Thompson was a "consummate gentleman," Sandler recalled, but he suspected the Wachovia CEO was a little angry. "Like, who am I to be talking to him like that?" Sandler told the *Observer*. "My obligation was to make Wachovia a better company."

Thompson listened to Sandler's concerns and acted on some. After the purchase closed, Sandler told the *Observer* he was disappointed that Wachovia rarely asked for help.

Despite the poor reception to the deal on Wall Street and even inside his own company, Thompson remained upbeat. Asked in an August 2006 interview about the slowing housing market, he said he was looking at the long term, not the next quarter or even the next year, when he bought Golden West.

"We bought it because strategically we think being in the mortgage business in the United States is a winning bet. We've got population growth, income growth, we have significant in-migration. Americans are going to buy houses. It's a great business long term. In the short term, we looked at Golden West's record over the last 25 years. They've been through quite a number of housing cycles and even in the most difficult housing cycle Golden West did extremely well. We think we got the right mortgage company."

Asked about Golden West's option ARMs, he added, "We like the product mix. I think you need to be conservative in the way you deal with ARMs and Golden West has done that. Again, in 1994, a period when California had 10 percent unemployment and housing prices had gone down by 20 percent, Golden West charge-offs were .18 percent of loans."

At a special meeting of Wachovia shareholders on August 31, investors approved the purchase after only a 30-minute session. Golden West shareholders gave their assent the same day. Now, all the bank needed was Fed approval.

A couple weeks later, *BusinessWeek* magazine ran a cover story entitled, "How Toxic Is Your Mortgage?" that raised eyebrows inside Wachovia. "The option adjustable rate mortgage (ARM) might be the riskiest and most complicated home loan product ever created," the story said, stirring worries among some employees about the company they were buying.

Wachovia had no way of knowing, but executives at one of Golden West's major competitors, Countrywide Financial, were also starting to worry about the potential for disaster with option ARMs. Countrywide, the California-based mortgage giant, had jumped into the product in 2004. By the middle of 2005, about one-fifth of its new loans were option ARMs. It was one of the competitors Sandler feared were corrupting the product. According to a complaint later filed by the SEC, Countrywide CEO Angelo Mozilo was concerned about payment shock among Countrywide's customers as early as April 2006, before Wachovia agreed to acquire Golden West. Borrowers were increasingly choosing to make only the minimum payment, adding to their principal and setting them up for big payment jumps later.

On September 25, 2006, Mozilo sent an e-mail to two of his top lieutenants: "We have no way, with any reasonable certainty, to assess the real risk of holding these loans on our balance sheet. The only history we can look to is that of World Savings [Golden West. H]owever their portfolio was fundamentally different than ours in that their focus was equity and our focus is fico [credit scores]. In my judgment, as a long time lender, I would always trade off fico for equity. The bottom line is that we are flying blind on how these loans will perform in a stressed environment of higher unemployment, reduced values and slowing home sales."

On September 29, the Federal Reserve Board approved Wachovia's proposal to buy Golden West. Several people who commented to the board "expressed concern about the financial impact of [Golden West's] adjustable-rate and nontraditional mortgage lending activities on the combined organization, asserting that interest rate increases and other economic uncertainties would increase the probability of borrower default," the Fed said. The regulator said it had reviewed the combined company's anticipated capital levels, financial resources, and risk management systems.

The deal, its final price tag falling to about $24 billion, closed October 1, 2006. More than a half-dozen of Wachovia's top mortgage executives soon departed the company, either because they were left without jobs in the merger or because they were uneasy with the unit's direction.

Chapter 7

BOOM TO BUST

I n February 2007, Bank of America invited analysts to a posh resort in Florida to lay out its plans for tackling the daunting but enviable task of topping 2006's record $21.1 billion in profits.

It was the second time the bank had held such an investor conference in Ken Lewis's tenure. The first, in November 2001, was staged at a Charlotte airport hotel as the economy shuddered after the September 11 terrorist attacks. Now, just over five years later, the bank was upgrading to the Ponte Vedra Inn & Club, an ocean-side conference center just down the road from where The Players Championship golf tournament was held every year.

It was a fitting location for a bank brimming with success.

In addition to the bank's record profits, its shares had hit an all-time high of $54.90 in November 2006, taking into account stock splits. Swelled by the rise in its stock price, Bank of America's total market value briefly eclipsed that of rival Citigroup, giving it the mantle of world's biggest bank.

Lewis had benefited personally as well. His compensation for 2006 totaled $97 million, including $77 million from exercising stock options accumulated over the years. That compared with $6.7 million in 2001, his first year as CEO.

For a change, 2006 had been a quiet year for acquisitions, Lewis's biggest move being a $3.3 billion deal to buy wealth manager U.S. Trust Corporation. The bank had mostly focused on its MBNA purchase, switching millions of accounts to a new system while sparking some gripes about account glitches.

During the integration, two New York–area executives grabbed attention when their reworded version of U2's ballad "One" hit YouTube. Sung with gusto and sincerity, the song—turned into a tribute to the MBNA deal—received an ovation from employees at a bank meeting but cackles from many who viewed it.

"And we've got Bank One / On the run. / What's in your wallet? / It's not

Capital One. / It's us. / So which card are you?" one of the executives sang while the other played guitar. "And we'll make lots of money. / Forever I can sing / About trusting and teamwork / And doing the right thing. / We'll live out our core values / While the competition crawls."

The performance put a spotlight on Bank of America's hard-core culture. Under Lewis, the bank indoctrinated employees with "spirit training," using terms like "onstage" to describe everything in view of customers and "offstage" for everything else. "We're delighted to have colleagues who can both carry a tune and be great bankers," Bank of America spokesperson Betsy Weinberger told the *Wall Street Journal.*

Investors wondered how Lewis could squeeze even more profits out of the behemoth he had helped create. The bank's stock slipped at the beginning of 2007, likely because investors were worried about the prospects of another big deal.

As he prepared for the conference, Lewis was working with his third chief financial officer since Jim Hance retired in early 2005.

Hance's replacement, Marc Oken, had lasted less than a year. A key player in the Fleet and MBNA integrations, Oken was known for his skill in hiring talented executives. But he wasn't the glib information source Wall Street desired. After a group of analysts complained, Lewis made a change in September 2005. Oken would later launch a private-equity firm with Hugh McColl.

The next CFO was Al de Molina, a capital markets aficionado who had helped the bank clean up the 1998 D. E. Shaw hedge fund mess. In another role, he had become known for producing big profits through his management of the bank's huge balance sheet. Later, he ran the corporate and investment bank. As CFO, the frank-talking native Cuban was a hit with analysts, dishing out financial information but leaving it to them to make their own earnings estimates.

In December 2006, de Molina surprisingly announced his resignation, saying he was looking for a more challenging job than being CFO of a well-run company. Behind the scenes, he had jousted with Lewis and other executives over strategy. After one disagreement, de Molina submitted his resignation, and Lewis accepted.

De Molina's successor was Bank of America veteran Joe Price. At an investor conference a couple of weeks after the departure, Lewis introduced Price as the right person for the job but acknowledged "too much turnover" at the CFO position. "Al is our friend, and we'll miss him," he added.

The weekend before the Ponte Vedra Beach conference, the bank kicked off a marketing campaign with TV commercials aired during the Oscars telecast. A new slogan, "Bank of Opportunity," aimed to highlight the products the bank could provide consumers and businesses. The previous "Higher Standards" campaign had signaled Lewis's aspiration to create the world's most admired company. But the tag line became a punch line whenever the bank faced regulatory issues or perturbed a customer.

Before the conference attendees sat down to a dinner of crab salad terrine and beef tenderloin, Lewis gave a speech emphasizing the bank's focus on internal growth. "We do not have to acquire to meet our financial goal," he told the audience of about 100 analysts, executives, and reporters. Still, he acknowledged it would be irresponsible to say he wouldn't do another deal, quipping, "You wouldn't believe me anyway."

Lewis said he was looking to create a new "paradigm" in American banking, one in which he could charge more for innovative products that stood out from rivals'. That went against the industry maxim that most banking services were commodities with little difference from company to company. Lewis cited examples such as the bank's "Keep the Change" savings program and a no-fee mortgage pilot.

The following day, Lewis and his lieutenants used a panoply of PowerPoint presentations to illustrate how the bank could increase revenues and profits without doing another big deal. Consumer banking head Liam McGee said the bank planned to say yes more often to customers seeking home-equity loans and add more credit card accounts. In a question-and-answer session, Lewis downplayed complaints about a new credit card that could potentially be used by illegal immigrants. "Nobody's profit plan has been changed because of this," he said of the blowback from a card that didn't require a Social Security number for enrollment.

In investment banking, executives planned to beef up areas such as collateralized debt obligations, complex investments based on assets such as subprime loans. In her presentation, chief risk officer Amy Woods Brinkley confidently expressed the bank's grasp on the risks it faced. "We are in the business of taking risk, and we are deliberate about the risk we choose to take," she said. "We believe our culture of measurement and accountability puts us out before our competition." She downplayed the bank's exposure to the subprime mortgage market but said the issue "bears watching very closely."

Closing out the conference, Lewis said he wanted to put the notion to rest "once and for all" that "size and scale don't matter." His big bank could reap efficiencies and plow its capital back into promising businesses such as investment banking.

Analysts left with thick binders jammed with new details about the bank. But the event didn't bump the stock price. A sell-off in overheated Chinese markets walloped American stocks on the last day of the conference, Bank of America's shares dropping nearly 4 percent. During the afternoon sessions, analysts scrambled to check their BlackBerries and laptops. Lewis thanked them for their attention "given the circumstances."

. . .

In mid-April, an international phone call short-circuited Lewis's plan to focus on internal growth.

Barclays, the British bank, was in exclusive negotiations to buy ABN AMRO NV when the Amsterdam bank's advisers started doubting the price Barclays was going to be able to pay. In particular, Barclays was valuing LaSalle Bank, ABN AMRO's Chicago-based American operation, at around $13 to $14 billion, which boded poorly for the overall offer.

John Cryan, a UBS investment banker advising ABN AMRO in London, called his partner in New York, Oliver Sarkozy. As the exclusive bidding period neared an end, Cryan feared Barclays' offer would be a dud, upsetting ABN AMRO shareholders and leading to a protracted fight.

Over the years, Sarkozy, whose half-brother Nicolas was about to become the French president, had worked on a variety of deals with North Carolina's big banks. He helped First Union on its restructuring when he worked at Credit Suisse, assisted Wachovia with its SunTrust proxy fight, counseled MBNA on its sale to Bank of America, and advised on the recent U.S. Trust sale. He suspected Bank of America would be willing to pay much more than Barclays to become the dominant bank in Chicago, a major hole in its United States franchise.

Sarkozy called Bank of America strategy executive Greg Curl at home and apprised him of the situation. ABN AMRO needed at least $20 billion for LaSalle and had to announce the deal by Monday, just a few days away.

"Can you do that?" Sarkozy asked.

"We absolutely can," Curl replied.

Curl flew to London for a meeting with ABN AMRO the next day and signed a confidentiality agreement. Bank of America dispatched its due diligence team to Chicago.

On Sunday, April 22, the UBS bankers informed Barclays of their gambit. They had found a way for Barclays to juice its bid. Bank of America was buying LaSalle for $21 billion in cash. That would pump capital into ABN AMRO and allow Barclays to pay more for the rest of the franchise, including the European bank branches and investment banking operations the British bank most coveted. Barclays executives were understandably upset by the move but didn't back out of the talks. CEO John Varley and Curl were both at ABN AMRO's headquarters that Sunday but never crossed paths.

Bank of America announced its deal on Monday, April 23, the same day ABN AMRO said it was selling the rest of its operations to Barclays for about $91 billion. The combination of European banks was "the largest merger ever in the global financial industry," Varley said. The developments surprised a consortium of banks led by Royal Bank of Scotland PLC that had also been eyeing ABN AMRO.

Back in the United States, analysts gave Bank of America's purchase a tepid response. Analyst Dick Bove of Punk Ziegel & Company called the agreement "shareholder unfriendly," questioning why the company would want to expand in the Midwest. In his opinion, "these guys are meaningfully hurting organic earnings growth." But analyst Gary Townsend of Friedman Billings Ramsey praised the move, citing the addition in the Chicago market and the fact that the deal would augment earnings immediately.

Most big bank deals were carried out by issuing new shares of stock to the takeover target's investors, but in this case Bank of America was paying cash. That was advantageous because the purchase didn't water down the holdings of existing shareholders and would boost earnings. The downside was that using it hurt the bank's capital cushion. Lewis told analysts that Bank of America would conserve cash for a while to get back to desired levels. "We'll be out of any acquisition of any size whatsoever through 2008," he said.

The move dragged Bank of America into a three-way international takeover fight for ABN AMRO that lasted into the summer. In the end, Bank of America prevailed in its bid for LaSalle, and the consortium scored the rest of ABN AMRO.

The battle conjured memories of the 2001 showdown over Wachovia. Part of the LaSalle spat played out during that May's Wachovia Championship, which grabbed national attention when Tiger Woods and basketball legend Michael Jordan played together in the pro-am event. Ken Thompson said he was glad he wasn't involved in the skirmish one year after he spent the tournament buying Golden West.

"I would imagine that [ABN AMRO chief executive] Rijkman Groenink has probably got a severe case of ulcers at this point," Thompson said while at the course. "He's got a lot of sharks swimming around him in the water."

Thompson had pledged to avoid big acquisitions by Wachovia until after digesting Golden West. But later in May, he agreed to buy St. Louis–based brokerage A. G. Edwards, Inc., for $6.8 billion, a deal Wachovia executives considered relatively modest in size. Boasting about 15,000 brokers, the combined firm would rival the number-two brokerage, Citigroup's Smith Barney. Merrill Lynch was number one. Wachovia Securities, based in Richmond, Virginia, would move its headquarters to St. Louis.

Wachovia had posted record profits in 2006 of $7.8 billion. But the post–Golden West slump in its shares persisted into summer. In a dubious milestone, the bank's shares had now stayed below their all-time high for nine years. On July 16, 1998, First Union shares had hit an all-time high of $65.69, taking into account stock splits.

Asked about the stock's long stay under $65, Wachovia CFO Tom Wurtz said the current-day company shouldn't be compared to First Union in 1998. Back then, the bank had just overpaid for three acquisitions and didn't have the profit potential to justify its high stock price, Wurtz told the Observer. He stressed the improvement the bank had made under the current management team. "What we'd like to communicate to folks is we've articulated a strategy, we've executed against it, we've provided industry-leading levels of transparency so investors can understand what their investment is doing, and we feel the strategy will produce very attractive returns," he said.

By late summer 2007, Wachovia wasn't the only financial company watching its stock fall.

Since the spring, delinquencies on subprime mortgages had mushroomed as the housing market peaked and borrowers found themselves stuck with unaffordable loans. Dozens of subprime lenders collapsed, and a growing cadre of borrowers faced foreclosures. The turmoil shook investors. Peeved lawmakers accused regulators of not doing enough to stem lax lending practices.

At a Senate hearing in July, Federal Reserve Board chairman Ben Bernanke, a former Princeton University professor appointed to his post in 2006, acknowledged that the problems were "likely to get worse before they get better." He said the Fed was reviewing possible actions to help consumers and pondering new rules, including restrictions on loans that didn't require borrowers to provide proof of income.

Soon, the subprime flu spread to hedge funds, banks, and other institutions with ties to complex securities backed by the unraveling mortgages. In June, investment bank Bear Stearns said it would bail out an affiliated hedge fund stocked with subprime-linked derivatives. On August 9, a French bank stopped withdrawals from some investment funds, saying it was unable to value them. Banks became increasingly nervous about lending to each other. Central bankers rushed to pump money into the skittish financial system. The Dow Jones Industrial Average sank 387 points.

By the next week, mortgage-lending giant Countrywide Financial Corporation was struggling to get the financing it needed to operate. Typically, the company borrowed money in the short term, loaned it to borrowers, then sold off the loans to investors. Countrywide also faced a demand for more collateral from Bank of New York Mellon Corporation.

Worried about Countrywide's impact on financial markets, New York Fed president Tim Geithner worked the phones late into the evening to find a solution. The next morning, Thursday, August 16, Countrywide announced it was tapping an $11.5 billion credit line with 40 large banks, allowing it to satisfy Bank of New York's collateral needs. The markets, however, went haywire, realizing a major mortgage player was in trouble.

That night, in a bid to flush more money into the financial system, the Fed decided to lower the interest rate it charged at its discount window. In normal times, the discount window was a borrowing option of last resort, carrying a stigma for banks that used it. But Geithner encouraged banks to use the window, making a call to Lewis and other CEOs. The New York Fed president, however, violated protocol by not checking in first with Jeff Lacker, the Richmond Fed president, whose bank supervised Bank of America. Bernanke had to smooth the rift.

Banks remained reluctant to access the window. But by Wednesday, August 22, Geithner persuaded the nation's three biggest institutions—Bank of America, Citigroup, and JPMorgan Chase—to borrow $500 million each. Wachovia heard about the move and called the Richmond Fed asking to join in. It was the nation's fourth-largest bank, though much smaller than the big three. It wanted to be seen as part of the club. When the four banks announced the move, they emphasized they were taking a leadership role and had plenty of liquidity on hand.

Bank of America had an even bigger move in the works. It began scoping out Countrywide's operations for a possible cash infusion. The two companies were familiar with each other. Countrywide CEO Angelo Mozilo had started the company in 1969 with a $75,000 Bank of America loan. And back in 2006, CFO Al de Molina had talked to Mozilo about a possible joint venture, although the deal never came to fruition.

After the markets closed on Thursday, Bank of America revealed it was taking a $2 billion stake in Countrywide. Although the lifeline was widely seen as the first step in an outright acquisition, the bank insisted it was a passive investment. Bank of America said it was providing a vote of confidence in the lender, while looking to make a profit. It was set to receive a 7.25 percent return on its investment. A securities filing would later reveal the bank had the right of first refusal if another suitor emerged for Countrywide.

To some, Lewis had made a J. P. Morgan–like move to soothe the markets. "We were able to do something which I do think is in the best interest of the country, but fortunately we also felt like it was a good deal on its own," Lewis said in an interview a month later.

With his LaSalle deal set to close on October 1, Lewis was the center of attention in the banking world. He was highlighted in national publications for leadership in a time of crisis and for building a consumer-driven profit machine. Detractors also surfaced, citing planned LaSalle layoffs and rising fees. The Service Employees International Union launched a website—bankofamericabadforamerica.org—that called the nation's number-two bank by assets "too big, too powerful." Illinois lawmakers, including Senator Barack Obama, the Democratic presidential candidate, decried cutbacks in LaSalle's Chicago headquarters. The bank, which would have 210,000 employees combined after the merger, planned to eliminate 4,000 positions in Illinois and Michigan over two years.

Although layoffs were "never pleasant," Lewis said the reductions were necessary to make the $21 billion deal work. "What I have said is that we will be incredibly good corporate citizens," he maintained. As to the union's broader criticisms, Lewis said the bank was the country's biggest taxpayer and corporate giver. He also noted it had introduced products that eliminated fees on mortgages and online stock trades.

In October, banks began disclosing third-quarter earnings for 2007—the first profit reports since the credit crunch erupted—and the news was ugly.

On October 18, 2007, Bank of America said its profits in the period fell by a third from a year earlier to $3.7 billion, marking the bank's first profit decline since the fourth quarter of 2005. Its corporate and investment bank was the big sore spot. Profits in the business plunged 93 percent to $100 million on trading losses and write-downs of loans tied to leveraged buyouts.

In a build-out initially led by Al de Molina, Bank of America had spent hundreds of millions to hire more traders, salespeople, and bankers in the United States and overseas. In 2006, corporate and investment banking generated $6.8 billion in profits, about one-third of the company's $21.1 billion in earnings. But the unit continued to be perceived by some as a second-tier player in many areas. Now, it was barely eking out a profit. Lewis said the bank would likely scale back. When an analyst asked if he would consider a merger to bolster the unit, Lewis gave a flip response: "I've had all of the fun I can stand in investment banking."

A week after the dour earnings report, the bank made its retreat official. It planned to slash 3,000 jobs, mostly in corporate and investment banking but also in the mortgage business. Vice chairman Gene Taylor, a nearly 40-year veteran who had led the corporate and investment banking unit since 2005, would retire at year's end, to be replaced by wealth management head Brian Moynihan.

Taylor's departure stunned some in the company and even brought tears. He had joined NCNB as a credit analyst in Charlotte in 1969, the same year Lewis arrived. Taylor became one of Lewis's closer friends at the bank, even buying hand-me-down sports cars from Lewis when he upgraded to new models.

Over the years, Taylor held key posts such as running Western operations after the BankAmerica deal. He was best known for his skill in dealing with big clients, forging relationships with corporate elite from Warren Buffett to General Electric Company CEO Jeffrey Immelt. While a surprise to some, the departure seemingly followed a well-worn pattern for Lewis. The CEO gave executives room to run their businesses. But if their results suffered or they made high-profile mistakes, they were likely to part ways with the company or have their jobs changed.

The earnings news at Wachovia wasn't any better. Third-quarter profits dropped 10 percent to $1.7 billion from a year earlier. The decline, the bank's first in six years, was worse than analysts expected.

The credit crunch wounded many of the capital markets businesses that Wachovia had been expanding, such as the packaging of commercial mortgages, loans for buyout deals, and the creation of complex securities known as structured products. The unit's profits swooned 80 percent to $105 million, mostly on $1.3 billion in write-downs. Wachovia planned to cut about 200 jobs in the unit by year's end.

In 2006, Wachovia's corporate and investment banking unit, now led by Steve Cummings, had brought in nearly $2 billion in profits, about a quarter of the bank's $7.8 billion in earnings. Most of the unit's 6,200 employees were based in Charlotte, but Wachovia had also expanded in New York, London, and Hong Kong. Thompson said his leaders had made "good strategic decisions" and not exceeded the company's risk appetite. Should markets tank, he said, the company's goal was not to lose more than one quarter's worth of investment banking earnings, a threshold it had neared.

In the coming weeks, executives at both banks would signal that more problems lay ahead in the fourth quarter. Both were being walloped by write-downs related to risky securities known as collateralized debt obligations, or CDOs, investment vehicles backed by pools of assets such as subprime mortgages. These holdings were losing value as borrowers began missing payments on the underlying loans, spurring the write-downs. Bank of America was braced for a $3 billion hit in the fourth quarter, while Wachovia expected more than $1 billion in write-downs, according to securities filings they issued.

The banks' difficulties revealed the need for better monitoring of risk in a financial world increasingly populated by ultra-complex products, experts said. "A lot of people didn't understand the risk they were taking," said Bert Ely, a Virginia-based banking consultant. Although the Charlotte banks weren't major players in making subprime loans, they were now paying the price for helping package them into investment products.

Back in 2001, Lewis had presciently stopped making subprime loans, only to take losses on the capital markets side of the business six years later. "I think we felt like it was a very good fee income opportunity," Lewis said of the decision to stay in that part of the business. "Having said that, in hindsight I wish we hadn't done that either."

Wachovia was cautious around subprime products, chief risk officer Don Truslow told the Observer, but also sought to meet client demand. Many of the investments carried sterling credit ratings that typically would have little chance of default, according to Truslow. He wished the bank's top mortgage experts had been more involved in examining investments. "What has happened here has been unprecedented, I think, in terms of market conditions," Truslow added.

Charlotte's financial giants weren't the only ones getting whacked by the credit crunch. Citigroup's third-quarter profits fell by 57 percent to $2.4 billion. And Merrill Lynch was getting ready to announce on October 24 a $2.3 billion loss.

In the week before Merrill's earnings report, CEO Stan O'Neal asked Greg Fleming, now Merrill's president, to place a call to Ken Thompson about a possible merger. Since things were getting tougher, it would be good to be tied to a bank, O'Neal explained. Fleming rang up Thompson, whom he had advised in the SunTrust fight. "I need to check with my board, but I absolutely would be interested," the Wachovia CEO said. Fleming told O'Neal he should follow up with Thompson. The Merrill president also called Wachovia CFO Tom Wurtz and talked about holding further discussions the next week.

O'Neal, however, had not run the idea by his own directors. When he disclosed the move at a board meeting on Sunday, October 21, the directors teed off on the unauthorized move. Fleming, a veteran deal maker, didn't understand why the board was so angry. These kinds of things happened all the time. CEOs sent out feelers, laying the groundwork for deals that might or might not develop over time. What O'Neal hadn't told Fleming was that he had approached Bank of America about a deal a month earlier. The Merrill board hadn't been pleased with that flirtation either.

In days, O'Neal was out as CEO. He was soon joined by Chuck Prince, Citigroup's CEO. High-flying bank executives were no longer safe in the unfolding credit crisis. Both, however, left with packages stuffed with stock holdings, pensions, and other awards.

For its next CEO, Merrill picked John Thain, the former Goldman Sachs executive who revamped the New York Stock Exchange. Citi chose Vikram Pandit, the head of its investment banking business. Both executives would play major roles in the future of Charlotte's banks.

In November 2007, the Charlotte Chamber landed a hot speaker for its annual meeting: Ben Bernanke. Having grown up in Dillon, South Carolina, the Federal Reserve chairman was to receive the business group's yearly "Citizen of the Carolinas" award.

Buoyed by the Bernanke buzz, the chamber sold nearly 2,400 tickets, close to the 2,445 dispensed for evangelist Billy Graham's appearance in 1999. Nearly 80 years after Treasury secretary Andrew Mellon commemorated the city's new Fed branch, the chamber was hosting another memorable gathering of financiers.

The bearded Bernanke arrived at the Charlotte Convention Center around 5:30 P.M., flanked by aides and security. He posed for photos with students involved in a financial literacy program and mingled with VIPs including Hugh McColl, Ken Thompson, and businessman C. D. Spangler at a closed reception.

Bernanke was joined in Charlotte by a host of family members. His parents and brother lived in the city. He hadn't been in the Carolinas much since taking over as Fed chairman in February 2006, although his hometown had feted him with a Ben Bernanke Day that included tales of his waiting tables at South of the Border, the campy I-95 landmark. During the market turbulence in August, he had missed a family trip to Charlotte and Myrtle Beach. "Ben's been a little busy," Bernanke's wife, Anna, said.

At the chamber program, Bernanke was treated to a video tribute that included pictures of him as a fresh-faced elementary-school student (who skipped the first grade) as well as a longer-haired high-school student. Duke Energy executive Jim Turner introduced the Fed chair as "a bit of a rock star."

In his 21-minute speech, Bernanke remembered visiting his grandparents' home on Charlotte's Cumberland Avenue, playing "very serious" games of chess with his grandfather, and appearing in an *Observer* photo accompanying a recipe for his grandma's blintzes. He also had been impressed by his trips to Freedom Park, which the young Bernanke thought was called Friedman Park. Friedman was his grandparents' last name.

As for the local economy, he said that, like many parts of the country, the Carolinas faced the challenge of replacing old-line manufacturing industries with new service sector jobs. He noted the importance of Charlotte's growth as a financial center, although he slipped up when he said three major banks, not two, were based in the city. He likely was referring to Winston-Salem's BB&T, which gave North Carolina three sizable institutions.

When it came to the national economy, Bernanke said the Fed was weighing data and anecdotes about inflation threats, a solid labor market, and weakening housing prices. "Needless to say, the Federal Reserve is following the evolution of financial conditions carefully, with particular attention to the question of how strains in financial markets might affect the broader economy," he said in a measured tone.

The world's most powerful central banker said uncertainty around the forecast was "greater than usual," adding that the Fed would "remain exceptionally alert and flexible as we continue to assess how best to promote sustainable economic growth and price stability."

After his speech, Bernanke stayed in town for a family visit. The *Observer* dug up his grandma's blintz recipe, which featured "dry-curd (not cream-style) cottage cheese."

Weeks later, the Fed cut a key interest rate by one-quarter point. Some policymakers had pushed for a bigger reduction in order to get ahead of the growing financial panic.

As the year wound down, Wachovia boasted of its success in converting 200 Golden West branches ranging from California to Illinois, giving it a true coast-to-coast presence like its much bigger Tryon Street neighbor. But uncertainty about the bank's mortgage operations continued to weigh on Wachovia's share price.

At an investor conference in November, general bank head Ben Jenkins expressed the bank's first public twinge of regret about the Golden West deal. "Our timing was not good" in light of the severe housing downturn, he said, but the bank continued "to feel that this acquisition will prove itself very positive when we get to the other side of the cycle."

Wachovia was closely watching its mortgage portfolio and monitoring unusual behavior such as credit-worthy borrowers eschewing their mortgage payments because their home values had fallen. The biggest trouble spots were California regions known as the Central Valley and the Inland Empire. But even if losses hit mid-1990s peaks, the Golden West portfolio would still make about $2 billion in pre-tax profits a year, Jenkins said.

In December, Lewis and Thompson made their annual appearance at the Charlotte Chamber's economic forecast luncheon. They were joined by the Richmond Fed's Jeff Lacker and Duke Energy CEO Jim Rogers. "It's good to be out of the bunker today," Thompson quipped.

The general consensus was that the economy was verging on recession but should pick up late in 2008. The panel's moderator, developer Henry Faison, pointed out the dismal performance of both banks' stocks in 2007 but told audience members they should be calling their brokers to buy at a good price. Lewis wasn't about to play along. "It is not my intent to have our stock price be a bargain for you guys," he deadpanned.

Lewis, however, wasn't above looking for bargains himself.

Since mid-November, Bank of America and Countrywide had been in discussions about a potential acquisition. Business conditions continued to deteriorate for Countrywide in early January, raising the possibility of debt-rating downgrades and regulatory actions. On January 11, 2008, Bank of America said it was buying Countrywide for $4 billion in stock.

In the deal, the bank would jump to number one in mortgages, with about a 25 percent market share. It would also take on billions in troubled loans and a slew of lawsuits seeking damages over allegations related to Countrywide's lending practices.

Over the previous month, about 60 bank officials had scoured Countrywide's books for potential loan losses and studied possible threats from lawsuits, CFO Joe Price said. Those risks were factored into the sales price, he said. In the past, critics had accused Lewis of overspending on acquisitions. But based on the previous day's closing prices, he would be paying $7.16 per Countrywide share, nearly an 8 percent discount.

The "compelling arithmetic" of the deal prevailed over the industry's "near-term challenges," Lewis said.

As was often the case, Bank of America's agreement spurred speculation of more deals by rivals. News reports had New York–based JPMorgan Chase in preliminary talks with Seattle's Washington Mutual, Inc., another major mortgage lender. "It's like musical chairs," banking consultant Bert Ely said. "When the music stops, we'll see who has a partner and who doesn't."

Chapter 8

"Moment of Truth"

On January 22, 2008, Bank of America and Wachovia delivered another round of grim quarterly earnings reports.

"Clearly, the past few quarters have been stressful for shareholders, management and associates, easily the toughest environment since I've been CEO of Bank of America," Ken Lewis said as he opened the bank's conference call. "At the same time, it is important to stay focused on strategic goals and to remember that our business model was designed to handle cyclical stresses, if not the extremes we are experiencing."

Early in 2007, the banks had been on pace for another year of record profits, but the credit crunch smashed those hopes in the second half of the year.

The big blow to profits in the quarter was a total of $7 billion between the two banks in write-downs for mortgage-related investments. Bank of America and Wachovia also set aside more money for bad loans in a shriveling housing market. Their suffering was shared by other major financial institutions. In 2007, banks around the world took more than $100 billion in write-downs from mortgage-related investments and other complex securities that plummeted in value during the housing meltdown.

Both banks barely managed to stay in the black in the fourth quarter of 2007, and their annual profits declined for the first time since the turn of the decade. Bank of America earned about $15 billion in 2007, while Wachovia made $6.3 billion.

Despite the carnage, both banks' stocks rose from 52-week lows after the Federal Reserve announced an emergency interest rate cut.

In his conference call with analysts, Ken Thompson struck a defiant tone about Wachovia's prospects despite a 44 percent drop in his stock price since the beginning of 2007. His bank had enough capital after raising $3.1 billion in recent months, he insisted:

> Based on recent action in our stock price, I'm certain that investors are anxious about several questions on Wachovia which I want to address now. The first question is, what is the level of losses in your Pick-A-Pay mortgage portfolio? And as we've said since the Golden West acquisition, we looked at the Golden West experience of the early 1990s. At that time, California had 10 percent unemployment and 20 percent house price depreciation, and charge-offs peaked in 1994 at 20 basis points. Based on our portfolio today, that 20 basis point peak would translate to about $250 million in charge-offs.
>
> Our expectations for this year are that charge-offs will exceed that historical peak, but even if charge-offs reach 3 or 4 times that peak, our Pick-A-Pay portfolio will generate very meaningful bottom line profits in 2008, and I do not believe that investors grasp that fact today.
>
> The second question, does Wachovia have enough capital? After our December preferred offering, Wachovia's capital levels were higher at year end, than at the end of the third quarter, in spite of the marks, and in spite of the reserve build that we did in the fourth quarter. And we're confident that those capital levels will increase as we go through 2008.
>
> And the third question, will Wachovia cut its dividend? And the answer to that question is, we have no plans to cut the dividend, because we do not need to cut the dividend. We're confident in our ability to meet our 2008 business plan, and that plan, as we have said before, will generate cash earnings that will cover our dividend.

In the question-and-answer session, analysts quizzed Thompson, CFO Tom Wurtz, and chief risk officer Don Truslow about the bank's commercial mortgage business—a big producer of mortgage-backed securities—and the continued deterioration in California housing markets. The $24 billion Golden West deal had become a sore point with some investors, especially after Bank of America agreed to buy Countrywide for $4 billion.

Truslow pointed to an unusual phenomenon banks were facing in the housing collapse: Borrowers capable of making payments were choosing not to when their homes dropped in value. "It's hard to know right now, but we may have seen somewhat of an acceleration of problem loans, as people have reached that conclusion, and we're just going to have to see how the patterns unfold here," he said.

Analyst Nancy Bush asked Thompson if he expected any new regulatory restrictions on option ARMs, which she said were increasingly seen as "evil instruments" by the press and in Congress. Thompson said the bank had long contended its product was different and shouldn't be lumped in with competitors' loans. "We think we're in good shape there, and we think our product will be attractive going forward," he said.

The bank was being conservative in determining loan losses and in its planning for the year, Thompson said. "That's why we feel comfortable giving the kind of guidance that we've given you, as far as covering the dividend, growing capital ratios, growing our business, and we're optimistic about Wachovia," he said. "Frankly, it's just hard for me to understand the impact that our stock price has taken over the last three months, because I look at how we compare to others, and I feel very good about where Wachovia is."

After the call, Wurtz in an interview echoed the regrets that Ben Jenkins had expressed in November. In hindsight, it would be "foolish" not to wish the bank had bought Golden West for less. But he said all of the due diligence was solid except for the anticipation of such a steep decline in housing prices in California. "Clearly, the impact of housing prices on the portfolio has been significant to us," Wurtz said.

In a sign of investor discontent, a group that represented labor union pension funds asked the four members of the bank board's risk committee to explain their efforts to protect investors from "excessive" mortgage investments. CtW Investment Group said it would urge shareholders to withhold votes for the four at the annual shareholder meeting that spring if it didn't get an appropriate response. Richard Clayton, CtW's research director, said it was "conceivable" the group could also call for withholding votes for Thompson, also a director. The group had made similar demands at firms such as Merrill Lynch, which posted a nearly $10 billion loss in the fourth quarter.

"Wachovia's risk committee has diligently monitored the company in accordance with its responsibilities, including risks associated with mortgage-related exposures," Wachovia spokeswoman Christy Phillips-Brown responded. "There is no basis for an election challenge."

In the summer of 2007, Wachovia had appointed one of its own as chief operating officer of the mortgage unit in anticipation of Jim Judd's retirement at the end of the year. David Pope, who succeeded Judd in January 2008, was a well-respected executive with a diplomat's touch. He had overseen some mortgage functions in the past but was known more for his experience in retail and business banking. While he might be able to ease tension among Wachovia and former Golden West employees, some questioned if Pope was the right person to navigate what had become one of the worst housing market collapses in history. "Do you want a nice guy or do you want someone who knows the industry and can get you through this environment?" one former Wachovia executive said.

Pope took steps to better merge operations and to craft a long-term mortgage strategy, but the environment inside the mortgage unit continued to deteriorate, according to insiders. Although his appointment initially appeared to be a sign Wachovia was reclaiming the business, "there didn't seem to be any action," according to a former mortgage employee. Two of Pope's top deputies, Tim Wilson and Rich Fikani, came from Golden West.

Going into 2008, Wachovia's continued focus on Pick-A-Payment loans was out of step with many of its industry rivals. Bank of America stopped doing option ARMs. Seattle-based Washington Mutual was tightening standards. Wachovia was diving in deeper.

Total mortgage volume had fallen from $2.9 trillion in 2006 to $2.4 trillion in 2007, according to *Inside Mortgage Finance*, a Maryland-based industry newsletter. But the category that included option ARMs had recorded an even steeper drop, total volume declining from a record $255 billion in 2006 to $111 billion in 2007. Washington Mutual was number one in 2007 with $23.7 billion in option ARMs, just ahead of Wachovia's $22.8 billion.

Golden West had specialized in selling Pick-A-Payment loans mostly through outside brokers, a type of sales force that drew criticism from some in the industry for pumping out mortgages with little regard to their suitability for borrowers. Now, in addition to using brokers, the goal was to sell the loans through Wachovia's more than 3,000 branches coast to coast.

In January 2008, Wachovia loan consultants began complaining that the bank was pressuring them to sell Pick-A-Payment loans over more traditional products. The bank also was awarding higher commissions for issuing the mortgages, an executive confirmed in an *Observer* interview.

Wachovia loan officers told the *Observer* their jobs were threatened for not selling enough Pick-A-Payment loans, which some felt weren't appropriate for most customers. The bank was requiring its loan officers to sell a minimum number of Pick-A-Payment, traditional, and other loans or face discipline, including termination, according to interviews and documents.

Some former Golden West executives suggested the complaining Wachovia loan officers simply didn't understand the product or were worried only about their personal compensation. But a former Wachovia mortgage consultant in Texas said he felt the loans weren't proper for most customers. In particular, he didn't think they suited first-time homebuyers, who might not understand their loan balances could increase. He was supposed to sell two Pick-A-Payment loans per month, a requirement he didn't meet. "That's all we heard about was Pick-A-Pay," said the consultant, who claimed he was dismissed for "production reasons." "If you sold a 30-year fixed [rate mortgage], they'd say, 'Why didn't you sell a Pick-A-Pay?' "

In a 14-page Wachovia training script for selling the loans, the first two pages emphasized the variety of products the bank offered. The rest was mostly about

Pick-A-Payment loans and how "savvy homeowners" could turn their mortgages into "smart financial planning tools."

The loan sellers' script included these lines: "If you're like us, there's more coming out than coming in some months, and we start putting more and more charges on our credit card. What can we do? Uncle Sam isn't going to take less. Or the car company. Or the credit card company. The children need to be cared for. You can't get along without insurance. Plus, you need to eat, and keep the lights on. That leaves your mortgage payment. What if you could pay a lot less on your mortgage some months when you need flexibility?"

The script instructed loan officers to tell customers that choosing the minimum payment option added to the loan balance. But the focus was on the extra "cashflow" customers could get by paying less per month.

Wachovia had training programs for all types of tasks as it tried to help its salespeople be the best they could be, according to spokesman Don Vecchiarello. The most important thing, he said, was "listening to the customer." While Wachovia dismissed employees from time to time for underperformance, "we have not terminated anyone for not selling enough Pick-A-Pay loans and will not in the future," Vecchiarello told the *Observer*.

Former Golden West mortgage executive Rich Fikani told the *Observer* that Wachovia offered higher compensation for loans—including Pick-A-Payment mortgages—that took more time to explain to customers. But he emphasized that the bank's loan officers were instructed to offer choices to customers and to provide the products that best fit their needs. "The company's philosophy is to reward incentives based on the best interest of customers and the company," Fikani said.

Pick-A-Payment loans benefited customers with variable incomes and those who wanted to stash more money in their 401(k) accounts, Tim Wilson, another David Pope deputy from Golden West, told the *Observer*. But he added that the bank offered a variety of loans because "it's not for everyone."

Wachovia's emphasis on the product triggered alarm bells with consumer advocates, who worried that higher incentives could encourage employees to sell loans that were not appropriate for borrowers. "Generally, institutions give incentives for products they want to be sold," said Kevin Stein, associate director of the California Reinvestment Coalition. In September 2006, regulators had issued alternative mortgage guidance that instructed banks to be careful about employee incentive plans because that could "produce higher concentrations of nontraditional mortgages" in their portfolios, potentially increasing default risk.

In general, consumer advocates didn't like the minimum payment feature of option ARMs because it could cause borrowers' loan balances to grow. Maeve Elise Brown, executive director of Housing and Economic Rights Advocates in California, said she had seen a rise in elderly clients who were having trouble paying former Golden West loans. In her opinion, "it was inappropriate for them to get these loans."

In its earnings report for the fourth quarter of 2007, Wachovia said delinquent Pick-A-Payment loans had grown to $2.8 billion, up 57 percent from the previous three-month period. In comparison, troubled traditional mortgages were up 36 percent to $257 million. Borrowers' "deferred interest"—the amount their loan balances had grown because they made just the minimum payments—climbed to $3.1 billion, although that remained a small portion of the $120 billion portfolio.

Wachovia continued to emphasize Pick-A-Payment loans' consumer protection features. The minimum payment could increase by only 7.5 percent per year. Borrowers' balances couldn't reach more than 125 percent of the original amounts. Borrowers had to make 20 percent down payments or take out mortgage insurance. The bank analyzed borrowers' ability to pay based on the full interest rate, not a low introductory rate. Like Golden West, Wachovia held onto the loans instead of selling them to investors, which gave the bank extra incentive to make them succeed.

In February 2008, Pope stood firmly behind the program. "We thought it was a good product at the time the decision was made to merge with Golden West," he said. "We think it's a good product today. We think it will be a good product in the future."

In January 2008, as the housing market continued to shudder, Wachovia launched an internal effort to take a closer look at its mortgage business. Thompson and general bank head Ben Jenkins assigned a pair of top executives—Peter Sidebottom and Walter Davis—to figure out ways to revamp the bank's overall strategy and reduce losses in the portfolio.

Sidebottom, a former consultant for McKinsey & Company and a UNC Morehead Scholar, was the bank's head of corporate development and strategic initiatives. Davis was a former Bank of America executive now running Wachovia's retail credit operations, which included a home-equity portfolio that was holding up relatively well compared to those of competitors. The bank also hired McKinsey consultants to help with the task, a move that bugged former Golden West executives, who eschewed paying expensive fees for outside advisers.

Publicly, the bank continued to downplay problems in the mortgage business. On February 13, chief risk officer Don Truslow told analysts that mortgages contributed "significant profits" at the bank and would continue making money even if losses from bad loans quadrupled from current levels.

That began to change at the end of the month. In his annual letter to shareholders on February 28, Thompson admitted the obvious about Golden West. The timing was "poor," he wrote, but the company maintained a high opinion of the franchise it had acquired, including "its underwriting and service model."

"We do believe this is a moment of truth for our company: We must execute superbly, manage risk and just plain out-compete in this environment," Thompson wrote. "We have every confidence we'll navigate the headwinds of the current business cycle and emerge as a strong company of proven mettle." Wachovia said it expected losses to exceed .75 percent of its loans in 2008, triple its losses in 2007. The bank blamed rapidly changing conditions in the housing market.

Thompson appeared to be feeling the pressure.

In February, he celebrated Wachovia's seventh year as number one in the American Customer Satisfaction Index rankings with a rally at headquarters. Sporting a touch more gray in his hair, he encouraged employees to take care of each other during another trying year.

In March, State Representative Ruth Samuelson, a Republican from Mecklenburg County, ran into him at the Charlotte Convention Center during the annual meeting of the Foundation for the Carolinas. Thompson was set to become the philanthropy's chairman. Samuelson, who had valued his counsel over the years, gave him a hug and told him she was praying for him. "It must not be working," he joked, adding, "This is the hardest thing I've ever had to go through."

Wachovia struggled in the spring of 2008, but it wasn't the most endangered institution. In March, government officials engineered a rescue of Bear Stearns Companies after mortgage-related woes brought Wall Street's fifth-biggest firm to the brink of collapse. The Federal Reserve initially agreed to provide emergency funding to Bear Stearns through JPMorgan Chase, but the arrangement soon became a takeover. Although JPMorgan CEO Jamie Dimon later raised his offer to $10 per share from $2 per share, the deal was seen as a major coup and raised hopes of more government-aided acquisitions. The firm's collapse also rattled financial markets and fueled concerns about other institutions.

Amid the gloom on Wall Street that March, the battered industry received a dose of levity when New York governor Eliot Spitzer, the former crusading attorney general, resigned over a prostitution scandal. His downfall cheered many at Bank of America, which had tangled with him in his mutual fund probe.

Inside Wachovia, risk managers began taking a closer look at the mortgage portfolio, using forecasting tools that the bank said did a better job weighing declining home values and changing consumer behaviors. The rate of deterioration in the portfolio caught some executives on the operating committee by surprise. One executive who would start asking more questions in the coming months was David Carroll, who now led the bank's brokerage and mutual fund operations.

With the risk models showing deeper deterioration, Thompson began considering raising more capital before reporting first-quarter earnings in mid-April. The bank brought in Goldman Sachs and lawyer Rodge Cohen as advisers. Around that time, executives also considered the possibility of a merger but never looked seriously at any particular deals. Instead, the bank decided to tap existing large shareholders in a securities offering.

Although Wachovia had announced plans to release earnings on Friday, April 18, executives rushed to line up investors in the stock offering before rolling out the bank's financial report early on Monday, April 14. Thompson held a conference call for his operating committee over the weekend. His message was that, with the offering, the bank had more capital than it needed.

Investors knew something was up when the bank announced Sunday night that it was moving up its earnings announcement to Monday. When fully unveiled the next day, the news was still stunning: Wachovia had lost $393 million in the first quarter, launched a $7 billion capital-raising effort, and clipped its quarterly dividend by 41 percent to 37.5 cents per share. The announcements constituted a major about-face from January, when Thompson had said the company had enough capital to maintain its lucrative dividend.

"I know these actions are not without costs, and I wish they were not necessary," Thompson told analysts. "But they are."

Wachovia also sprung news of 500 job cuts in its corporate and investment banking unit, which continued to reel from the credit crunch.

Raising capital was a blow to existing shareholders and an acknowledgment that Wachovia's loan losses were spiking. Putting the best face on the move, the Wachovia CEO said the bank was now one of the industry's best-capitalized institutions, allowing it to weather losses and invest in existing businesses. "We think this is more than enough to get us through the crisis," Thompson told reporters.

The quarterly results included $2 billion in additional write-downs from the falling value of mortgage-related investments and loans made for buyout deals. The bank had now taken write-downs of about $4.7 billion in the credit crunch. The other big problem was rising loan losses spurred by the deepening housing crisis. The bank set aside $2.8 billion to cover problem loans in the quarter, including $1.3 billion for Pick-A-Payment loans. It had set aside just $1.5 billion for bad loans in the fourth quarter.

Wachovia's new models now estimated 7 to 8 percent lifetime losses on the Pick-A-Payment loan portfolio. The company hadn't previously signaled losses of this size to the markets. The bank also disclosed more details about the makeup of the portfolio. For one, about a third of the $122 billion in loans had originated in 2007 and 2008, after the acquisition closed.

The bank revealed that borrowers who received the loans in 2005, 2006, and 2007 had lower credit scores than customers in previous years. The figures gave new insight into the creditworthiness of the borrowers, although Golden West had long considered credit scores unreliable.

Analysts said Thompson's job didn't appear to be in immediate danger but that he could be on a "short leash." Before Golden West, he had worked to boost customer satisfaction rankings and shed the bank's reputation of overpaying for deals. But he had lost credibility with some investors after the Golden West deal and his January statement about dividends, said Gary Townsend, now with Hill-Townsend Capital. "If I were a shareholder I would be asking for his replacement," he said.

In an interview after the report, Lanty Smith, the bank's lead independent director, said Thompson had the board's backing. Such a statement, akin to an athletic director's backing of a struggling football coach, was unusual in corporate America. But Wachovia's dramatic announcement almost required public comment from the board that had approved the Golden West deal. "The board very much stands behind the management team," Smith said. "Now is an important time when continuity of management and a strong working relationship between the board and management is imperative."

When it decided to buy Golden West, the bank had vetted the quality of the portfolio, including its performance during past downturns, Smith said. During a historical peak for delinquencies, Golden West had posted losses of about .18 percent of loans, he reiterated. In the first quarter, Pick-A-Payment losses were more than four times that much. In retrospect, the timing of the deal was bad, and management and the board had to "take the ultimate responsibility," according to Smith. In the long term, he said, the branches Wachovia gained would be strategically important and successful, but the mortgage portfolio would be "very expensive."

Thompson said he was confident he could continue to lead the bank. The same management team had resurrected First Union in 2000 and boosted shareholder value until the recent downturn. He took responsibility for the Golden West deal and its fallout. "I'm accountable," he said. "I understand that."

The company was analyzing its mortgage business strategy, Thompson added. Days earlier, Wachovia had said it was tightening underwriting standards on Pick-A-Payment and other loans, including adding minimum credit score requirements. But the company expected to continue offering a broad array of products including option ARMs, he said. Asked about the bank's practice of paying extra to loan officers who sold those loans, Thompson said companies needed to motivate employees to learn and sell new products. "I would not describe them as quotas," he added. "We were emphasizing the product where appropriate."

After dropping 8 percent that day, the bank's shares, now at $25.55, were down about 57 percent since the Golden West announcement.

A week later, shareholders crammed into an Uptown Charlotte hotel ballroom for a chance to vent their fury during the bank's annual shareholder meeting. Thompson began his presentation by again acknowledging the bad timing of the Golden West deal. He said Wachovia's big mistake was not foreseeing the coming plunge in home values in markets such as California. "I'm not here to sugarcoat things," he said. "I'm not here to make excuses. I'm not here to tell you we're a victim of circumstances."

The first shareholder to speak in the question-and-answer session said Thompson and the board should step down. Others criticized executive pay and even compared the bank's acquisition of Golden West to the messy American invasion of Iraq. "If I had made a mistake like this I'd be out of a job," said investor Tim Vorick, a retired small businessman from Tampa, Florida, who commenced the grilling before a bigger-than-usual crowd of about 400 shareholders and employees.

Many of the shareholders said they felt betrayed by statements from management in January and February that the company had enough capital to maintain the dividend. Thompson defended the bank's actions, saying they were needed only after loan losses spiked. The moves would benefit shareholders in the long term, he added.

When criticized about his compensation, Thompson bristled. Management, he said, had taken "severe" pay cuts. He received about $2 million in total pay in 2007, after not receiving a bonus or any restricted stock. That compared to total compensation of $16.4 million in 2006, counting salary, bonus, stock awards, perks, and exercised options.

Charlotte shareholder activist John Moore, a bow-tie-wearing insurance firm owner who often spoke at the banks' annual meetings, steered his questions to Lanty Smith, the lead independent director. "At what point would you not be in lockstep with management?" Moore asked, noting that directors were charged with protecting shareholders.

Smith said the board stood behind management and that continuity was important in the current environment. He took offense at Moore's "lockstep" question, calling it an insult to the directors. "The board is supportive of management and will continue to be constructively supportive of management," Smith said.

Despite the vitriol, shareholders reelected all 17 directors, including Thompson, by an overwhelming percentage. More than 60 percent of the company's shares were held by institutional investors such as mutual funds, so the anger of smaller holders wasn't enough to force change. Perhaps the biggest compliment Thompson received during the hour-and-a-half session was unintended. "We'll see you at next year's annual meeting," one of the speakers said as he departed the lectern.

Speaking to reporters after the meeting, Thompson said he had expected the tension. "Our shareholders have suffered, they've got questions, they deserve to have those questions answered," he said.

Chapter 9

"I Didn't Throw in the Towel"

Bad news continued to deluge Wachovia.

Over a 12-day period in April and May 2008, the bank agreed to a $144 million settlement over its ties to telemarketers, faced a media report that it was under investigation for alleged money-laundering violations related to Mexican money exchange houses, disclosed a $1 billion charge to earnings over controversial leasing transactions, and revealed an additional $315 million insurance loss that nearly doubled the bank's first-quarter red ink.

The insurance loss came after Wachovia said it reviewed agreements related to its bank-owned life insurance portfolio. Bank-owned life insurance, or BOLI, is a sometimes-controversial type of insurance a financial institution can take out on its employees. It can serve as an attractive investment and provide a payout when employees die. In Wachovia's case, the life insurance premiums had been invested in a Citigroup-run hedge fund that was now faltering. Another bank, Cincinnati-based Fifth Third Bancorp, also invested premiums in the fund but had begun taking write-downs a quarter earlier.

In a brief escape, Ken Thompson attended a Wachovia Championship party for bank clients and other VIPs. He appeared to be in a good mood, one attendee said. That would soon change.

On May 8, Wachovia's board voted to strip Thompson of his chairmanship. Lead director Lanty Smith would assume the title, while Thompson remained CEO. In a statement, Thompson said giving up the chairman's post freed him to "focus 100 percent of my time and attention on guiding the company through the current environment." Analysts suspected his grip on Wachovia was slipping.

Board members were increasingly rattled by a cascade of events that suggested poor risk management. In the telemarketing case, which developed inside the general bank, the bank's regulator found that allegedly fraudulent telemarketers and payment processors obtained bank account information mostly from elderly customers and withdrew money from their accounts. The bank didn't admit wrongdoing but agreed to pay restitution and change practices. In the corporate and investment bank, directors were agitated by potentially risky Asian real-estate investments and write-downs related to a reinsurance business. Directors began talking to Thompson about a plan to hire a third-party company to review Wachovia's procedures and controls.

On May 12, just four days after losing his chairmanship, Thompson spoke at an investor conference in New York. He offered his first public remarks since the contentious shareholder meeting and the string of negative news that had followed. Normally, these conferences featured relatively relaxed presentations by CEOs who highlighted their successes and fielded a few questions. Thompson took a much more serious tone. He said Wachovia had some "self-inflicted" wounds but denied the company was in crisis. "My job is to address the problem head-on, and that's absolutely what I intend to do with 100 percent commitment," he pledged.

Thompson disclosed the plan to hire an outside firm to review the bank's "systems, controls, processes, procedures and people." The analysis would be coordinated by management and the board's audit committee. Management was examining each incident that had plagued the company so that it could come back to investors with a "clean bill of health," he said. And the bank was already pursuing "detailed strategies" to "remediate" concerns with the mortgage unit and the corporate and investment bank. Recent negative news did "not reflect the company we built, nor does it reflect the company we want to be in the future," he said.

Before losing his chairmanship, Thompson had asked a number of top executives to film a video designed to inspire the leadership ranks in difficult times. "Lead the business. Lead yourself. Lead the team" was the catch phrase that opened and closed the presentation. By the time it was played in May for about 200 top executives, Thompson was out as chairman.

In the video, the executives spoke frankly of the tough period Wachovia was enduring and the disappointment they felt. Corporate and investment banking executive Ben Williams said the company was making painful decisions like eliminating one-third of the staff in the fixed income division and one-fourth of the employees in the markets and investment banking unit. "If you're going through hell, keep going," Williams said, quoting Winston Churchill.

Managers needed to be out in the field with their employees, consoling them, encouraging them, and motivating them, the executives preached. Walter Davis, the executive helping to analyze the bank's mortgage unit, said this was the time for employees to roll up their sleeves and dig into details. Employees had no reason to suit up unless they were playing to win, he added. The team would emerge stronger from the crisis, said corporate and investment banking executive Jonathan Weiss. "We're going to be forged by fire," he said.

In his effort to stabilize the company, Thompson began looking to tap executives outside Wachovia for help.

He approached former Bank of America CFO Al de Molina, who had become CEO at GMAC Financial Services, about a possible role, but it didn't work out. He also talked to Chris Marshall, a former Bank of America executive and Fifth Third Bancorp CFO, about possibly taking on the post of chief financial officer or chief risk officer. Thompson told Marshall he planned to revamp the bank's finance and risk management organization, a move he would outline to the board in coming weeks. Marshall even chatted with CFO Tom Wurtz, who appeared comfortable with a possible change.

At the same time, Lanty Smith, the new chairman, sought his own counsel. One of the people he called was former Wachovia CEO Bud Baker. Baker didn't ask if the board was considering a CEO change but said it was "a decision they would have to make." "At the end of the day," he told Smith, "the board works for the shareholders and not management." Like other shareholders, Baker had watched the value of his stock holdings plummet over the past two-plus years. Thompson was "in a situation where he made some moves that didn't work out," Baker later told the *Observer*. "Sometimes in life that happens. We all make decisions that don't work out."

Other former CEOs who had sold companies to Wachovia were also growing frustrated. Former SouthTrust CEO Wallace Malone said he "almost had a heart attack" when he first heard about the Golden West deal. He didn't like the company's focus on real-estate lending, especially in California. He also wasn't impressed with its branches. Thrifts typically focused on collecting deposits to fund loans, rather than selling a range of banking products "I knew it was an accident waiting to happen," he said. As the bank's stock faltered, he peppered several board members with detailed letters outlining his complaints.

Another high-profile Wachovia critic was Ben Edwards III, the retired A. G. Edwards CEO. His successor, Robert Bagby, had forged the sale to Wachovia. Edwards had criticized the deal at the 2007 meeting in which shareholders approved it. In a later interview, he said he had heard dissent within both companies. "I think it was an ill-advised thing from the get-go," he said.

On Thursday, May 29, Smith called Thompson into his 40th-floor office in the bank's headquarters. Still focused on fixing the company, Thompson didn't know what was coming. When he left Smith's office, he was out as CEO. His three-decade career at the company had ended.

Thompson signed his retirement agreement Sunday, June 1, the same day Wachovia's board met in New York to formally install new leadership. He left with $1.45 million in severance, plus $7.2 million in restricted stock that immediately vested, $4.8 million in deferred compensation, and other stock holdings. His stock options were worthless. In one of his last acts, he reviewed the language in the news release announcing his departure. He wanted it clear that he had been asked to step down. "I didn't throw in the towel," he stressed.

Before the news came out, Thompson talked with North Carolina governor Mike Easley, the boyhood friend from Rocky Mount who regularly sought his economic advice. Easley knew Thompson had driven himself hard over his career. "You need to take a break," he told Thompson.

Early on Monday, June 2, Wachovia announced the unsettling news. Smith would serve as interim CEO and Ben Jenkins as interim chief operating officer. Smith attributed the move to a series of missteps, not just one incident. Sometimes, there came an "inflection point" in an organization when new leadership could be an energizing force, he said. In an interview, he said the decision was difficult because Thompson was a friend. But board members had a "higher obligation to the company, its shareholders and its employees." The bank would consider both internal and external candidates in its search for a new CEO, Smith said.

The move saddened employees who had known Thompson for years and raised questions about the bank's future, including the possibility of a takeover. Smith said Wachovia remained strong and didn't require a major restructuring. "The board very much believes it's best for shareholders if the company [is] independent," he said.

Some analysts questioned whether or not Smith was the right person to take charge. A board member for more than 20 years, he was one of the directors who had approved the Golden West deal. He had experience in a range of industries, including textiles, law, medical device research, and merchant banking. But he had never been in charge of a company as large and complex as Wachovia. The ouster of Thompson without a successor rattled investors and heightened concerns about Wachovia's future, critics of the move said. Some even wondered if Smith was interested in the job.

By the end of the week, Wachovia's shares had fallen more than 15 percent to $20.13, a level last seen in late 1994.

With Thompson gone and no new CEO in place, Wachovia executives and employees found themselves in a strange interim period. Some employees were shell-shocked over Thompson's departure. Others were increasingly angry at him for buying Golden West. Some dove deeper into their work. Others found themselves unmotivated. Almost no one knew the new interim CEO, Smith, a longtime director but never a major presence inside the company.

"We're all working hard," a tired-looking Ben Jenkins said in late June. "Everybody is pulling together to get through this time."

One problem that wasn't going away was the Pick-A-Payment portfolio. Even without a permanent boss, executives continued to wrestle with ways to reduce losses. One step they took at the end of June was to stop making new loans. Wachovia also looked at means of trimming the size of the existing portfolio.

Randy Robertson, an executive in the corporate and investment bank, advocated refinancing Pick-A-Payment customers into traditional loans. The idea was to contact the borrowers and offer them alternatives to their current loans. The plan was trickier than it sounded. Wachovia had more than 400,000 Pick-A-Payment customers. Some preferred the loans and their low minimum payments. Others couldn't qualify for new loans because of poor credit scores or because the value of their homes had plunged.

Robertson had run the idea by Thompson before he left, and the initiative became known as Project Green Earth because it was approved on Earth Day. Robertson, Walter Davis, and Peter Sidebottom began meeting regularly with CFO Tom Wurtz as the program was implemented.

Former Golden West executives were upset with the plan. They didn't think the Pick-A-Payment loans were going to perform as badly as feared over time, meaning Wachovia was trading more profitable assets for less profitable ones. Inside the mortgage unit, the division among employees hardened. The Wachovia side blamed Golden West for harpooning the company. The Golden West faction felt Wachovia had mismanaged a once-lucrative product and was now blaming Golden West for the result.

By June, Wachovia brought in more outside help, hiring Goldman Sachs to analyze the Golden West portfolio and evaluate alternatives.

The mortgage business wasn't Wachovia's only problem. It still needed to fix risk management lapses exposed by the rash of problems that had emerged in late April and May.

Thompson had announced a plan to examine the bank's operations. It appears that regulators also weighed in on the issue. The Federal Reserve keeps certain supervisory actions related to banks confidential, but an e-mail later released in an unrelated investigation indicated that Wachovia faced a crackdown on its risk management practices. The e-mail, sent by Mac Alfriend, senior vice president of banking supervision and regulation in Richmond, listed requirements that included the hiring of an outside consultant to review the effectiveness of the bank's corporate governance and risk management. The Fed declined to comment on what actions it took.

To fill the vacant CEO post, the Wachovia board hired an executive search firm.

Meanwhile, Smith worked his own contacts. At the top of his list was Bob Steel, a former Goldman Sachs vice chairman now at the United States Treasury. Steel was working for his old Goldman boss, Henry Paulson, as undersecretary for domestic finance. Smith had known Steel for more than 15 years, serving with him on the Duke University Board of Trustees. Steel also came recommended by former Wachovia CEO John Medlin, who knew him from their work with the Research Triangle Park–based National Humanities Center. Smith called Steel at his Washington home on Sunday, June 1, the evening before Thompson's ouster was made public. Steel, a Durham native, told him the timing wasn't right. He was busy dealing with the financial meltdown and didn't plan on leaving Treasury until a new administration arrived in January 2009. He thanked Smith for the call and suggested a few other names.

Other bankers also talked with Wachovia. Al de Molina chatted with Smith but didn't get a good sense of where the search was headed. Bob Kelly, the former Wachovia CFO who had merged Mellon Financial with Bank of New York, got a call but didn't express interest. Smith told other board members he wasn't interested in the job on a permanent basis.

After the first contact with Smith, Steel gave a heads-up to the Treasury Department's general counsel, Bob Hoyt, who said Steel had no recusal issues to worry about because he had turned Wachovia down. At the end of June, Paulson and Steel caught up for a late-afternoon chat in the Treasury secretary's office. Steel was about to go on a short vacation to Colorado, and Paulson was headed to Russia for some meetings. Steel mentioned the Wachovia entreaty, not wanting his boss to hear from another source. Paulson, a former CEO himself, didn't want to lose his lieutenant but noted that the George W. Bush administration was winding down. Steel should think about the job if it intrigued him.

Over the July 4 weekend, Steel met with the bank's search committee. The interview went well. After talking with Wachovia executives and auditors, he officially accepted the job following a July 9 board meeting. Steel called Thompson and told him it was an honor to succeed him. Smith later said Steel was the bank's "first and only" choice.

Wachovia announced the news that evening, following reports during the day by the *Observer* and other outlets that Steel had emerged as a candidate. The bank had found a CEO with a résumé that seemed almost too good to be true. A 56-year-old North Carolina native with a wave of dark hair and an easy smile, Steel had a Goldman Sachs pedigree and Washington connections. His appearance and personality allowed him to move easily among the top circles of finance and politics. He quickly picked up the names of people he met, eased tension with self-deprecating jokes, and carefully laid out his thoughts in a few easy-to-digest steps.

The new CEO's first day, July 10, started with conference calls with analysts and reporters eager to hear about the bank's financial condition. For the most part, Steel demurred on details but promised Wachovia would be forthcoming when it disclosed second-quarter earnings on July 22. Asked how long he planned to stay, he said that was up to Smith, who would remain chairman. "I now have two bosses—my wife and Mr. Smith," he quipped. "I'll follow orders from both like I usually do."

Next came Steel's debut with employees. In recent years, Wachovia workers had come to the atrium in the bank's headquarters complex to celebrate customer service accolades. Now, they were meeting their new leader at a time of major uncertainty for the company and the financial services industry.

Following a medley of pop music including U2's "Beautiful Day," Smith introduced Steel to a roar of applause. Leaning on the Wachovia-branded lectern, Steel peered into the crowd, absorbing the moment. "This is pretty intimidating," he said, earning his first laugh in the new post. "What a way to start your first day at work."

Steel made it clear he had taken the job to right the ship, not sell it to the highest bidder. "We're going to make Wachovia great, and that's the plan," he said.

Robert King Steel, the new boss of 120,000 Wachovia employees from Connecticut to California, grew up in a traditional middle-class neighborhood just a short walk from the Duke University East Campus.

Steel's father had a vending machine business before later selling life insurance. His mother worked part time in a Duke psychiatry lab where children with cleft palates were studied. The family's driveway and basketball goal were where Steel and his two brothers often gathered with other neighborhood children.

When he was old enough, Steel mowed lawns and had a job at the Young Men's Shop less than a mile from home. A Boy Scout, he earned the prestigious rank of Eagle Scout. He rooted for the Duke Blue Devils sports teams and later went to his parents' alma mater. "He enjoyed his college experience," older brother Charles Steel said. "You would not have found him in the library every night."

Steel got his first taste of the financial world in Chicago when he landed a job at a bank that eventually became part of JPMorgan Chase. He went to graduate school at the University of Chicago, where he got his MBA. He also met his future wife, Gillian, who earned a graduate degree in journalism from Northwestern University in nearby Evanston, Illinois.

He joined the Chicago office of Goldman Sachs in 1976. The office was relatively small, fostering collegiality in an industry known for its competitiveness. Steel worked in securities but became close with an investment banker who had joined the firm about two years earlier: Henry Paulson. Steel moved to London in 1986 to found the equity capital markets group for Europe. In 1994, he transferred to New York, where he served as head of equities, a key stock-trading business. By 2001, he climbed to vice chairman. He retired in 2004, reportedly leaving as eventual CEO Lloyd Blankfein consolidated power.

Steel was a senior fellow at Harvard University when he got a call from Paulson and signed on as one of his lieutenants at Treasury. As Bear Stearns imploded in March 2008, Steel was among the regulators weighing an unappetizing choice: Let the firm's demise possibly unravel the global financial system or engineer a rescue sure to be labeled a government bailout. From his New York hotel room, Steel dialed in to a 5 A.M. conference call in which he, Paulson, Bernanke, and others finalized steps to prop up the firm. Later that day, it was Steel's job to brief President Bush.

"He thrives under adversity," Paulson told the *Observer*. "I watched him at Goldman Sachs when we went through tough times. I watched him deal with others on the team, people inside and outside. He is cool under fire. He is measured. He knows how to pace himself, how to motivate others around him."

Since leaving Duke, Steel had kept close ties to his alma mater. He had served on the board of trustees since 1996 and assumed the chairmanship in 2005. He led the search for a university president in 2003, chaired the university's endowment during a time of strong returns, and guided the administration when basketball coach Mike Krzyzewski toyed with leaving for the Los Angeles Lakers. He also was at the helm when the 2006 lacrosse scandal polarized the campus and community. Some praised Steel's steady hand in the crisis, while others criticized him and other university officials for not standing behind the players accused of raping an exotic dancer. The players were later exonerated, and the prosecutor was disgraced.

Steel's move from the public sector to Wachovia raised questions about a potential conflict of interest. A Treasury spokeswoman said Steel had recused himself from Wachovia issues when discussions about the job heated up in June. Under his employment agreement with Wachovia, Steel was to receive up to $22.1 million per year—$1.1 million in salary, a target bonus of $6 million, and "target long-term incentive" pay of $15 million. His pay would depend on the company's performance. He didn't receive a signing bonus.

In his United States Treasury post, Steel had made a salary of $158,500. But he had accumulated significant wealth at Goldman Sachs before entering government. His final Treasury financial disclosure form valued his stock, bonds, and other financial interests at somewhere between tens of millions and less than $300 million. The family owned homes in Greenwich, Connecticut; Washington, D.C.; and Aspen, Colorado. In a sign of commitment to the new job, he'd soon buy a home in Charlotte's Eastover neighborhood, ironically just down the street from Ken Thompson.

Wachovia shareholders weren't likely to hold Steel's wealth against him if he could rescue the company.

Steel's first big jobs were to announce second-quarter earnings for 2008 and to start laying out plans for a recovery.

On July 22, he revealed that the bank had lost $8.9 billion in the April-to-June period. Part of the damage was caused by a $5.6 billion provision for loan losses, driven mostly by the deteriorating Pick-A-Payment portfolio. Now, the bank was expecting lifetime losses of 12 percent, up from 7 to 8 percent. It had also incurred a $6.1 billion goodwill-related charge as its stock price continued to fall.

Steel's plan for stabilizing the bank was largely to build capital by spending less money and fine-tuning Wachovia's business mix. By the end of 2009, the bank hoped to accumulate $5 billion by slashing the dividend, cutting more than 10,000 jobs, and selling off assets and businesses.

Wachovia also promised to whittle down the mortgage portfolio. It would ramp up the effort to contact Pick-A-Payment customers and refinance them into new loans.

The mortgage unit formed by the Golden West deal was being dramatically downsized. Ultimately, Wachovia planned to eliminate 5,000 of the 11,000 jobs in the division. Since closing the deal in October 2006, the bank had announced plans to eliminate a total of 8,100 mortgage positions. Golden West had about 10,500 employees when Wachovia bought it. The top two former Golden West executives still at Wachovia, Tim Wilson and Rich Fikani, would soon depart. The Pick-A-Payment portfolio would be moved out of the mortgage unit and put under the direction of David Carroll, who would be charged with the effort to refinance borrowers into new loans. The initiative once known as Project Green Earth was now called the Distressed Asset Resolution Team, or DART. Except for the bank branches, most of Golden West was being wiped away.

Steel also had concerns about other areas. After years of expansion, Wachovia's corporate and investment bank still was a second-tier player that didn't match up to major investment banks like his former employer, Goldman Sachs. He preferred a business model that focused more on customers and put less of its own capital at risk through lending or trading. Wachovia also had a $48 billion commercial real-estate portfolio whose losses were spiking.

Steel's initial plan was well received on Wall Street, the bank's stock rising 27 percent on the day of the earnings report. The new CEO gave his own vote of confidence when he bought 1 million of the bank's shares, initially valued at $16 million.

As he redrew strategy, Steel also began assembling his management team.

Hired back in May by Thompson, general counsel Jane Sherburne had worked in the Clinton White House, where she was in charge of damage control for Whitewater-related matters. She later served as the top lawyer for Citi's global consumer group. Before starting at Wachovia, Sherburne was driving from New York to her family's home in Maryland when Smith called to tell her that Thompson had been let go. She drove only a couple more exits on the New Jersey Turnpike before deciding she wanted to start earlier than planned.

Later, when the board picked Steel as CEO, Sherburne started hearing good things about him from friends and former colleagues. Shortly after he arrived at the company, she met with the new CEO in his office, which had belonged to Thompson only months earlier.

"I can understand if you want to find your own general counsel," she said.

Steel wasn't looking to make a change. "I've checked you out and like what I've heard, as I'm sure you've checked me out," he said. "I'd like to see if we can make it work."

Two key players under Thompson—CFO Tom Wurtz and chief risk officer Don Truslow—announced their retirement in quick succession after the earnings report. Before they left, they provided some of their thoughts on the Pick-A-Payment portfolio to analysts from research firm CreditSights. It was a surprisingly candid exit interview for two executives heavily involved in the Golden West deal and its troubled aftermath.

Wurtz and Truslow told the analysts that Golden West's policy of making mid-sized loans backfired because it led to a heavy concentration of mortgages in California's Inland Empire and Central Valley regions. As home values skyrocketed, Golden West was priced out of expensive coastal areas and made more loans in the state's interior. Those markets became ground zero for the housing crisis, experiencing big runups in home values, followed by major crashes.

They said Wachovia was caught off guard by the steep decline in home values. They also pointed to what they saw as a major weakness in the Pick-A-Payment product. "It seems that borrowers who choose a mortgage with the option of lower minimum payments may in fact be indicating to the lender that there is more likelihood that they will not have the resources to cover the [full] payment," the CreditSights analysts wrote.

Wurtz and Truslow also noted that the bank had failed to shed the portfolio before the financial crisis flared up. They were frank in saying they believed Wachovia missed an opportunity to aggressively "sell down" the portfolio in early 2007, when the loans may have still been attractive to investors, the analysts wrote.

Chapter 10

FROM LEHMAN TO MERRILL

As Bob Steel began his effort to resuscitate Wachovia, Bank of America turned to absorbing Countrywide. It had officially bought the lender on July 1, 2008, for $2.5 billion, the price declining along with Bank of America's stock.

In May, Ken Lewis put one of his top executives in charge of rehabilitating the tarnished franchise. Barbara Desoer, the bank's former technology and operations executive, would lead the combined mortgage unit from Countrywide's Calabasas, California, headquarters, the new base for the company's mortgage operations. It was a California homecoming for Desoer, a BankAmerica alumna who once served as an aide to two of the San Francisco bank's CEOs.

Desoer's appointment recalled the BankAmerica deal because Lewis had originally planned to make Countrywide president David Sambol the head of the combined unit but reversed course a few months later. By June 2009, the SEC would charge Sambol, Countrywide CEO Mozilo, and another executive with civil fraud for misleading shareholders about Countrywide's financial situation. All three would deny the allegations.

Unlike the 1998 merger, the California company's name didn't stick around this time. The combined mortgage business would be rebranded Bank of America Home Loans. The Charlotte bank also stopped originating subprime loans and option ARMs and pledged to provide $35 million in grants and low-cost loans to help nonprofit organizations stem foreclosures. Consumer advocates remained wary of the takeover but were hopeful that Bank of America could rehab one of the most damaged companies in the mortgage meltdown. "It will be a significantly different company," Lewis told shareholders at the bank's annual meeting in April 2008. To cut costs, the bank planned to eliminate 7,500 jobs over two years.

At an analyst conference in June, Lewis faced questions about possibly buying Countrywide at the wrong time. He said he "personally" worried the housing market could fall dramatically farther but added "from everything we know, we think we got it right." Speaking on the same day Wachovia announced Thompson's departure, he appeared to allude to his counterpart's much more costly purchase. "Obviously, there is a risk to it," he said, "but we are not paying $22 billion, either."

In taking on Countrywide, Bank of America was tackling one of the financial industry's biggest trouble spots, a relief to government officials scrambling to prevent more Bear Stearns–like blowups. But after a seemingly calm summer, the financial crisis was about to boil over again.

On Sunday, September 7, Treasury secretary Henry Paulson announced the government was placing mortgage giants Fannie Mae and Freddie Mac into conservatorship, injecting them with capital, and ousting their CEOs. It was another dramatic sign that the government wasn't done with intervening in the private sector. "We examined all options available, and determined that this comprehensive and complementary set of actions best meets our three objectives of market stability, mortgage availability and taxpayer protection," Paulson said.

Fannie and Freddie had long played a central role in the mortgage market by buying home loans from banks and packaging them into bonds for investors. Charlotte's banks lauded the move to stabilize the entities, and their stocks rallied when the markets opened on Monday, September 8. "This action should lead to an increased availability of mortgage financing, which will help achieve stability in housing, a critical element in the health of our economy," Bank of America's Lewis said. Wachovia's Steel said the agency had developed a "very constructive plan that should be encouraging to the financial markets [and] restore confidence to the housing industry while being sensitive to taxpayers."

Optimism about the markets didn't last long. After the dramatic steps taken with Freddie and Fannie, financial markets homed in on the next potential victim in a domino effect that would continue for weeks. Lehman Brothers, a 158-year-old investment bank that had once been part of American Express Company, was the smallest of the big-four Wall Street investment banks following the demise of Bear Stearns in March. For months, Lehman had been searching for new capital to absorb its real-estate-related losses. Now, word leaked that talks had broken down with the state-owned Korea Development Bank, perhaps ending the investment bank's chances of getting the cash infusion it needed to survive on its own. On Tuesday, September 9, Lehman's shares plummeted 45 percent to less than $8.

Even as its prognosis worsened, Lehman held its annual financial services conference that week in New York, bringing together the leaders of top banks for reports on their performance and strategy. Steel made his presentation on Tuesday, providing an update on plans to chip away at Wachovia's option ARM portfolio. "We believe we've accomplished a great deal in a short amount of time," he said. "I'm very confident that we're moving in the right direction and making the tough decisions." He added later, "To tell you that I had it all buttoned up and raised my right hand . . . would be disingenuous. But we're on the case."

A day later, Bank of America's Brian Moynihan, who had replaced Gene Taylor as head of corporate and investment banking, told analysts that his unit had been able to gain market share even as it completed a restructuring that purged 3,400 employees. He stressed the bank's "capital strength and stability" and noted the company was investing in its businesses even in the face of challenging economic times.

While other banks used his firm's conference to lay out future plans, Lehman CEO Dick Fuld made a major move of his own. His resistance to selling Lehman was ebbing, and Bank of America was at the top of the list of potential buyers. Bank of America's commercial bank could bring stability to Lehman, and Lehman could offer the Charlotte bank big-time investment banking capabilities, at perhaps a depressed price.

Bank of America was still considered a lesser Wall Street player, especially in the glamour businesses of underwriting stock and advising on mergers. Lewis hadn't helped his firm's standing with the crack about having "all of the fun I can stand in investment banking," which raised questions for some about the company's desire to be a serious player. In June 2008, at a *Wall Street Journal* conference, he made another quip at Wall Street's expense: "We wouldn't use our petty cash to buy an investment bank."

Lewis turned down an entreaty from Fuld in July. A new courtship began on Tuesday, September 9, when Fuld called his outside lawyer, Sullivan & Cromwell's Rodge Cohen, who would be a key adviser for a number of firms during the nation's escalating financial drama. Cohen took the call in his New York financial district office, which offered a commanding view of the Statue of Liberty and the harbor lapping at her feet. Fuld's instructions: Get in touch with Greg Curl, Bank of America's strategy executive.

Since this would be a critical call, Cohen took time to write a brief script. When he reached Curl, he delivered his prepared pitch: "We have two considerations. One is the company and one is the people. As you will notice price is not one of them. Of course there is a price where we could not go forward." Curl said he would check with his boss, Lewis, and get back with Cohen.

Treasury and Fed officials were eager for Fuld to find a contingency plan for his faltering firm. Since brokering JPMorgan Chase's purchase of Bear Stearns, Paulson and Ben Bernanke had been preparing for the possibility of another crisis. But they knew their tools to deal with major blowups were limited. When a traditional bank failed, the FDIC had the power to take it over and sell off its deposits and loans. But regulators didn't have similar authority to deal with other types of large financial firms. In the case of Bear Stearns, the Fed had used authority stemming from a 1932 law to lend "to any individual, partnership or corporation" if five Federal Reserve Board members in Washington determined "unusual and exigent" circumstances.

Bailouts were already becoming unpopular. Congress wasn't likely to hand regulators any new powers in a contentious presidential election year. That's why Paulson wanted a stronger institution like Bank of America to scoop up Lehman. On Tuesday, the former Dartmouth football player dialed Lewis in Charlotte to prod him to take a look. The Bank of America CEO expressed interest but didn't commit. Paulson's schedule later showed the Treasury secretary made six calls to Lewis between 4:30 P.M. and 6:55 P.M. that day, plus another on Wednesday.

Later on Tuesday, Curl told another Treasury official about a stumbling block. One of the company's primary regulators, the Federal Reserve Bank in Richmond, had been pressuring Bank of America to build its capital levels since buying Countrywide. That would make it tough for the bank to tackle another deal.

As in most big bank mergers, the Federal Reserve Board of Governors in Washington had to approve an acquisition by any holding company it regulated. After Bank of America announced the Countrywide acquisition in January, Fed staff in Washington, as well as examiners in Richmond, reviewed the proposal. They recommended approval but expressed concern about the amount of capital the combined company would have to absorb future losses, especially if the economy weakened. The board backed the merger June 5 by a 5–0 vote, a move that regulators believed placed troubled Countrywide in safer hands. The order approving the acquisition said the bank had "sufficient financial resources to effect the proposal."

But officials including Richmond Fed president Jeff Lacker began to press the bank to pad its capital cushion, which had already been trimmed by the 2007 LaSalle acquisition. Traditionally, Bank of America rebounded from deals by pumping out more profits and rebuilding its reserves. This time, Richmond examiners told the bank to come up with a specific plan for accumulating capital, including steps such as cutting its lucrative dividend or selling assets. That irked some at Bank of America, who felt they were getting conflicting orders from Fed officials. Now, with the government eager to find a bidder for Lehman, the bank perhaps had a chance to win some wiggle room on capital requirements. It hadn't publicly announced to investors the regulatory push to trim its dividend.

On the morning of Wednesday, September 10, Lehman rolled out a grim earnings report earlier than expected, disclosing a $4 billion third-quarter loss. In a bid to regain market confidence, the firm announced plans to spin off up to $30 billion in troubled real-estate loans and sell a stake in its prized asset management business and potentially sell the whole company. Fuld, the longest-serving chief on Wall Street, acknowledged his firm's days as an independent company might be over. "If anybody came with an attractive proposition that was compelling for shareholder value, it would be brought to the board, discussed with the board, and evaluated," Fuld said on an analyst conference call.

Lehman's plans did little to assuage investors. Its stock continued to plunge during the day, falling another 7 percent to $7.25. At Paulson's bidding, Bernanke placed a call to Lewis to try to smooth things over. He urged the CEO to take a look at Lehman and said the Fed could work with the bank on capital. Lewis agreed to send a team to New York Thursday morning. Back in Richmond, officials stood by their assessment that the bank needed more capital, though they wouldn't play a major role in the Lehman negotiations. Later, some officials would believe they should have pushed Bank of America harder to cut its dividend, considering the problems that lay ahead.

Lehman's troubles didn't worry the government only. Rival investment banks also feared the fallout.

Merrill president Greg Fleming caught Lehman's earnings report on CNBC at a hotel in Dallas, where he was leading a town hall meeting for Merrill employees before heading back to New York for a gathering with brokers that evening. That summer, Merrill, led by new chief executive John Thain, had made big strides in cleaning up a balance sheet riddled with mortgage-related assets and skimpy on capital. But Fleming, a 16-year company veteran, worried that the markets wouldn't give the firm credit as yet another investment bank unraveled. Merrill was likely next on the hit list.

If Lehman were up for sale, Fleming assumed Bank of America was a potential buyer. That was a big worry because he had always seen Bank of America as a premier partner for Merrill. If the Charlotte bank snapped up Lehman, there would be one fewer dance partner for his firm.

Fleming checked in with Ed Herlihy, a lawyer with the New York firm of Wachtell, Lipton, Rosen & Katz who had long represented Bank of America in merger deals, to see if he could glean any intelligence. Herlihy said the bank was looking at its options but didn't let on to its plans. If Merrill wanted to talk with Bank of America, CEO Thain needed to call Lewis, Herlihy said. Fleming surmised something was up with Lehman and knew he needed to persuade Thain to make the call. Once a deal maker for clients such as First Union, Fleming now might have to call on his skills to sell his own company.

On Thursday, September 11, the Bank of America team, led by strategy executive Greg Curl, convened in Sullivan & Cromwell's offices in Midtown Manhattan's Seagram Building, a Park Avenue landmark. Curl, a bespectacled former naval intelligence officer, had summoned Chris Flowers, a former Goldman Sachs banker who had founded an eponymous private-equity firm known for its bank deals. Flowers would provide an extra set of eyes and could become a potential co-investor if he liked what he saw.

Curl and Flowers had known each other for years. Only a year earlier, Bank of America had joined Flowers's bid to buy education lender Sallie Mae. That deal, however, unraveled amid the credit crunch and changes to education laws. Flowers's consortium had triggered the deal's "material adverse change" (or MAC) escape clause in an effort to abandon the buyout. Later, the parties reached a legal settlement. It was a rare setback for a self-proclaimed "grave dancer" who pounced on chances to invest in ailing institutions. When he scored, he scored big, earning him a regular spot on *Forbes* magazine's list of richest Americans.

Although the list of potential suitors was slim, Bank of America wasn't the only bank mulling a Lehman overture. Barclays, looking to expand in investment banking and in the United States, was also mulling the idea. Wachovia CEO Bob Steel had helped feed the British bank's interest when he was at Treasury. He knew Barclays president Bob Diamond from a stint serving on the Barclays board and encouraged him to consider the prospect when Lehman's problems were building in the spring of 2008.

Little more than a year after the ABN AMRO takeover fight, Barclays and Bank of America were now paired in another financial drama. Both banks' due diligence teams dug into Lehman's books and came to the same conclusion: They would need government help to absorb Lehman's troubled real-estate loans. Bank of America officials figured they might need assistance covering $40 billion or more in losses.

By Thursday afternoon, word leaked that Bank of America was in the mix to buy Lehman. Gary Townsend of Hill-Townsend Capital wondered why Bank of America would want to add another battered institution to its crowded plate but said such a takeover wasn't unthinkable. "Ken Lewis has always struck me as someone incapable of passing by a deal," he said. Tom Brown, the hedge fund manager, said a takeover would give Bank of America some needed muscle in investment banking, where it was considered "mediocre." "It's not a niche player, and it's not one of the major investment banks," Brown said. "That's not a position Ken Lewis likes to be in."

On Friday, Lehman's shares slumped another 13 percent to $3.65, leaving them down 94 percent for the year. Lehman wasn't likely to survive the weekend without a deal or a rescue package. But CNBC reported Friday morning that the government wasn't looking to provide another bailout, a line in the sand that would be difficult to erase. Paulson had leaked the message to the news outlet through spokeswoman Michele Davis.

That morning, Merrill's Thain held a conference call with his board to update directors on the situation. One of the board members, John Finnegan, asked why Merrill's fate would be different from Lehman's. Thain pointed out that Merrill owned half of respected money manager BlackRock, Inc., and also had its well-known brokerage arm. To some Merrill insiders, this served as a sign that Thain didn't understand how dire the financial crisis had become.

That afternoon, Paulson instructed the heads of the nation's major banks to convene at the Federal Reserve Bank of New York's fortress-like headquarters in Manhattan. Thain hoped to get out of the city early to beat traffic home on a rainy Friday, but a Fed official told him to be at the meeting by six that evening. Soon, shiny black luxury cars were depositing Wall Street chieftains at the Fed. The three main players in the drama—Lehman, Bank of America, and Barclays—were conspicuously absent. Moynihan, Bank of America's investment banking head, was on his way to the meeting when a Treasury official told him he shouldn't attend because Bank of America was in the mix to buy Lehman.

In a call that afternoon, Curl and Flowers, however, had told Paulson that the bank couldn't do the deal without massive government help. Bank of America didn't officially pull out, but a transaction was looking less likely with no commitment from Paulson to provide assistance. The Treasury secretary pushed Bank of America to keep looking at a possible deal even though it was obvious the Charlotte bank was losing interest.

Inside the New York Fed, Paulson and Tim Geithner laid out the problem: Lehman was headed to bankruptcy unless they worked out an alternative. It probably wouldn't be able to open for business on Monday. And then came the kicker: No government aid was in the offing.

Back in 1998, the New York Fed had hosted a similar gathering when hedge fund Long-Term Capital Management was on the brink. Banks grudgingly chipped in capital to allow an orderly winding down for the firm. But this time, the problem assets were much bigger and the players in the room had major issues of their own. The prospect of patching up Lehman only to have it sold to a rival such as Bank of America or Barclays wasn't appealing. The executives were to report back Saturday morning to begin working on a solution, including analyzing the depths of Lehman's problems and the potential fallout.

At Merrill Lynch, Fleming, treasurer Eric Heaton, and lawyer Pete Kelly were increasingly worried about the firm's prospects and growing frustrated with Thain's inaction. Late into the night, they called and texted each other about the need to persuade Thain to contact Lewis.

It was a delicate situation. Thain, an outsider with a Goldman Sachs pedigree, and Fleming, a Merrill veteran long seen as a potential CEO candidate, weren't exactly close. Tension had simmered inside the company as Thain recruited former Goldman Sachs colleagues such as Peter Kraus and Tom Montag to top positions and handed them huge pay packages. Thain and his Goldman peers were already wealthy from their previous jobs, while their Merrill counterparts, although well compensated over the years, had much of their net worth tied up in Merrill stock. Merrill insiders weren't eager to sell the 94-year-old firm. But they also didn't want it to become another Bear Stearns or Lehman.

After a fretful night at his Bedford, New York, home, Fleming called Thain around 6:30 A.M. on Saturday, September 13. He wanted to catch Thain before he headed back to the New York Fed. Since it was to be one of the most important calls of his life, he wrote out three bullet points to emphasize: The deal made strategic sense whether it was under duress or not; Thain would be considered a hero for protecting the firm; and executives had a fiduciary duty to shareholders and employees to consider their options. Thain was getting out of the shower and said he would call back.

When Thain returned the call from the road, Fleming again urged him to contact Lewis. They at least needed to lay the groundwork for a deal. They needed options.

"You're panicking," Thain said.

"I don't think so," Fleming fired back, saying it might be the biggest regret of their lives if Merrill didn't reach out to Bank of America. If the weekend passed without a deal, that meant five more harrowing trading days before the next weekend.

Thain said he wasn't ready to make the call, and the conversation ended.

Fleming didn't give up. He continued to buzz Herlihy and Curl, who were meeting that morning at the New York Fed with Paulson and Geithner. Bank of America had already decided it wasn't going to buy Lehman and started sending its team home to Charlotte. Herlihy in turn had a message for Fleming: Lewis wasn't going to get on a plane to New York unless Thain called him first.

Back at the New York Fed, Lehman's troubles crystallized during meetings of the Wall Street chiefs. The firm might need at least $20 billion in capital, an almost impossible hole to fill without government help. Thain began thinking Merrill could be next and decided it was time to meet with Bank of America. He made a call to Fleming. The Merrill president had lined up a meeting in New York for 2:30 P.M., but Thain still needed to call Lewis, Fleming reiterated. Bank of America wanted to know Thain was on board before making a move. Fleming's assurances weren't enough.

"He wants to hear your voice," Fleming said. "Tell him the weather is nice and you're looking forward to seeing him."

Thain worried that talking with Bank of America could end up hampering a Lehman deal, which could in turn hurt Merrill. He also knew a sale would end his short stint as Merrill's CEO. Still, he knew he had to make the move.

"Get me the phone number," the Merrill CEO said.

Standing on the street outside the Fed, Thain placed the call to Lewis, who was home in Charlotte.

"Ken, I think we should talk about a strategic arrangement," Thain said.

Lewis said he could be in New York in a couple of hours.

Bank of America's corporate apartment in the Time Warner Center offered a commanding view of Central Park and beyond. But Lewis and Thain had little time to absorb the scenery when they met Saturday afternoon. The two CEOs quickly got down to business. Thain said he wanted Bank of America to take a 9.9

percent stake in Merrill and provide a credit line to stabilize the firm. Predictably, Lewis was thinking bigger.

"I'm not interested in a 9.9 percent stake," he said.

"Well, I didn't come here to sell the company," Thain responded.

"That's what I'm interested in," Lewis said.

The Bank of America CEO launched into the strategic rationale of the deal, which would turn his company into an instant force on Wall Street. He had never been excited about a Lehman pairing because that firm was bigger in the bond business, which was already a strength for Bank of America. Merrill, however, had a well-rounded investment bank in the United States and overseas, plus its renowned brokerage unit. When the meeting ended, the two CEOs agreed to pursue two tracks: A whole-company deal and a minority investment. The two Gregs—Curl and Fleming—would lead the negotiations.

As they parted, Thain said he probably should tell Paulson about the talks. Lewis said that was fine. "We've already told him that we're done with the Lehman deal," he said.

Back at Lehman, the grim reality that Bank of America wasn't going to be a savior started to sink in. For hours, Rodge Cohen, Lehman's lawyer, had been hearing rumors of talks between Merrill and Bank of America. At the New York Fed, he pressed Geithner and other officials to assist Lehman for the good of the financial system. "If you guys blow this one and don't help there will be no firebreak for Merrill Lynch," Cohen said. The officials said they were working on something. That wasn't a good sign for Lehman.

Later in the weekend, Fuld even tried phoning Lewis at home, but Lewis's wife, Donna, politely told him to stop calling. From Lewis's perspective, taking the call didn't make sense. He was negotiating with the government, not Lehman.

Around five on Saturday afternoon, Fleming and Curl connected at Wachtell Lipton's Midtown Manhattan office, housed inside the imposing granite CBS headquarters building known as "Black Rock." During the negotiations, each company would have its own floor as a base for due diligence teams and negotiators.

"We want a deal done to announce before the market opens Monday," Fleming said.

"That's fast," Curl responded. They had only about 36 hours to pull a deal together.

Fleming said he would provide whatever Bank of America needed—numbers, documents, people. To kick off the rapid-fire review, he began calling Merrill employees around the world, rousing some who were asleep in London and Asia and apologizing to spouses who picked up the phone. One Merrill executive didn't mind the late-night call. "Thank God you're doing this," he told Fleming.

Bank of America began calling its troops back to New York. Most hadn't even unpacked after returning to Charlotte from the Lehman due diligence work.

Some had gone straight to the office to start preparing for the fallout from a Lehman bankruptcy. Now, they headed back to New York, most not knowing the reason for the return trip. Some suspected a Lehman deal might be back on.

After meeting Lewis, Thain returned to the New York Fed, where the other CEOs were still huddling. He caught Paulson for a moment and told him about his conversation with Lewis. "Good," the Treasury secretary said.

Merrill also got feelers from other firms interested in talking. Morgan Stanley CEO John Mack approached Thain and suggested they meet later that evening. Goldman executives sidled up to Merrill's Peter Kraus, their former colleague, setting up a meeting for Sunday. The New York Fed was practically becoming a financial industry singles bar.

After leaving the Fed, Thain connected with Mack at a Morgan Stanley executive's Manhattan apartment. It was clear that the Mooresville, North Carolina, native wasn't operating on the same timetable as Merrill. Mack suggested they start working on something the following week. By the end of Saturday, Bank of America and Goldman were Thain's two best hopes.

Bank of America assembled its due diligence team at Wachtell Lipton's office as flights arrived from Charlotte. Some members didn't get there until as late as 10 that night. Most had been up since early Saturday morning after working long hours earlier in the week analyzing Lehman. Besides its own analysts, the bank brought in Flowers's team again. Flowers, who was also working with faltering insurance conglomerate American International Group over the weekend, had reviewed Merrill's books in the past year as he weighed investing in the firm.

Even with Flowers's head start, it was going to be a long night.

Around eight in the morning on Sunday, September 14, Thain and Lewis met for breakfast back at Bank of America's corporate apartment.

They reviewed preliminary due diligence reports. When Lewis again pushed for a purchase of all of Merrill, Thain told him it couldn't be a lowball price. They agreed talks should continue.

Thain's next stop was the New York Fed. It was increasingly clear that neither Bank of America nor Barclays was going to rescue Lehman. The nation's fourth-biggest investment bank was headed toward a bankruptcy filing. Paulson took Thain aside, urging him to cut a deal. "I'm working on something," Thain told Paulson.

While Fleming and other Merrill executives negotiated with Bank of America at Wachtell Lipton, Merrill strategy executive Peter Kraus was still cultivating a possible Goldman investment. The former Goldman executive called Fleming and asked him to send some of his people to Merrill's downtown headquarters to help with due diligence.

"That's not happening," Fleming said. He felt Bank of America was the better deal. It wasn't worth scaring off Bank of America by sending part of his team.

"You're president, and it's your decision, but you're making a mistake," Kraus responded.

Minutes later, Thain called to repeat the order to send some staff down to Merrill headquarters. Fleming said Goldman would buy a stake in Merrill only if was good for the rival firm. But he relented, dispatching Merrill treasurer Eric Heaton. By the time Heaton's car navigated street festival traffic and made it downtown, he didn't find anyone from Goldman to meet with.

Back at Wachtell Lipton, Fleming and Curl negotiated price. Fleming said he wanted something in the $30-per-share range. Bank of America was getting a once-in-a-lifetime chance to buy a great business that had been worth a lot more just weeks earlier, he argued. Curl noted the difficult environment both firms faced but left open the possibility of a premium over Merrill's Friday closing price of $17.05.

As Fleming battled for the best price he could get, some of his friends in the firm told him to be careful not to blow the deal at such a precarious time. They'd be happy if he got half the firm's market price. Eventually, Curl gave Fleming an ultimatum of $29, for a total of $50 billion. Bank of America was concerned about the "optics" of paying any more for the struggling firm.

"A 70 percent premium," Curl said. "That's as far as we'll go."

Fleming called Thain, who still wanted $30. Fleming said Curl's figure was the best they were going to get, and eventually Thain agreed.

While price was a big issue, Fleming and Curl also negotiated other key provisions. Merrill wanted a material adverse change clause, which would give Bank of America little room to escape the deal should market conditions or Merrill's performance fall off before the deal closed. If the sale to Bank of America collapsed, Merrill was likely dead.

The two sides also agreed to allow Merrill to pay year-end bonuses up to the same level as 2007. That amounted to a total bonus cap of about $5.8 billion, to be paid 60 percent in cash and 40 percent in stock. Lawyers for Bank of America and Merrill included the bonus provision in a "disclosure schedule" that accompanied the merger agreement. Both sides felt the bonuses were needed to retain employees. The agreement didn't determine bonuses for top Merrill executives.

Later on Sunday, Bank of America held a board meeting to consider the deal. Company executives and Flowers presented their findings. Flowers's namesake firm and another firm affiliated with him, Fox-Pitt Kelton Cochran Caronia Waller, were willing to vouch for the $29-per-share offer for Merrill. Such fairness opinions provided boards with an outside examination of a purchase price but were widely viewed as potentially conflicted because of the big fees firms received for rendering them. Bank of America agreed to pay the two firms a total of $20 million, $15 million of which would come after the deal was completed.

During the board's deliberations, director Chad Gifford, the former Fleet CEO, questioned the purchase. In particular, he said he was worried about the timing of the deal, coming as it did amid the Lehman Brothers bankruptcy and the coming blowup at AIG. Bank of America likely could have paid less by waiting until Monday, after Lehman's demise rocked Merrill's share price. In the end, the board voted unanimously to approve the purchase.

Merrill's board meeting started after Bank of America's and went smoothly. Considering the circumstances, the firm was getting a good price. After the session, Thain and other Merrill executives walked the short distance from the firm's Midtown office to Wachtell Lipton's location. It was the first time Thain had been to the scene of the furious negotiations to sell his company.

The two sides hadn't clinched the deal yet. Lawyers continued to haggle over final details in the merger. At one point, an antsy Lewis and Thain waited in the same room to sign off on the agreement.

A Federal Reserve Bank of Richmond official checked in with Bank of America's chief risk officer, Amy Brinkley, and was told the deal was "solidified" but legal issues needed to be finalized. Brinkley said Bank of America had a "much higher level of comfort" buying Merrill than Lehman, Lisa White, a vice president at the Charlotte branch of the Richmond Fed, told her colleagues in a 9:49 P.M. e-mail. "While Amy acknowledged that it may look to the outside world as if BAC [Bank of America] is paying a bit of a premium for Merrill, BAC's estimate of Merrill's asset values indicate they are getting the firm at a 30–50% discount," White wrote. "Chris Flowers, the prominent private equity guru, has done extensive due diligence on Merrill over the past few months for potential equity investors, and I got the impression that BAC is at least partially relying upon this work."

Around midnight, Lewis, Thain, and other top executives, exhausted from the frenzied weekend, gathered for an awkward, anticlimactic toast. The champagne had warmed during the wait. Lewis had long craved buying Merrill. Now, his Southern bank had scored a hallmark Wall Street firm. But he wasn't particularly happy after days of tense negotiations. Thain felt like he had done the best he could for his shareholders, but his future was uncertain after less than a year on the job. Other Merrill executives were relieved the company was saved but were annoyed that former Goldman-turned-Merrill executives like Tom Montag and Peter Kraus were part of the moment, having done little to forge the deal.

"No one was happy," remembered one participant. "It was like an awkward Thanksgiving at the in-laws'. People were tired. There was remorse over selling. People were scared of what the next day would bring."

Chapter 11

FOR SALE: WACHOVIA

The morning of Monday, September 15, 2008, brought a swarm of stunning—and stomach-churning—headlines: Lehman Brothers had filed for bankruptcy protection, Merrill had fallen into the arms of Bank of America, and insurance giant AIG was on the brink.

Ken Lewis was the most obvious victor in the chaos sweeping Wall Street, having rescued a renowned company from failure. But in a conference call with analysts, he had to face tough questions about the $50 billion price and how the deal came together.

Asked if he paid too much, Lewis said he probably could have rolled the dice and tried to buy Merrill for less but didn't want to risk the firm's surviving on its own or receiving a possible investment from a rival. "I don't know anybody who's perfect at picking the absolute bottom," he said.

Knowing that Bank of America had also looked at Lehman Brothers over the weekend, UBS analyst Matt O'Connor quizzed the bank on its due diligence of Merrill's books. CFO Joe Price said the bank knew Merrill as a competitor and also had help from Chris Flowers, "who had pretty extensive knowledge of the company" from his past review. The bank had more than 45 people on site during the due diligence, plus others off site and outside counsel.

NAB Research analyst Nancy Bush prodded the Bank of America CEO about his much-expressed distaste for the investment banking business. Lewis said the bank likely would have been "frustrated for quite some time" trying to build an investment bank on its own. The Merrill deal, he said, "changes that." Recalling his "all of the fun I can stand" remark, he added, "I like it again."

Back at Merrill, John Thain held a town hall meeting for employees shocked by the sale of their firm to a smaller competitor in the investment banking and brokerage business. Hundreds of employees packed the third-floor conference room where the firm held its annual meetings and other events. Employees also watched a video feed.

Thain was tired and still coming to grips with the deal. He choked up a couple times as he talked.

With Wall Street in crisis, investors weren't sure about the deal—or anything else going on in the financial world. Bank of America shares fell more than 21 percent to $26.55. Merrill shares jumped early in the day but ended almost flat at $17.06.

When Lewis got home from New York, a congratulatory message from Hugh McColl awaited him. There wasn't a more symbolic victory of a Southern bank over the New York establishment than Bank of America's buying Merrill Lynch.

At "Mother Merrill," views on the deal were divided. While some employees worried about job cuts and the loss of a culture built over 94 years, others were pragmatic in light of the financial system's disarray. Lehman peers were gathering their belongings in cardboard boxes. "They probably saved us," one employee said. In a restaurant at the base of Merrill's headquarters, other investment bankers took the news as expected. "They're drinking," the general manager said.

In a case of extremely bad timing, a luxury car show had taken over the plaza behind Merrill's offices that week. Browsers seemed scarce, although an Aston Martin bore a "Sold" ticket. Suggested price: $265,000. Surveying the odd scene was a former Merrill investment banker who had come to meet a colleague still at the firm. On an otherwise pleasant autumn day, with a view of the Statue of Liberty in the distance, he was there to provide "grief counseling" in the aftermath of Bank of America's stunning purchase of the firm.

Reflecting the cultural divide that would add to the merger's challenges, the banker dismissed the Charlotte institution's Wall Street pedigree. Bank of America "is a commercial bank that owns an investment bank," the banker said. He nodded in the direction of Merrill's headquarters: "This is a real investment bank. It's a big difference."

On Tuesday, September 16, the same day the government announced a major rescue package for AIG, Wachovia chairman Lanty Smith called a telephone board meeting for six in the evening. From a conference room next to his office, Bob Steel briefed a faceless audience of directors calling in from around the country about the nation's financial crisis. Only a day after projecting confidence on the *Mad Money* show, the Wachovia CEO described a grim picture for the bank as the industry reeled from the Lehman Brothers collapse and other market turmoil.

The rapidly moving crisis had significantly affected the market's perception of Wachovia, as investors fretted about the next potential victim, he told them. This could cause a potentially severe liquidity crisis for the bank—meaning the bank might struggle to find the readily available financing it needed to fund its daily operations. The panic was showing that even if financial institutions had enough capital to cover their losses, they could fail if depositors began rapidly withdrawing funds or if other banks stopped lending to them.

Ahead of the meeting, Steel had written out six potential steps the bank could take. He outlined them for the board: Wachovia could continue cutting costs and reducing risk inside the company; sell businesses or assets; raise $10 to $15 billion in capital; pursue a combination of capital raising and asset sales; find a company or investor to take a 20 to 40 percent stake in the company; or pursue a sale or merger. Board members, realizing the stay-the-course option was no longer viable, told Steel to start exploring the other strategies, with a preference for keeping the bank independent.

Steel's Wachovia makeover was about to get much more dramatic.

In the coming days, Wachovia lined up law firms and investment banks to help with its next move. Lawyers began drawing up documents for raising capital. Wachovia also set up a virtual data room to allow outside parties to review its financial data. For the next two weeks, bank executives would juggle multiple merger scenarios and capital-raising possibilities.

As part of the company's contingency planning, Wachovia's legal team researched an FDIC procedure known as "open-bank assistance." While the government had little authority to rescue or even to safely wind down investment banks, the FDIC had extensive procedures for dealing with failing commercial banks. In most cases, it would close a bank and parcel out its assets and deposits to a healthy institution. But the FDIC board, with the assent of other agencies, also had the capability to broker a deal or provide loan-loss assistance without formally closing the bank. The bank's lawyers wanted to be up to speed on the applicable legislation but saw the likelihood that such a situation would happen at Wachovia as extremely remote.

Unsolicited calls came in from Citigroup. The New York banking giant had been struggling with mortgage-related losses for more than a year and was eager for the salve of Wachovia's stable deposit base. Steel was noncommittal in a conversation with Citi CEO Vikram Pandit, whom he had known for years as a competitor and from industry forums.

Wachovia general counsel Jane Sherburne also heard from two of her former colleagues at Citi, vice chairman Lewis Kaden and general counsel Michael Helfer. When she was at Citigroup, the company had scaled back its retail banking operations. They wanted to make sure she knew the company was serious about reversing course.

By Wednesday, September 17, Steel was in touch with another big-bank CEO, fellow Duke University alumnus John Mack of Morgan Stanley. In such a marriage, Wachovia would provide Morgan Stanley with deposits, while Morgan Stanley would offer the Charlotte bank a better-known investment banking operation.

Earlier that summer, Mack had flown down to Charlotte to have lunch with Steel. The mission was mainly to pitch Morgan Stanley's services as an investment bank. But at the end of the lunch, Mack mentioned that maybe someday, under the right circumstances, the two banks might want to consider a combination. That proposal hadn't gone anywhere until now. The two CEOs decided to dispatch teams to check out each other's financials.

By Wednesday evening, word leaked about the discussions. When Wachovia executive David Carroll arrived at Morgan Stanley's Times Square headquarters on Thursday, TV trucks were waiting outside. Morgan Stanley officials slipped Carroll and his team inside through an employee entrance.

The talks got off to a rough start when confusion developed over Morgan Stanley's access to Wachovia's electronic data room. Morgan Stanley officials were eager to comb through Wachovia's Pick-A-Payment loan portfolio, a trouble spot that could quickly squelch the deal. Gary Lynch, Morgan Stanley's chief legal officer, dialed up Wachovia general counsel Jane Sherburne, who was back in Charlotte. "Our guys need access," he said.

The answer was simple. "Sign the NDA," Sherburne responded. The nondisclosure agreement would ensure the information remained confidential and clear the way for the due diligence to begin.

While Wall Street executives worked on last-ditch efforts to save their companies, the financial crisis gripped Manhattan. Newspapers blasted the turmoil. Lunchtime conversations darted among the latest merger possibilities. Employees trudged grim-faced from the subway stops to the office towers. Downtown in the financial district, one construction worker at the World Trade Center site offered his support, calling, "Good luck, guys."

At Morgan Stanley headquarters, workers ducked reporters when they emerged for smoke breaks and treks to the coffee vendor. Around the corner, amid the cacophony of Times Square, tourists gawked, double-decker buses idled, and a kangaroo mascot distributed fliers. Up above, the ticker read, "Morgan Stanley talking to Wachovia, others."

By Friday, the discussions moved to the Midtown Manhattan office of Morgan Stanley's outside lawyers, Wachtell Lipton. But the talks were clearly starting to fizzle. Morgan Stanley was balking over Wachovia's option ARM portfolio. Wachovia wasn't all that enamored with Morgan Stanley's holdings either. Analysts studying the deal weren't even sure who would be considered the buyer and who would be considered the seller. For the banks, that was a critical question because the buyer received the benefits of taking write-downs on troubled assets. Soon, executives at the law office realized that many of the key players needed to seal a merger weren't even involved. The deal was going nowhere.

The government's effort to stem the crisis also helped cool the conversations.

On Friday morning, Henry Paulson announced a plan that would be called the Troubled Asset Relief Program, or TARP. If approved by Congress, the proposal would potentially allow banks such as Wachovia to off-load their worst assets to the government. The idea was to clean up bank balance sheets so the institutions would start lending again to individuals and businesses, juicing the economy. News of the program eased some of the pressure on Wachovia to do a deal quickly.

The TARP and merger news also helped stabilize both companies' share prices, which had fluctuated wildly during the week. Starting on Friday, September 12, the last trading day before Lehman's undoing, Wachovia shares swung from $14.27 to as low as $9.12 the following Wednesday to $18.75 by Friday, September 19. Morgan Stanley shares vacillated from $37.23 to $21.75 on Wednesday to $27.21 on Friday.

While juggling the Wachovia talks, Morgan Stanley also began eyeing a possible investment from Japanese bank Mitsubishi UFJ Financial Group, a move that could ease worries about the firm's capital and liquidity. Morgan Stanley's Mack, whose stock had been under pressure for most of the week, told Steel he was interested in Wachovia but needed to focus on the Mitsubishi deal first. The two CEOs agreed to end their talks. Mack later said he was attracted to the Charlotte bank's deposit base but that the hole at Wachovia "was just too large for us to get comfortable with. We were very disappointed."

Heading into the weekend, banking regulators continued to worry about the prospects of the industry's weaker players. Investment banks such as Morgan Stanley and Goldman Sachs were under pressure because they didn't have deposits to provide a stable source of funding.

Wachovia was one of the commercial banks the Federal Reserve was tracking, largely because of its mortgage troubles. Keeping a particularly close eye on the Charlotte bank was Federal Reserve governor Kevin Warsh. The 38-year-old former Morgan Stanley investment banker became the youngest Fed appointee in history when he was selected in 2006. Now, the former Bush administration economic adviser emerged as a key player in the government's response to the financial crisis. He became a point person for Steel because the Wachovia CEO couldn't talk to Paulson, his former boss, about Wachovia business. The Fed was privy to the Morgan Stanley talks, but regulators remained skeptical that the deal made sense.

On the night of Friday, September 19, Warsh was in New York to powwow with Tim Geithner about recent events. Sullivan & Cromwell's Rodge Cohen called up the Fed governor to float another merger combination, a pairing of two of his longtime clients: Wachovia and Goldman Sachs.

It was an idea that others in the government and the industry had been mulling. The deal would give Goldman critical retail banking deposits, while Wachovia would win the imprimatur of one of the world's most respected investment banks. The big drawback was the "optics," or public perception, of a government-arranged deal with Goldman. The firm had long been nicknamed "Government Sachs" for its tradition of landing former executives in political positions in Washington and elsewhere. Goldman's tendrils—including Steel's and Paulson's past ties to the firm—would be hard to miss in this one. Another question was whether or not Goldman, a risk-taking investment bank, really wanted to enter the staid business of commercial banking.

At a time when merger combinations that normally evolved over years were happening in days, it became an idea worth exploring.

After a roller-coaster week, Steel flew to Aspen, Colorado, early on the morning of Saturday, September 20, to participate in an annual conference hosted by private-equity giant Teddy Forstmann. The Wachovia CEO made it just in time for his appearance on a panel with former Treasury secretary Larry Summers, CNBC's Larry Kudlow, and the CEO of asset manager PIMCO, Mohamed El-Erian. Steel had planned to stay in Aspen for a few days but now was going to leave as soon as the discussion ended.

Slipping out after his panel, Steel bumped into Dick Kovacevich, the Wells Fargo chairman. Kovacevich noted the tough times and suggested they talk sometime. "It probably makes sense to talk sooner rather than later," Steel said. He asked Kovacevich to call Wachovia's investment banker, Peter Weinberg of the firm Perella Weinberg Partners. Wells had long been seen as an ideal merger mate for Wachovia. The San Francisco bank remained one of the country's healthier institutions in the financial morass.

On his way to the airport, Steel noticed an e-mail from Warsh and gave him a call. The Fed governor had a request: Call Lloyd Blankfein, Goldman's CEO and Steel's former colleague. The government had another marriage partner in mind for Wachovia. Steel called Blankfein. They agreed to meet in New York later that day.

After Steel flew into Westchester County Airport outside New York City, Blankfein gave him a ride to the headquarters of Goldman Sachs at 85 Broad Street in the city's financial district. Steel had good memories of his time at Goldman, but it was still an odd feeling to be back. Late into the evening, they discussed the possibility of a combination.

Back in Charlotte, Wachovia general counsel Jane Sherburne was moving into a new condominium. Her primary home was still in the Washington area, but she spent her workweeks in Charlotte. Out shopping with her husband and daughter for kitchenware and hardware, she kept getting interrupted by phone calls.

On the line was Bob Hoyt, the Treasury Department's general counsel. "Is there someone Paulson could talk to?" he asked Sherburne.

Because of Steel's post-government employment restrictions, he and Paulson weren't allowed to discuss Wachovia business, although they could have personal conversations and talk about other issues such as Barclays' interest in Lehman. The two longtime friends exchanged calls on September 8, September 10, and twice early on Monday, September 15, Paulson's calendar later showed. The schedule didn't disclose the nature of the brief calls.

Reluctantly, Sherburne gave Hoyt contact information for one of Wachovia's board members, Joseph Neubauer, the chief executive of ARAMARK Corporation, a provider of concessions at stadiums and other services. Neubauer also knew Paulson.

"This is crazy," Sherburne said to Hoyt. "You can't have a Goldman deal with Treasury brokering it. You'll never get TARP passed. This is political suicide."

"I know. I know," Hoyt responded.

Soon, Sherburne gave up working on her move and told her husband and daughter she had to go to New York.

On Sunday, the Wachovia team gathered at Goldman headquarters. Joining Steel and Sherburne were David Carroll, who had quickly become a key Steel lieutenant, and some of the bank's top number-crunchers. Chairman Lanty Smith and Neubauer also made the trip.

Knowing Sullivan & Cromwell's longstanding ties with Goldman, Sherburne had hired another law firm as outside counsel. Wachovia was also working with investment bank Perella Weinberg Partners. Goldman Sachs had been helping Wachovia analyze its loan portfolio since the summer but obviously couldn't assist on this potential match-up. But in a world where Goldman ties seemed inescapable, Peter Weinberg, half of his firm's eponymous name, was a former Goldman banker and grandson of a prominent partner.

In conversations with Goldman and Wachovia, Warsh told the two sides to see if the combination made economic sense before wrestling with social issues such as what type of job Steel would hold in the combined company. As the talks went on, Goldman struggled with whether or not it really wanted to get into the commercial banking business. The firm also was concerned about the depth of Wachovia's loan troubles.

By afternoon, the two banks started framing a possible price for Wachovia—$18.75 per share, equivalent to Wachovia's closing price on Friday. But Goldman wanted government help to proceed. In particular, it desired some protection on Wachovia's $120 billion in option ARMs. A weekend earlier, the government hadn't stopped Lehman's slide into bankruptcy, but assistance didn't seem as far-fetched now. That was because Lehman's fallout was bludgeoning the financial system, because the government had already doled out a massive aid package for AIG, and because officials appeared to favor this tie-up.

While Steel was in another room with Goldman executives, the rest of the Wachovia team holed up in a conference room on the 30th floor of Goldman's headquarters. There was a sense a deal might come together that night, although it remained unclear if the government would cough up another aid package with TARP pending in Congress.

Wachovia board member Neubauer heard from Paulson Sunday afternoon.

"Joe, I just want to make sure you have the right sense of urgency," Paulson said.

"Why does this have to be done so quickly?" Neubauer asked.

"Wachovia is likely to fail soon," the Treasury secretary said. "The market is very nervous about your mortgage portfolio. It's much better to get ahead of this."

Paulson also called Goldman Sachs CEO Blankfein a number of times, urging him to be "aggressive and creative" but advising him that the deal wouldn't receive much assistance from the federal government.

Inside the Fed, officials continued to debate a way for the central bank to facilitate a transaction. But in the end, the answer was no. Paulson, Ben Bernanke, and Geithner decided they couldn't back the deal. The incestuous nature of the government's aiding Goldman Sachs was too much to overcome. The potential political backlash began to sink in for Paulson. The Treasury secretary also worried about the implications for Morgan Stanley if Goldman Sachs found a safe harbor and Morgan Stanley didn't. Warsh delivered the news to an exasperated Steel.

Goldman president Gary Cohn, who was in the room, suggested he should leave to allow Steel and Warsh to talk further, but the Wachovia CEO told him to stay. They didn't have any secrets after hours of merger talks. "You've been bouncing me around here," Steel said to Warsh. "This going back and forth is not constructive to my company."

The exhausted Wachovia team packed up and left Goldman headquarters. Sitting in traffic on their way to the airport, Sherburne and others checked their BlackBerries. An unexpected headline popped up: The Fed had granted Goldman Sachs and Morgan Stanley permission to convert into bank holding companies.

The Wachovia team now realized why Goldman backed off the deal. The Fed's move would subject Goldman and Morgan Stanley to tighter regulation and capital requirements but would also give them access to all of the Fed's various lending facilities, a crucial lifeline amid their liquidity crunch. The final two major Wall Street investment banks had been transformed.

Chapter 12

THE PASSING OF A GREAT INSTITUTION

W hile the Morgan and Goldman deals waxed and waned, Wachovia considered other options as well.

On Thursday, September 18, 2008, Spanish bank Banco Santander, which had first approached Wachovia back in August, began conducting due diligence on the Charlotte bank with an eye toward taking a 20 to 40 percent stake in the company. The talks never got off the ground.

Wachovia also hadn't given up on raising fresh capital, which could stabilize its balance sheet and potentially alleviate investor concerns about its burgeoning loan losses. The rebound in the bank's stock price made raising capital more attractive for the company because it could issue fewer shares to raise the same amount, making a stock offering less dilutive to existing shareholders.

From Friday to Sunday, Wachovia talked to private investors about a potential private placement offering that would then be followed by a public stock offering. One of the potential investors was Warren Buffett, whose investment touch would have been seen as a major vote of confidence. Earlier in the year, the bank had sold billions in troubled auction-rate securities to a subsidiary of Buffett's Berkshire Hathaway Incorporated investment vehicle. The move came in the wake of a regulatory settlement over the bank's sale of these investments, a type of security that had blown up for many institutions in the credit crunch and left investors with holdings they couldn't redeem.

David Carroll, who led Wachovia's brokerage and Evergreen Investments mutual funds, spearheaded the talks with Buffett. "The Oracle of Omaha" was willing to invest $5 billion if Wachovia raised billions in additional capital from other sources. But the recovery in Wachovia's stock actually helped spike the deal. Up to $18.75 by Friday, September 19, Wachovia's shares grew too expensive for Buffett's taste. On Tuesday, September 23, another financial institution—Goldman—said it was getting $5 billion from Buffett.

The other item on Bob Steel's checklist was selling off business units or assets to bolster capital. Executives got close to a sale of Wachovia's insurance unit, but that deal was sidetracked as bigger moves took precedence.

While the Fed's emergency conversion of Goldman and Morgan Stanley might have stabilized those firms, it didn't calm financial markets. Seeing his stock slide again, Steel sought more potential merger partners.

In the week after the derailed Goldman deal, the Wachovia CEO and adviser Peter Weinberg followed up with Wells Fargo's Dick Kovacevich, encouraging him to consider a combination on a rapid timetable. On Wednesday, September 24, Steel tried Citi's Vikram Pandit but couldn't reach him.

On Thursday, September 25, events in Washington, D.C., and Seattle piled more stress on Wachovia. That afternoon, an apparent agreement to approve the Bush administration's $700 billion TARP proposal disintegrated during a bipartisan meeting at the White House. House Republicans said they could no longer support the unpopular bailout without significant changes. Democrats blamed Senator John McCain, the Arizona Republican, for flying in from the presidential campaign trail and upsetting the tenuous compact. Republicans said Democrats were trying to ram a deal through before McCain arrived.

In a surreal moment, Henry Paulson, the Republican Treasury secretary, bent down on one knee to ask Nancy Pelosi, the Democratic House speaker, not to shatter the deal by pulling her support. "I didn't know I was going to be the referee for an internal GOP ideological civil war," Barney Frank, the Massachusetts Democrat leading the negotiations, quipped afterward. By Thursday evening, the talks were scheduled to start again on Friday, leaving the bailout plan in jeopardy.

On Thursday evening, another major bank collapse rocked the financial system. The Office of Thrift Supervision closed Seattle-based savings and loan Washington Mutual, and the FDIC sold its deposits and some operations to JPMorgan Chase for $1.9 billion. It was the nation's biggest-ever bank failure. Since September 15, WaMu's customers had pulled $16.7 billion in deposits, about 9 percent of the thrift's deposits as of June 30. Closing the bank on a Thursday instead of the typical Friday sent a signal to the markets that the banking system still had problems.

The outflow of deposits left WaMu with insufficient liquidity to meet its obligations, placing it in an "unsafe and unsound condition to transact business," the OTS said. The bidding process had taken place the previous two or three days, with some potential buyers eyeing bailout talks in Washington, OTS officials later said.

In a press release Thursday night, FDIC chairman Sheila Bair emphasized the protection of depositors and the agency's insurance fund in the transaction. "For all depositors and other customers of Washington Mutual Bank, this is simply a combination of two banks," she said. "WaMu's balance sheet and the payment paid by JPMorgan Chase allowed a transaction in which neither the uninsured depositors nor the insurance fund absorbed any losses."

For JPMorgan CEO Jamie Dimon, it was another deft move, expanding his retail banking franchise on the West Coast at little expense. Now, the New York giant would have branches in 23 states, eclipsed only by Bank of America's 31 states.

WaMu's collapse drew more attention to Wachovia's mortgage woes. JPMorgan said it would mark down the value of WaMu's $50.3 billion option ARM portfolio by $8.2 billion, or about 16 percent. Over time, the bank projected total losses of $10.3 billion in the portfolio. That sent a message that Wachovia's own Pick-A-Payment loan book potentially faced bigger losses.

The way the WaMu failure was handled unnerved some investors. After the JPMorgan transaction, holders of WaMu's more than $30 billion in debt and preferred stock had little hope of recovering their money. In a report the next day, analysts at research firm CreditSights said the deal seemed "unprecedented" in how it was structured. "As of this early writing, it seems that WaMu's major debt holders have been stranded by regulatory intervention and have access to the limited assets at the [holding company] and non-bank subsidiaries holdings," the report stated. "The worse case developed for the major credit instrument holders."

That Thursday night, Pandit, the Citi CEO, was in Philadelphia participating in a lecture series at the University of Pennsylvania's Wharton School. While predicting more volatility in the coming year, he encouraged the overflow audience to learn from the crisis. "We live in times that will serve as lessons for future generations," Pandit said.

At 4:27 A.M. on Friday, back home in New York, Pandit sent Steel an e-mail in response to the Wachovia CEO's call earlier in the week. Steel was awake. "I'm free," he responded. The two CEOs had a short phone conversation and decided to kick off the due diligence process.

When markets opened on Friday, Wachovia's shares nosedived. CNBC, newswires, and websites tracked the slide, spurring worries about the next bank to fall. Credit analysts at Goldman Sachs downgraded their rating on Wachovia to "trading sell" from "outperform." In a research report, the analysts expressed concern about a "silent run" on deposits like the one experienced at Washington Mutual. If Wachovia ended up taking write-downs similar to WaMu, it would be on the edge of being considered "well capitalized."

In a research note Friday, Kevin Fitzsimmons, an analyst with Sandler O'Neill & Partners, said Wachovia's stock likely was suffering from "guilt by association" as investors worried about the toxic assets of other banks following WaMu's collapse. "While we acknowledge that [Wachovia] is facing a number of daunting challenges, particularly the burden of a deteriorating $122 billion option-ARM portfolio, we do not necessarily agree that [Wachovia] and [WaMu] represent an apples-to-apples comparison," Fitzsimmons wrote. He noted that WaMu was a forced seller that had to write down its portfolio in the wake of a purchase. The proposed government bailout was a potential boon for Wachovia, he added. "If the bailout gets approved and details emerge that WB has the option to offload some of its Pick-a-Pay portfolio at prices more favorable than today's 'fire sale' prices, this would likely provide investors with a sense of relief," he wrote. Still, the company might have to take more dramatic action, including selling off a major business, raising capital, or seeking a merger, he said.

In an effort to comfort employees, customers, and shareholders, Steel emphasized Wachovia's financial and business strengths in internal memos and a note on the bank's website. Bankers passed along the CEO's sentiments to their customers. "Financial markets and our industry are undergoing unprecedented change," Steel wrote in the note. "We are watching these events carefully and must plan and remain flexible. Therefore, we are strategically protecting and managing liquidity and capital in this challenging environment."

Despite these assurances, deposits started pouring out of the bank. Inside Wachovia, executives saw withdrawals lighting up their computer screens beginning Friday morning. Customers, for the most part, weren't closing accounts. Instead, businesses and institutions yanked enough money to lower their balances to the federally insured $100,000 limit. The bank lost as much as $5 billion in deposits on Friday alone. That was a big number, although still a small piece of its more than $447 billion in total deposits.

If deposits kept flowing out, the bank might have trouble coming up with the money it needed to cover its obligations. Since Lehman's collapse, banks had all but stopped lending to each other. On Friday, financial institutions started turning the bank down for normal financing transactions. The cost of credit default swaps—a type of insurance against a default on Wachovia's debt—spiked, making it more risky for banks to lend to Wachovia. The bank briefed credit-rating agencies, which signaled plans to downgrade Wachovia's debt ratings in the near future.

During the day, Wachovia reviewed its liquidity position—the cash it had to meet obligations—with the Fed and the Office of the Comptroller of the Currency, whose staffers remained on site at the bank's offices. OCC examiners thought the company was more valuable than the market perceived it but knew the bank was worried about its liquidity amid roiling financial markets. The fact that Wachovia was shopping itself—and not finding any takers so far—also didn't help confidence in the company.

In a conference call at two in the afternoon on Friday, the OCC told the FDIC that Wachovia would be okay through the weekend. But later in the day, FDIC staff heard about problems from the regulator. Comptroller John Dugan was overseas in Amsterdam at a meeting of international banking regulators but made plans to leave early and fly home Saturday morning.

By the end of the day, Wachovia's shares had fallen 27 percent to $10. The plunge would have been worse if news hadn't leaked that the bank was talking to Citi and Wells Fargo.

That evening, Wachovia's board members dialed in for a telephone update on the bank's condition. Wachovia executives said that the bank's funding would be "questionable and unpredictable" starting Monday and that it might have to tap the Federal Reserve's discount window, the funding source of last resort. Raising capital was no longer a viable option, and the bank had begun talks with Citi and Wells, Steel told the board. If a deal couldn't be reached by Monday, the FDIC would place Wachovia in receivership.

An institution formed by two North Carolina banks that had survived the Great Depression was on the brink of failure.

Wachovia executives started flying up to New York on Friday night. For a bit of relief, they watched the presidential debate between McCain and Democratic hopeful Barack Obama. After saying he would suspend his campaign until an agreement on TARP was reached, McCain had reversed course and flown to Mississippi for the sparring match. Members of Congress had renewed negotiations on Friday but hadn't yet reached an accord.

On the morning of Saturday, September 27, the Wachovia team, led by Steel and Carroll, met in a conference room at the Regency Hotel on Park Avenue before beginning a weekend of negotiations that would likely mean the end of Wachovia as an independent company.

Since July, the bank's leadership had been dramatically remade with the hiring of a new CEO, CFO, and chief risk officer from outside the company. Carroll, a North Carolina native and company lifer once seen as a possible successor to Ken Thompson, now served as the bank's most conspicuous tie to its past. In his smooth Southern drawl, the increasingly silver-haired executive gave the equivalent of a pregame speech before a contest his team had no hopes of winning. He talked about what a special company Wachovia was and the quality of its people. In the coming days, they would need to be as professional as possible. Tears spilled down the cheeks of normally austere bankers.

The group of about 30 then walked the eight blocks down Park Avenue to the Seagram Building, where Sullivan & Cromwell, Rodge Cohen's firm, had a Midtown office—the same one where Bank of America analysts had scoured the books of Lehman Brothers two weekends earlier. Wachovia's corporate and investment bank also had offices in the building.

The law firm had a series of conference rooms complete with a kitchen, designed for marathon merger talks and due diligence sessions. Citi, which had its headquarters across the street, sent over its personnel. The two sides divided up their teams by areas such as credit, legal, and balance sheet management and split into separate conference rooms. Citi's representatives, led by vice chairman Ned Kelly, reiterated that the New York bank was interested only in Wachovia's banking subsidiaries and would do a deal only with government assistance. Wachovia negotiators said they were worried about the viability of the business units that Citi didn't want to buy. They pressed Citi executives on why they preferred such a deal structure but never felt they got a satisfactory answer. After completing a round of talks, the Citi delegation left to confab back across the street.

Things went better with Wells. On Saturday, Steel talked with Kovacevich, who indicated the San Francisco bank was interested in buying all of Wachovia in a stock purchase. The deal wouldn't need government assistance and could be announced by Monday morning. The due diligence team from Wells had started examining Wachovia's books, accessing the virtual data room remotely. Kovacevich was flying to New York and planned to meet Steel for breakfast on Sunday.

Meanwhile, regulators from the Fed and the OCC tracked the talks. Tim Geithner, from the New York Fed, served as a main contact for Citi, while Kevin Warsh was on the phone with Steel and Kovacevich. The various agencies often had competing agendas and weren't always on the same page. Tension was particularly palpable at times between Geithner and the FDIC's Bair. On a number of occasions, the FDIC felt it wasn't being provided the information it needed.

On a conference call Saturday with other regulators, Geithner said that the New York Fed had been approached by Citi about a possible government-backed deal to buy Wachovia's banking operations. Regulators on the call felt Geithner favored the proposal. Citi had a weak United States retail banking franchise, and Wachovia would instantly give it a massive East Coast deposit base. Citi was the biggest bank supervised by the New York Fed and a potential trouble spot as it struggled to overcome mortgage-related losses.

Bair had heard from the OCC that Wachovia was talking to Wells about a non-government-assisted deal and that Steel had lined up a breakfast with Kovacevich. It was news to her that Citi had talked to the New York Fed about a government-aided deal that might require money from her FDIC fund. She was incredulous that she hadn't been consulted earlier and worried that an assisted Citi deal could disrupt an unassisted Wells purchase.

It wasn't the first time Bair had tangled with her fellow regulators. Since joining the FDIC in 2006, she had sparred with other agencies on issues ranging from higher bank capital requirements to the need for more aggressive efforts to help struggling mortgage borrowers. As the bank crisis deepened, the Kansas native became an ardent defender of the FDIC fund that salvaged depositors when banks failed.

To Bair, allowing Wachovia to pursue an unassisted deal with Wells was a no-brainer. She thought it was premature for the New York Fed to push a government-backed deal, particularly when it required assistance from the FDIC's insurance fund. In addition, to receive open-bank assistance for a Wachovia deal, Citi needed formal approvals from the Fed, the FDIC, and the White House before anything could be put in place. She also reminded Geithner that the FDIC would follow its procedures and analyze the least costly offer for Wachovia—if it came to that.

Back in Charlotte, employees knew the bank was in merger talks because of media reports but had to wait like everyone else to see how the weekend would unfold.

While the drop in the bank's stock Friday had been severe, it wasn't clear how dire a situation the company faced. Analysts said the bank likely had to do a deal or raise capital, but they also noted that the government bailout plan still could be an attractive alternative. Some Wachovia investment bankers worried that if the company ended up in bankruptcy like Lehman, their deferred compensation accounts would be wiped out. Others were increasingly angry about the damage they thought was caused by the Golden West purchase. Before the deal, Wachovia had run a traditional mortgage shop with little California exposure.

"I guess the lesson here is to stick with what you know and stick with your principles," a former Wachovia executive said that Saturday. If Wachovia had not bought Golden West, he felt the bank "could be out there taking advantage of this market instead of being a victim. It's a shame."

Adding to the surreal feeling in Charlotte was a gas supply seriously drained by two Gulf Coast hurricanes earlier in the month. Officials promised more gas was on the way, but the shortage forced some workers and students to stay home, spurred long lines at pumps, and even sparked fights.

Back in New York on Saturday evening, Kelly brought his Citi team across the street for another meeting with Steel and the Wachovia team. Rodge Cohen, able to advise Wachovia again, was also on hand, along with Peter Weinberg and advisers from Goldman, also back on the team.

Citi was willing to pay $1 per share for Wachovia's banking subsidiaries but still didn't want the brokerage unit or other parts of the company. It already had thousands of financial advisers in its Smith Barney unit and didn't need Wachovia Securities, which offered the same services. Citi also needed government assistance to do the deal.

Wachovia executives pressed Citi to buy the whole company, explaining how difficult it would be to disentangle the various units, but Citi didn't budge. The two sides agreed to talk more on Sunday.

Wachovia executives still weren't sure the government would be willing to offer aid, but they got a sense that Citi thought something was possible. And it was obvious that Citi was drooling over Wachovia's retail banking franchise. Still, Wells remained the company's best hope with a little more than 24 hours left in the weekend.

Left: *Bank of America CEO Hugh McColl, Jr., against the backdrop of one of the three Ben Long frescoes gracing the lobby of the bank's Uptown tower*

Below: *Ed Crutchfield above Charlotte in First Union's headquarters building*

Above: *Wachovia CEO Bud Baker (left) and First Union CEO Ken Thompson leaving the Wachovia shareholders' meeting in Winston-Salem after a 2001 vote on their proposed merger passed by a wide margin*

Below: *Herb Sandler, co-CEO of Golden West Financial, discusses his company's history in May 2006 after agreeing to a sale to Wachovia. Listening from right to left are Golden West co-CEO Marion Sandler and Wachovia executives Ben Jenkins and Bob McGee.*

Above: *Wells Fargo CEO John Stumpf* (center) *stands with Wachovia CEO Bob Steel* (left) *and general bank head Ben Jenkins before an employee gathering in October 2008.*

Below: *The stock ticker on One Wachovia Center shows "N/A" for Wachovia after the Wells Fargo deal became official.*

Above: *Incoming Bank of America CEO Brian Moynihan (right) applauds the work of retiring CEO Ken Lewis at an employee meeting in December 2009.*

Below: *The Duke Energy Center (left), once set to be Wachovia's headquarters, and the Bank of America Corporate Center (tallest building on right) book-end the Charlotte skyline.*

Chapter 13

SYSTEMIC RISK

Bob Steel and David Carroll met early Sunday morning with Dick Kovacevich in his suite at The Carlyle, an Art Deco hotel on Manhattan's Upper East Side that had hosted notable guests from United States presidents to Princess Diana.

Kovacevich was one of the most respected bankers in the industry, and his reputation continued growing as rivals cratered. After selling a toy company he had founded to General Mills, the Pacific Northwest native jumped to Citicorp in 1975 after meeting Citi executive John Reed on a Virgin Islands vacation. Kovacevich led the bank's implementation of ATMs in New York and gained a reputation as a marketing whiz, but he lost out in a management shakeup in the 1980s. He left for Minnesota's Norwest and in 1998 bought San Francisco's Wells Fargo, kept its name and headquarters, and won respect for gradually merging operations. Since then, he had eschewed mega mergers and risky capital markets businesses and was now reaping the rewards. In perhaps the biggest sign of his success, Warren Buffett was Wells Fargo's largest investor.

In 2007, Kovacevich had handed the CEO title to his longtime number two, John Stumpf, but stayed on as chairman. He was set to off-load that title at the end of the year and fully retire. This would be his chance at one more game-changing deal.

At the Sunday-morning meeting, Kovacevich again told Steel he thought Wells could make a stock offer for all of Wachovia without government help, pending the bank's review of Wachovia's books. Wells Fargo's price wouldn't be in the $20-per-share range, Kovacevich said.

Steel and Carroll left the meeting optimistic. The debate inside Wachovia was whether the offer from Wells would be in the high or mid-teens per share. Wachovia's advisers drafted a merger agreement and sent it to Wells Fargo's lawyers at Wachtell Lipton, which was playing a role in yet another major deal in the financial crisis.

By the afternoon, Wells was growing comfortable with Wachovia's option ARM portfolio, but the credit team was starting to worry about some of the bank's commercial loans. Wells was experienced in the mortgage business but had little background in corporate and investment banking. Wachovia officials tried to assuage any concerns but started to worry about Wells Fargo's waning enthusiasm.

Kevin Warsh, at the Fed in Washington, talked with both Steel and Kovacevich during the weekend. On Sunday after the breakfast meeting, Steel seemed positive about a possible Wells deal. To Kovacevich, Warsh repeated the message he had sent to Goldman: If Wells was willing to pay a positive share price, the Federal Reserve could help facilitate the talks, especially since it was the primary regulator that approved these types of bank deals. But if the bank wasn't, Kovacevich needed to talk to Sheila Bair, whose agency had procedures for dealing with failing banks.

As Wells did more due diligence, the price Kovacevich told Warsh he was willing to pay kept coming down. By the afternoon, he was no longer willing to do the deal without government help. Inside the Fed, a debate raged over whether or not Wachovia should be turned over to the FDIC if an unassisted deal couldn't be worked out. Officials kicked around the idea of some type of bridge loan if Wachovia needed help staying afloat until a deal could be reached, but that idea didn't go far. In the end, Fed officials decided Wachovia's resolution should be handled by the FDIC.

That afternoon, Bair waited at home to see if Wells agreed to buy Wachovia, but word never came. She called Warren Buffett to get a number for John Stumpf, the Wells Fargo CEO. The deal was off, Stumpf told her.

Around four o'clock, she started notifying her staff and drove to the FDIC's headquarters in Washington a short distance from the White House. In a couple months, the agency would open an exhibit in the lobby celebrating the FDIC's 75th anniversary. The agency was created in 1933 in response to a rash of bank failures and hadn't lost an insured deposit since then.

Shortly after reaching her office, Bair got a call from Ben Bernanke. The Fed would be willing to make a "systemic risk" determination related to Wachovia, the designation required to allow an open-bank assisted transaction.

The FDIC was required to use the "least costly" method to the deposit insurance fund to resolve failed banks. Assistance to open banks was generally barred because it would benefit shareholders. But a 1991 law allowed the FDIC to make an exception to this requirement in the case of systemic risk to the financial system. The provision required the recommendation of two-thirds of the Fed board and two-thirds of the FDIC board, plus the approval of the Treasury secretary after consultation with the president. To date, regulators had never used this exception.

After Bernanke's call, Bair heard from President George W. Bush's chief of staff, Josh Bolten, a former Goldman Sachs banker. The White House supported a systemic risk determination as well. The Federal Reserve had approved Wachovia's purchase of Golden West, and the OCC had been the Charlotte bank's primary regulator. But now the FDIC had to deal with Wachovia's collapse. The FDIC's receivership staff called Citi and Wells to let them know it was going to take bids that night for a government-assisted transaction. A deal had to be arranged by Monday morning.

Around seven o'clock that night, Kovacevich called Steel, who was waiting with the Wachovia team at Sullivan & Cromwell's offices. Wells wasn't prepared to do a deal on such a short timetable without government assistance, the Wells Fargo chairman told Steel.

It was a wrenching blow for a group that had thought it was close to an agreement after watching deal after deal fall apart in the past two exhausting weeks. Most of the executives had been up since early Saturday. Few had found time for showers or naps. They were surviving on takeout food and adrenaline.

Now, some executives thought they might be out of options. They knew Citi was still out there, but government assistance wasn't a sure thing. The unthinkable was happening. The bank might fail.

Not long after that, Bair called Steel, whom she knew from his days at Treasury. The government had determined that Wachovia was a systemic risk to the financial system, and the FDIC planned to use its open-bank assistance powers. The FDIC had contacted bidders and would call back with the results. This doomsday scenario was actually good news for Wachovia.

At some point that evening, Bair, continuing to review all options, considered a more severe outcome for Wachovia.

The FDIC chairman mulled failing the bank and disposing of its assets without an assisted transaction. Such a move could wipe out shareholders and damage bondholders. But this approach could also potentially result in zero losses to the deposit insurance fund, as in the WaMu transaction. FDIC accountants also worried that if the agency booked an unexpected loss from an assisted transaction, it would be legally required to levy special assessments on other banks, adding more stress to the financial system.

Officials at the Fed and the OCC pushed back. Failing Wachovia would be a disaster for a financial system already reeling from the collapse of Lehman and WaMu. The Charlotte bank was far bigger and much more complicated than the Seattle thrift. Seeing the resistance, Bair continued with the bidding process.

Around nine that night, Wachovia held a board meeting to update its directors. A decision was likely in the next several hours. Around 11, someone in the conference room with Steel, Rodge Cohen, and Jane Sherburne said they should revive a proposal they had set aside earlier in the weekend: A request for government aid as a stand-alone company. The idea had lost traction when it appeared Wells was going to do an unassisted deal. Around the same time, bankers from Goldman and Perella Weinberg burst into the room with the same idea.

This brief moment of hope gave the demoralized team something to do while Wachovia awaited the FDIC's decision. In the offer Wachovia crafted, the FDIC would share losses on $200 billion to $225 billion of the bank's worst assets. Wachovia would take the first $25 billion in losses, issue the government $10 billion in preferred shares, and raise another $10 to $15 billion in capital.

Wachovia thought the offer was less expensive than Citi's, which would call for the FDIC to cover $312 billion in assets, with Citi taking the first $42 billion in losses. The other positives: It would require no shareholder vote, it could be done in seven to 10 days, and it would keep the company in one piece. Cohen e-mailed Bair with the proposal around 12:30 A.M.

The FDIC considered the proposal but rejected it based on economics and a concern that financial markets wouldn't perceive Wachovia as a viable standalone institution even with the aid. Bair thought Wachovia needed to be paired with a stronger institution. The FDIC wasn't in the business of rescuing banks that made bad business decisions.

As the night went on, Bair became increasingly exasperated by Wells. It was taking hours for the San Francisco bank to deliver its bid. Wachovia executives didn't even know Wells Fargo was still in the running.

The other regulators were also frustrated with Bair, whom they felt was still resistant to pulling the trigger on an assisted deal. The FDIC, however, had to weigh the merits of two deals and was analyzing if it might be forced by law to levy the special assessment on the rest of the banking system, which would hurt the earnings and capital levels of other struggling financial institutions.

The logjam finally broke when FDIC analysts determined the cost of the Citi package was likely zero. That was because Citi was taking the first losses on a pool of assets and paying the government $12 billion in preferred stock and warrants. The analysts decided the expected losses wouldn't exceed those amounts and that the FDIC wouldn't have to start putting anything on its books as a loss. In the Wells offer, the FDIC would share in the first loss on a pool of assets, guaranteeing that it took a hit.

At four in the morning on Monday, September 29, Bair declared Citi the winner of the auction. She called Steel with the news. He asked why the independent plan didn't win out and was told Wachovia needed a partner. The explanation made Wachovia officials wonder if Citi was also in need of help.

Wachovia had only a few hours to assent to a nonbinding "agreement-in-principle" that laid out the basic terms of the transaction. In the document, Citi was code-named "Crimson" and Wachovia "Wednesday."

Under the offer, Citi would acquire Wachovia's banking operations for $2.16 billion in Citi cash and/or stock—essentially $1 per share—while the FDIC would assume up to $42 billion in losses on $312 billion in assets. Citi later said the "protected portfolio" comprised $156 billion in residential mortgages, $100 billion in commercial real estate, and $56 billion in other assets. Vikram Pandit said the agreement included Wachovia's riskiest assets. Wachovia executives wondered if Citi was also looking for protection for some of its own holdings.

Wachovia continued to push Citi to buy all of the company but was rejected. An independent Wachovia holding company comprising asset management and brokerage businesses would remain after Citi plucked out the banking operations. How to break up the company remained subject to negotiation. Citi would keep a "substantial presence" in Charlotte, according to the document.

The agreement-in-principle would be a starting point for the final merger agreement to be hashed out in the coming days. A final pact would need the approval of Wachovia shareholders. If a definitive agreement was reached but later not consummated, Citi would have an option to purchase certain Wachovia branches in California, Florida, and New Jersey.

At 6:04 A.M., Bair presided over an FDIC board meeting to give approval for the agreement. More than two dozen officials participated either in person or by telephone. Normally much more formally dressed, the officials and staff members wore blue jeans and other casual clothes during the hectic weekend in the office.

Bair was stationed in her normal position on the dais at the front of the agency's wood-paneled boardroom. Comptroller John Dugan, also an FDIC board member, phoned in from home. He had gone straight to the office after flying back from Amsterdam on Saturday. But on Sunday, he tapped into conference calls remotely. Since staff advised that Wachovia's banking units were "in danger of default," the five FDIC board members unanimously agreed to approve the Citi deal, finding Wachovia's failure would have "serious adverse effects on economic conditions or financial stability."

Treasury secretary Henry Paulson, limiting his contact with Wachovia, had gone to bed thinking the bank would be sold to Wells. That meant one of his deputies, David Nason, had to call Josh Bolten at the White House to officially get the president's systemic risk consent. The Fed also signed off on the decision, meeting the legal requirement for a systemic risk determination.

The Wachovia board met by telephone at 6:30 A.M. Steel had made a quick trip to his home in Greenwich, Connecticut, for a shower and a change of clothes and looked more refreshed than the others gathered in the Sullivan & Cromwell conference room. He explained the situation: Wachovia needed to sign the agreement-in-principle with Citi and the FDIC or face the prospect of being placed in receivership, resulting in a likely bankruptcy filing. The board didn't have much of a choice. The directors backed the Citi deal unanimously.

The board meeting lasted until about 7:30 A.M., leaving only a half-hour until the FDIC planned to publicly announce the deal. Lawyers from Citi's outside law firm, Davis Polk & Wardwell, e-mailed over the nonbinding agreement-in-principle, plus a second document.

Sherburne signed off on the agreement-in-principle but asked about the second document. A lawyer on speaker phone said it was an exclusivity agreement barring Wachovia from talking to any other parties about a deal.

"I have to read it," Sherburne said.

"Just sign it. Just sign it," the lawyer said.

"I'm not signing something I haven't read," she snapped before flipping through the pages.

Sherburne noticed the exclusivity agreement had no end date. She penned one in for a week later—October 6, 2008—and scribbled her initials.

At 7:55 A.M., Sheila Bair sent an e-mail with only a subject line to the FDIC board: "Wachovia and Citi Boards have approved the terms of the transaction."

Chapter 14

"You're Not Going to Believe This"

L ate on Sunday, September 28, 2008, reports began leaking that regulators were pressing Wachovia to sell itself and that Citi and Wells Fargo were the top candidates. "Regulators urge sale of Wachovia," was the bold headline across the top of Monday's *Observer*.

A little after eight that morning, the FDIC posted the first official statement declaring Wachovia's fate:

CITIGROUP INC. TO ACQUIRE BANKING OPERATIONS OF WACHOVIA

FDIC, Federal Reserve and Treasury Agree to Provide Open Bank Assistance to Protect Depositors

Citigroup Inc. will acquire the banking operations of Wachovia Corporation, Charlotte, North Carolina, in a transaction facilitated by the Federal Deposit Insurance Corporation and concurred with by the Board of Governors of the Federal Reserve and the Secretary of the Treasury in consultation with the President. All depositors are fully protected and there is expected to be no cost to the Deposit Insurance Fund. Wachovia did not fail; rather, it is to be acquired by Citigroup Inc. on an open bank basis with assistance from the FDIC.

"For Wachovia customers, today's action will ensure seamless continuity of service from their bank and full protection for all of their deposits," said FDIC Chairman Sheila C. Bair. "There will be no interruption in services and bank customers should expect business as usual."

Citigroup Inc. will acquire the bulk of Wachovia's assets and liabilities, including five depository institutions and assume senior and subordinated debt of Wachovia Corp. Wachovia Corporation will continue to own AG Edwards and Evergreen. The FDIC has entered into a loss sharing arrangement on a pre-identified pool of loans. Under the agreement, Citigroup Inc. will absorb up to $42 billion of losses on a $312 billion pool of loans. The FDIC will absorb losses beyond that. Citigroup has granted the FDIC $12 billion in preferred stock and warrants to compensate the FDIC for bearing this risk.

In consultation with the President, the Secretary of the Treasury on the recommendation of the Federal Reserve and FDIC determined that open bank assistance was necessary to avoid serious adverse effects on economic conditions and financial stability.

"On the whole, the commercial banking system in the United States remains well capitalized. This morning's decision was made under extraordinary circumstances with significant consultation among the regulators and Treasury," Bair said. "This action was necessary to maintain confidence in the banking industry given current financial market conditions."

About an hour later, Wachovia issued a press release that added details about its fate. The leftover Wachovia Corporation would remain based in Charlotte, with its Wachovia Securities brokerage group staying headquartered in St. Louis. Citigroup would base its combined retail banking group in Charlotte while keeping the investment bank in New York.

The sale to Citi was expected to close at year's end. In the meantime, the company's customers should continue doing business as normal, Wachovia urged.

"During recent weeks, the financial landscape has changed significantly and presented us with unprecedented challenges," Bob Steel said in a statement. "Today's announcement is the best alternative for the company, enabling a resolution on the Golden West portfolio."

In its press release, Citi said the combined company would be the nation's largest in deposits and noted the New York bank would assume Wachovia's senior and subordinated debt. Citi held a conference call with analysts, but it was devoid of the typical friendly banter between the two CEOs who had forged a fresh deal. Vikram Pandit was in on the call, but Steel was not.

Pandit praised the know-how and customer service reputation of Wachovia's larger retail banking operation and reiterated plans to keep the unit based in the Southern bank's hometown. He also said the company was considering keeping the "respected" Wachovia brand. "It's essential to have a strong presence in Charlotte, North Carolina," he added. Pandit lauded Steel as a colleague and competitor he had known for decades.

Commentary soon poured in from Charlotte dignitaries and business leaders, Hugh McColl perhaps providing the most stark assessment. "It's very, very much a body blow to the city," he said.

Former Wachovia and First Union CEOs also lamented the loss of the company.

"I'm both sad and mad," said John Medlin. "Wachovia didn't deserve to go down. It had a very viable and strong retail, commercial banking and wealth management operation. It could have worked its way out of the Golden West losses over time. I think Bob Steel was on the right track. The marketplace just didn't give it a chance to survive."

Bud Baker, Medlin's successor, said his reaction was one of sadness. "One of the great companies of America . . . now it's not going to exist anymore," said the former Wachovia CEO, who would face criticism in Winston-Salem and elsewhere for selling the bank to First Union. Baker remembered a 102-year-old woman he once met whose family had placed its money in Wachovia during the Great Depression. She told him the bank had saved the family's money, adding, "We owe everything we have to you."

An upset Ed Crutchfield could only say, "It's not a very happy day."

After years of buying other cities' banks, one of the two Charlotte financial giants had fallen. Inside Bank of America, its rival's collapse was not a cause for celebration. For most, the realization of how fast a big bank—especially one just down the street—could fall was sobering. Friends and neighbors worried about their jobs. A longtime collaborator on civic causes had been hobbled. The other major employment option for job-jumping bankers had been severely jarred.

The city's anxiety ricocheted from slashed bank jobs to damaged prestige to an unfinished arts complex still under construction on South Tryon Street. Wachovia's planned new headquarters building anchored the project.

Bob Morgan, president of the Charlotte Chamber, kept a stiff upper lip. "We have a first-class cultural facility, and that's not going to change," he said. "I'm watching out my window and the crane is still moving on the Mint Museum and the Bechtler Museum and the new tower."

Some observers painted Charlotte as having arrived at a crossroads. "Something significant and historic just happened here about which we can't even begin to predict the consequences," said Jeff Michael, director of UNC Charlotte's Urban Institute. "On the one hand, we may have just witnessed the beginning of the end of Charlotte's upward trajectory, or alternatively, we may be getting ready to see just how resilient this city really is."

The general consensus among analysts was that Citigroup had grabbed sought-after retail banking operations for a good price and not too much risk. How Wachovia fared was trickier to determine because neither the bank nor regulators had released details on how dire the bank's situation was over the weekend. Rob Bliss, a business professor at Wake Forest University, called it another example of a creative and unusual effort by regulators to aid an ailing financial institution. "Now the FDIC has an equity stake in a major bank," he said, referring to the preferred shares the FDIC would receive from Citi. "It's mind boggling."

While the deal preserved much of Wachovia, the transaction likely meant major layoffs, especially among highly paid top executives and investment bankers, as Citi cut costs. Analysts also suspected the remaining pieces of the company—the brokerage and asset management businesses—were likely to be sold off, portending even more turmoil for the city. UNC Charlotte professor Tony Plath estimated the city could lose 4,000 jobs.

Early on Monday, small groups of employees clustered in the company's headquarters atrium to discuss the stunning news. "Whatever it is, it will be gory," one employee waiting to buy coffee told a coworker. Outside, another employee said tersely, "There is no positive spin."

For investors, it was a horrific landing for a stock that had fallen from about $60 per share in the spring of 2006 to $1.84 by the end of Monday, September 29. A company once worth more than $100 billion in market value was now worth less than $4 billion. Many shareholders had held the stock for decades, watching shares in smaller banks around the Southeast morph into holdings in a national giant. Thanks to its lucrative dividend and solid reputation, Wachovia stock was the foundation of many retirement plans.

"They gave away the bank," said Marc Newell, a retired pilot who with his wife had held stock for 30 years. "They gave it to Citi for nothing. . . . I don't understand how you can give away a bank, but that's what they did." Because of Wachovia's problems, he said, the couple's retirement fund of roughly $400,000 had largely vanished. He said he planned to vote against the sale.

Others weren't sure how they would vote. "It's irrelevant whether the deal goes through or not," shareholder Chuck Johnson said. "We've gotten crushed. The shareholders have gotten crushed."

On his *Mad Money* show that evening, Jim Cramer affixed Steel to his "Wall of Shame" for selling the company at such a low price. He apologized to his viewers for letting them down and for not being more skeptical of Wachovia's prospects. He trusted Steel and had told his viewers to do the same. Now, the CEO was selling the company for "a pittance."

Some employees and investors felt betrayed by Steel's comments on CNBC, as well as by the memo he put out on Friday noting the bank's challenges but also stressing its strengths. "We had a plan. I really believed him," said a Wachovia employee in Winston-Salem. "A lot of employees had a really good feeling." Now, the employee had lost $30,000 on his Wachovia stock holdings and was worried about losing his job in the Citi acquisition.

Adding to the turmoil in the banking sector, the United States House of Representatives later on Monday voted down Henry Paulson's bailout package. Even as Charlotte's hometown bank was falling into the arms of Citigroup, all North Carolina Republicans voted against the bill. The state's Democrats were split.

Over the weekend, Paulson had signaled to lawmakers that a major bank was about to go down. Even on Monday, after the Wachovia news, members of Congress didn't seem to grasp the financial system's troubles, Paulson felt. Wachovia's lobbyists had worked with the industry's trade associations to press North Carolina lawmakers to support the bill, arguing its importance for all financial institutions but not letting on to Wachovia's particular problems. The bank's lobbyists knew Wachovia faced a critical situation but weren't privy to the negotiations in New York. They also didn't want to highlight Wachovia as a troubled bank.

"We need to go back to the drawing board and come up with other solutions," said Charlotte Republican Sue Myrick after voting against the bill. In a 2010 interview, she said she didn't recall being lobbied to vote for the bill over the weekend and said she had concerns when Paulson wouldn't explain how he planned to spend the TARP funds.

While Charlotte tried to digest the massive change to one of its lifeblood industries, exhausted Wachovia and Citi executives and lawyers still needed to finalize the deal.

On Tuesday afternoon, Citi officials delivered a draft proposal to jump-start the negotiations. Citi's chief administrative officer, Don Callahan, visited Charlotte to start assessing Wachovia operations and employees. On the trip, he met with local officials worried about the deal's impact. Citi liked what it saw and reiterated its promise to base the combined retail bank in Charlotte, executives told Mayor Pat McCrory.

"They're bullish on Charlotte," McCrory said after the meeting. "They're very impressed with Charlotte and the talent of the Wachovia employees."

While questions still swirled about the bank's future, Wachovia put out a statement saying the company was "well capitalized" and that it could support the stand-alone brokerage and asset management company that would remain after the deal. Citi also issued a statement saying it remained committed to the deal and that it continued to conduct normal business with Wachovia.

From the beginning of the talks, Wachovia executives stressed how difficult it was going to be to chop up the company. Computers were interconnected, jobs crossed division lines, and business units worked closely together. For example, some Wachovia Securities brokers worked inside bank branches. Wachovia executives worried about the viability of the pieces that would be left behind and continued to argue for the purchase of the entire company, instead of just the banking operations.

After hearing these concerns, Citi offered to pay an additional $2.16 billion in Citi stock to Wachovia to buy additional assets not part of the original agreement. With the extra payment of Citi shares, Wachovia would be able to make a tender offer to buy back outstanding preferred shares owned by investors. Before the deal closed, Wachovia also wanted a solvency opinion affirming the viability of the remaining company.

As the negotiations proceeded, employees and executives continued to deal with the emotional side of the company's unraveling.

On Wednesday, Wachovia retail bank head Cece Sutton posted a recording for employees thanking them for their dedication to customers during trying times and espousing optimism about a Citi deal that would spread Wachovia's platform to more customers.

But even top executives remained rattled by the deal. "To have your whole life change in a matter of literally a couple of weeks, not even weeks, a weekend, is tough," wholesale banking executive Carlos Evans told the *Observer*. An emotional Evans confirmed the outflow of deposits the bank had faced over the weekend, providing a dramatic glimpse of the depths of its troubles. "The so-called silent run on the bank—it's real," Evans said. "When Congress failed to pass the [$700 billion bailout] proposal, when WaMu collapsed, you could see the money flowing. My computer screen was lighting up."

Wachovia shareholders also grappled with the deal. Some were starting to revolt over what they saw as a fire-sale price for one of the nation's biggest retail banks. Charlotte businessman Mark Beck started a website, www.wachoviavoteno.com, to urge fellow shareholders to register their displeasure. "I'm mad as hell," said Beck, whose family had held Wachovia shares for 60 years. "That deal is so abusive. . . . They have apparently made a bad decision or were forced into it."

Since no merger agreement had been signed, some employees began wondering if the sale was ironclad. Communication from Steel had been conspicuously absent since Monday's initial announcement. An e-mail circulated speculating that Steel had brilliantly forged a deal with Citi to buy the company time until a congressional bailout was approved and accounting laws changed. All shareholders had to do was vote down the Citi deal, the e-mail said.

As the week progressed, the two sides and their lawyers continued to haggle over the final merger agreement. While Wachovia expressed concerns about the terms, Citi on Wednesday said it aimed to finish the talks by Friday, October 3. That would allow Citi on Monday to launch a $10 billion stock offering it needed to finance the deal. Regulators also pressed both sides to wrap up the discussions.

Early in the morning on Thursday, October 2, FDIC chairman Bair responded to a Citi official's e-mail regarding changes to the proposed agreement: "This is probably fine though we would like a little more info on the risks you are taking on with the investment group. Given our stake in the game [we] would appreciate continued consultations on any changes in the deal."

That same Thursday morning, Steel talked to Pandit by phone and agreed to fly up to New York to discuss how to keep top Wachovia executives at the combined company. In a Citi conference room, Steel, Jane Sherburne, and Wachovia human resources executive Shannon McFayden went through the list with Pandit, Citi vice chairman Lew Kaden, and chief administrative officer Don Callahan. After the meeting, Steel headed to the airport and Sherburne returned to the Midtown office of Davis Polk, Citi's outside law firm.

Wachovia officials were camped out in a large conference room at the law firm, breaking off to other rooms to negotiate specific pieces of the agreement. Sherburne didn't like what she heard. Disagreements continued over details Wachovia thought had been settled, including the solvency opinion provision. Citi officials would later say they thought they were close to an agreement, but Wachovia executives would contend numerous issues had to be resolved.

Sherburne realized it would be another long night if they were going to finish the document by the next day. The former White House lawyer was disappointed she wouldn't be able to catch the debate that night between Republican vice presidential candidate Sarah Palin and Democrat Joe Biden.

As the Citi negotiations dragged on, Wells Fargo was lurking.

On Tuesday, Wells chairman Dick Kovacevich rang Fed governor Kevin Warsh at his Washington office. Kovacevich had what he called good news. Wells was prepared to make an offer for Wachovia—without government help. After the call, Warsh went down the hall to see Ben Bernanke, who was in his office with Fed vice chairman Don Kohn.

"You're not going to believe this," Warsh said.

Boosting Wells Fargo's bid was a change in tax law quietly announced on Tuesday by the Treasury Department. In the past, the government had limited the ability of an acquiring company to shelter its income from taxes by counting an acquired company's losses. The new tax ruling, however, removed those limits for banks. The Treasury Department later said the change had been in the works for a while and was designed to boost bank consolidation, although officials said it wasn't meant just to help Wells. The change was a factor in Wells Fargo's ability to return to the table, but regulators also suspected that Wells hated being outbid by Citi in a once-in-a-lifetime auction for Wachovia. During the week, Wells continued to analyze the data it had received over the weekend on the Charlotte bank.

Around 7:15 P.M. on Thursday, October 2, Bob Steel was at the Teterboro, New Jersey, airport waiting for his plane to take off. He was flying to Durham, North Carolina, to chair a Duke trustees' meeting the next morning. His phone rang. It was FDIC chairman Sheila Bair. "Have you heard from Kovacevich yet?" she asked. Steel said he hadn't talked with him since a brief, awkward congratulatory call on Monday morning.

Earlier on Thursday, Treasury secretary Paulson told Bair he had heard reliable rumors that Wells was considering coming back with an unassisted offer worth about $7 per share. The FDIC chairman hadn't yet talked to Kovacevich but was trying to find out if it was true. With his plane about to take off, Steel asked Bair to give Sherburne a call.

In her conversation with Sherburne, Bair agreed that the new offer sounded better than Citi's. But both were wary of dealing with an offer that wasn't totally buttoned up, especially after Kovacevich's previous 11th-hour withdrawal.

Later that evening, Bair talked with Kovacevich, who told her the tax ruling had helped Wells make its bid. Bair told him that any offer had to be signed and binding. Later, she called Sherburne to tell her the Wells chairman planned to deliver such an offer.

Bair didn't feel sorry for Citi because she felt the bank had dragged out negotiations with Wachovia that week. One of the hitches that came with open-bank assistance was that a deal had to be finalized and then approved by boards and shareholders. In closed-bank assistance, the FDIC was in control as receiver of the failed bank.

While Steel flew back to North Carolina, Sherburne also heard from a Treasury Department official who encouraged her to give serious consideration to the Wells offer. When he landed, Steel called Bair back to learn more about the proposal. She told him it required no government support and carried no risk to the FDIC fund.

Around nine that night, the Wachovia CEO got a call from Kovacevich confirming that he was sending an e-mail with a signed, board-approved agreement to buy all of Wachovia. At 9:04 P.M., the e-mail landed in Steel's in-box. It was essentially the same merger agreement Wachovia had prepared for Wells Fargo over the weekend.

Steel consulted with Sherburne and Rodge Cohen about the various alternatives and the potential consequences for each. They decided they had a fiduciary duty to bring the offer to the board. "You're going to get sued no matter what you do," Cohen said. Steel and Cohen also checked in with Warsh and other major regulators. Reading from a prepared script, they said Wachovia had a fiduciary duty to go forward with the offer unless they were told to stop. No one called them off.

Back at the Davis Polk law offices, Sherburne dialed in to Wachovia's 11 P.M. board meeting from one of the bank's conference rooms. The Wachovia team had retreated during a break in the negotiations.

In the meeting, Steel, who had made it to a Durham hotel, updated the board on the situation. An agreement with Citi had not been finalized, and he had concerns about the company's viability under the terms the New York bank proposed. Wells Fargo had returned with a new bid, and Kovacevich planned on announcing his proposal Friday morning, regardless of whether or not Wachovia acted on it, he told the board.

One caveat to Wells Fargo's offer was that it was contingent on the Wachovia directors' approval of an agreement that handed a substantial voting stake to the San Francisco bank before the deal closed. This provision, which would not be put up for shareholder approval, would give Wells a 39.9 percent voting interest, all but guaranteeing a successful shareholder vote on the deal.

Wells had initially asked for a voting stake of more than 50 percent, but Wachovia negotiated the number down. Wells wanted the agreement because it would send a strong signal to markets that the merger was going to get done, preventing further deterioration in the bank's financial condition. Wells was not asking for a material adverse change clause, a provision that could allow Wells to escape the deal if Wachovia's condition or the economy slipped farther. That gave Wachovia assurance that it would not be jilted again.

The directors didn't have a lot of time to make up their minds. The bank was under pressure to come up with a deal by Friday, and its financial condition remained shaky. As of that evening, it wasn't clear whether or not the House was going to approve TARP. As the discussion continued, the view of executives and directors became clear: The Wells offer appeared to be the better proposal, and it faced fewer hitches in getting done.

After midnight, the board unanimously voted to approve the agreement, contingent on receiving fairness opinions from the bank's advisers, Goldman Sachs and Perella Weinberg. The firms declared the price offered by Wells Fargo to be fair, although they didn't perform all the analysis they would normally do, such as making comparisons to similar transactions. Such comparisons were meaningless under extraordinary circumstances, they determined. After the meeting, the audit committee approved the bank's decision to grant Wells the 39.9 percent voting stake without a shareholder vote, deciding any delay could jeopardize the company.

With the offer approved, Steel and Sherburne called Kovacevich. The Wells chairman had trumped his old employer, Citigroup. Steel also called Bair on her cell phone, trying not to wake her two children. Bair suggested they call Pandit together in the morning, but Steel wanted to do it right away with the FDIC chairman on the line. It was around three o'clock Friday morning, but Steel preferred waking the Citi CEO to having him hear about the new deal elsewhere.

Steel wrote out bullet points for the conversation. "There have been some unexpected and important developments with regard to Wachovia," he told Pandit. "We were advised by regulators first and then informed directly that Wells Fargo wanted to and has subsequently made an offer for the entire company at a higher price with no government support, and our board voted to accept that offer."

Clearly upset, Pandit reminded Steel that the bank had signed an exclusivity agreement. Steel said he was aware of that. Pandit appealed to Bair. "Sheila, you know this is not just about Wachovia," he said. "There are bigger issues here." Bair told him they should have a separate conversation, and Steel and Sherburne dropped off the line. Pandit's remarks would bolster the feeling at Wachovia that Citi needed a deal as much as Wachovia did.

In the early-morning hours that followed, Bair's phone line burned with angry calls from Pandit and other Citi executives and lawyers. Bair said the FDIC didn't have the ability to intervene in a deal that did not require government assistance. But she said she would stand behind the original Citi deal if that offer for some reason prevailed. The Federal Reserve, not the FDIC, approved bank holding company acquisitions, she reminded Citi. She also turned down Pandit's request to back a sweetened offer for Wachovia—a higher share price, with the same FDIC protection against losses.

Pandit called Steel back. The Wachovia CEO said he was uncomfortable having the conversation without his advisers on the line and told Pandit he needed to hang up. Citi executive Ned Kelly also called, and Steel said the same thing. Steel would skip the Duke trustees' meeting and head to Charlotte Friday morning.

Back at Davis Polk, Sherburne had to confront Citi executives in person. Wondering why the negotiations had mysteriously stopped, the Citi executive leading the talks, deputy counsel Andy Felner, went looking for the Wachovia team. "We got to get going," he said when he found a group in a conference room. "We got to pick up the pace and start discussions again."

Felner noticed the Wachovia team members were putting on their coats and packing up. Then he saw Sherburne, who asked her colleagues to wait in the hall. She gave Felner, a friend from her days at Citi, the news about Wells Fargo.

"We just signed at seven bucks a share, for the whole company, no government assistance," she said. "It's a done deal, and we're leaving."

"You can't do that," Felner exploded. "You had an exclusivity agreement."

"I know," Sherburne said.

"We will sue you for billions," Felner said.

"I know," Sherburne said.

Around seven in the morning on Friday, October 3, Wachovia and Wells Fargo issued a joint news release announcing their deal.

"Today's announcement creates one of the strongest financial firms in the world and is great for all Wachovia constituencies: our shareholders, customers, colleagues and communities," Steel said in a statement. "This deal enables us to keep Wachovia intact and preserve the value of an integrated company, without government support."

The announcement stunned employees and the city. Normally, Charlotte would be reeling from the sale of one of its banks, but this time the reaction was largely joy. In an ironic twist, a San Francisco bank was riding to Wachovia's rescue 10 years after Charlotte's NationsBank had snapped up San Francisco's BankAmerica.

"Everyone is kind of numb," one Wachovia employee said. "It's been such a long few months." Another summed up the flip-flop in emotions: "I'm jubilant. On Monday, I was suicidal." The headline in the next day's *Observer* captured the city's emotions with one word: "Whiplash."

Adding to the unreal feeling of the day, Charlotte's gasoline situation had begun to return to normal on Friday after the hurricane-imposed shortage. It was almost confirmation that a shell-shocked city's equilibrium had been righted.

Although details were still sketchy, the general consensus in Charlotte was that Wells was a better partner and that keeping the company together was better than breaking it up. Both Wells and Citi were likely to whack the bank's work force of more than 20,000 employees in Charlotte, but neither had given specific numbers. Citi was likely to slash more investment banking jobs; Wells might cut deeper into the retail banking unit.

For most investors, $7 per share sounded better than Citi's $1 per share. By the end of the day, CNBC's Jim Cramer apologized for slamming Steel earlier in the week and ordered his staff to gin up a "Wall of Acclaim." "You are the Man of Steel," Cramer said of the Wachovia CEO to his *Mad Money* audience. Wachovia shares on Friday climbed 59 percent to $6.21.

In a conference call with investors that morning, Kovacevich said Wells had needed the extra time to get familiar with Wachovia's loan portfolio. "We have to be comfortable before we will ever make a decision," he said. "And it took this much time to be that comfortable."

In combining the two companies, Wells said it planned to mark down Wachovia's loan book of $498 billion by $74 billion. The value of Wachovia's $122 billion in Pick-A-Payment loans would be slashed by $32 billion, taking into account lifetime losses and "market value adjustments." In July, Wachovia had said it expected losses of about 12 percent on the portfolio, or around $15 billion.

Steel was in Charlotte but joined the Wells executives on the conference call, unlike when Citi had announced its deal on Monday. Kovacevich praised his new partner's leadership in difficult times. "We can't wait to get to know you and think you'll enjoy the stagecoach," Kovacevich said, referring to his bank's Wild West–themed emblem. "Let's ride together."

In an interview that morning, Wells CEO John Stumpf said executives at both companies were elated but bushed by all the late nights. "I've come to believe sleep is overrated," he joked. "It's been around the clock for a number of days. But it's so well worth it."

Wells trumpeted the fact that its deal didn't need government assistance. But tax experts told the *Washington Post* that the acquisition would likely be more expensive for the government because of the potential reduction in Wells Fargo's tax bill. Experts said Wells might be able to shelter up to $74 billion in future profits—the amount of losses the bank was predicting on Wachovia's loan portfolios. In a CNBC interview that day, Kovacevich acknowledged that his bank had analyzed the tax change. But in a later securities filing, Wells said that, by its analysis, Wachovia's built-in losses had "substantial value" regardless of the new tax ruling. The tax change was not expected to have a "material impact" on future results of the combined company, according to the filing.

As the day went on, regulators began chiming in on Wells Fargo's announcement. But it wasn't initially clear which bank they backed.

In a joint statement, the Federal Reserve Board and the OCC said they had extensively reviewed Citi's proposal but hadn't yet examined Wells Fargo's. "The regulators will be working with the parties to achieve an outcome that protects all Wachovia creditors, including depositors, insured and uninsured, and promotes market stability," the agencies stated.

At the insistence of the Fed, the FDIC issued a statement reminding people that under either proposal "all banking customers of the merged institutions would be fully covered with no disruptions in service." But it also sent a confusing signal about which deal it favored. While saying it would be reviewing "all proposals and working with the primary regulators of all three institutions to pursue a resolution that serves the public interest," the FDIC added that it "stands behind its previously announced agreement with Citigroup."

Some interpreted the statement as favoring Citi. United States representative Robin Hayes, a North Carolina Republican, ripped off a letter assailing the agency's position. "I cannot understand why the FDIC would stand in the way of Wachovia entering into an agreement that seems better for their employees, shareholders, customers and the community around them," he wrote. "And since FDIC is not part of this merger, it would seem that it's better for the taxpayer as well."

The FDIC's intended message, as Bair had assured Pandit, was that it would back the original Citi offer—if the new Wells Fargo agreement didn't come to fruition or was not approved by the Federal Reserve.

On Friday, regulators dialed in to a conference call in which New York Fed president Tim Geithner and Bair clashed again. Geithner said the government would lose credibility if it welshed on the Citi deal, making it harder for the officials to broker future rescues. The FDIC's process had no integrity, he claimed. Bair fired back that with open-bank assistance, a deal was in doubt until an agreement was finalized and shareholders gave their approval. Bair said she was standing by the original proposal if needed, but that she didn't see how she could support an offer that posed more risk to her FDIC fund. And the Fed, of course, had the ability to derail either merger because it approved acquisition proposals, she noted.

Enraged Citi executives went on the offensive, issuing a statement demanding Wells and Wachovia terminate the transaction. Wachovia's agreement with

Wells Fargo was "in clear breach of an exclusivity agreement between Citi and Wachovia," the bank said. Citi officials reiterated their commitment to Charlotte.

Charlotte Chamber president Bob Morgan forwarded Citi's statement to other local business leaders. "Would caution all of us that it appears we are only in the third or fourth inning of what will likely be a long game," Morgan tapped out in his e-mail. "We should make no assumptions about the outcome and keep our comments guarded to every possible outcome."

In another turnaround from Monday, Congress on Friday approved a modified version of the TARP legislation, and President George W. Bush signed the bill into law. Around 6:30 P.M., a Citi lawyer sent an e-mail to Bair explaining how a provision slipped into the bill overruled all or most of the Wells-Wachovia deal. "In short the section invalidates provisions in non-assisted deals (like Wells) that interfer[e] with/impede the consum[m]ation of transactions that are FDIC-assisted (us). Happy to discuss with you or staff anytime. Thanks for all your time, day and night recently!"

Bair's response was less than encouraging: "This is in the [Federal Reserve Board] and OCC court. We have no role in the Wells application as they are not seeking assistance from us. I assume you are sharing the same thoughts with them."

The FDIC chair, however, didn't shut out Citi entirely. Over the weekend, Bair continued to e-mail Citi lawyers about possible changes in the bank's agreement to buy Wachovia.

Chapter 15

LIKE A FUNERAL

On the afternoon of Saturday, October 4, 2008, Jane Sherburne got a call from Citi general counsel Michael Helfer: "We're filing a TRO." As Wachovia had expected, Citi was seeking a temporary restraining order in its bid to block the deal.

Citi launched its fight in state court in New York, even sending lawyers to a judge's Connecticut home in its attempt to obtain the TRO. The initial complaint alleged that Wachovia had violated the exclusivity agreement that barred it from talking to other suitors. Echoing the e-mail to Sheila Bair, Citigroup also contended the Wells agreement violated a provision in the TARP bill.

The lawsuit also questioned the self-interest of Wachovia executives in switching merger partners. That deal triggered golden parachutes worth $225 million for Bob Steel and other Wachovia executives, the suit stated. The number would be oft-quoted in the brewing legal battle, but in reality Steel wasn't eligible for severance, and the total payout owed other executives ended up being smaller. Wachovia officials also thought the argument was odd because they believed the Citi deal would trigger the same provisions.

In a counterattack, Wachovia and Wells lodged their own suit against Citi, asking a federal judge to prevent Citi from interfering in the Wells transaction. Wachovia, represented by high-profile New York defense lawyer David Boies, argued that the TARP bill provision cited by Citi actually *favored* Wachovia because the intent of the law was to protect taxpayers. At a hearing Sunday, a United States District Court judge said Wachovia appeared to have been permitted to consider merger offers other than Citi's, but he did not make a decision. Another judge would take up the issue at a hearing scheduled for Tuesday, October 7.

On the legal front in North Carolina, former Wachovia chief executive Bud Baker and another shareholder, Mary Louise Guttmann, on Sunday asked a

Mecklenburg County Superior Court judge to grant a temporary restraining order barring Citigroup from enforcing its exclusivity agreement. Hating the idea of Citigroup's winning Wachovia, Baker had agreed to join the effort. Judge Robert Johnston temporarily approved the request, pending another hearing.

Vikram Pandit continued to seethe on Monday, October 6, lashing out against Wells and Wachovia at a Citi town hall meeting. His bank needed to be compensated for bailing out Wachovia in its time of need, he argued. "If Wells Fargo prevails, nobody will ever step up on Sunday night at 12 A.M. and/or Monday morning at 4 A.M. to say, 'I'm here for you[,] government[,] when you need us,'" he said.

"Our claims are large, they are rightful, and we will go after them with every bit of strength we have," Pandit added. Later in the day, Citi announced it was seeking $60 billion in damages.

Analysts and investors debated which deal was better and what would become of Wachovia. In one presentation, Pershing Square Capital Management suggested that Citi and Wells might up their offers. The firm also speculated that another buyer might step in to buy the pieces of Wachovia that would be orphaned in the Citi deal. In another report, Stifel Nicolaus analyst Christopher Mutascio estimated that the offers would be roughly equivalent if another buyer purchased the Wachovia "stub" for $6 per share.

As the legal spat escalated, regulators cringed at the invective flowing between the parties—and the uncertainty it was fostering for Wachovia, Citi, and the financial system as a whole. If the fight continued, Wachovia was likely to hemorrhage deposits, and customers and investors might develop deeper doubts about Citi.

Fed governor Kevin Warsh called up Dick Kovacevich and Pandit. Both banks asked him to help negotiate a truce. Later in the day, the banks announced they had agreed to a legal cease-fire until noon on Wednesday, October 8. Warsh, who was home in New York, began brokering a possible split-up of Wachovia's retail banking franchise and other assets.

As the talks proceeded, Wachovia executives, employees, and shareholders were virtual bystanders to the potential dismemberment of their company. Deposits continued to seep out of the bank, $2.4 billion disappearing on Monday alone. Wachovia human resources executive Shannon McFayden sent an e-mail to managers urging them to take care of themselves, their teams, and their clients. A Charlotte restaurant began providing a special discount to Wachovia workers.

As the talks progressed, Warsh was able to arrive at an outline for dividing up customer deposits, but not a price each institution would pay. The banks extended the truce until Friday at eight in the morning. But on the evening of Thursday, October 9, Citi walked away. The New York bank would continue to seek damages but wouldn't stand in the way of Wells Fargo's acquisition.

Wachovia and Wells scrambled to issue a joint press release declaring their deal would move forward. Kovacevich reiterated that the two companies had a firm, binding merger agreement and that he was confident the merger would be completed. The deal was "simply an incredible fit that will result in an immensely strong, stable financial services company that will carry on Wachovia's proud tradition of being one of the very best financial institutions in the world," he said.

The combined company would create a major rival for Charlotte's Bank of America and New York's JPMorgan Chase. Wells-Wachovia would be number one in branches with 6,600 in 39 states and number two in deposits with a total of $774 billion.

In its statement, the Fed praised the efforts of Citi and Wells Fargo but said an accord couldn't be reached. The Fed would immediately begin considering Wells Fargo's proposal to buy Wachovia. Bair said the announcement brought "needed certainty to the process."

A little after 10 that night, Steel sent an e-mail to employees saying "the people of Wachovia have demonstrated firsthand that we always put the interests of our shareholders, customers and clients ahead of our own—even in the most difficult of times. While we reiterate our great respect for Citigroup and its senior management and wish them well, we are now focused on the bright future of the combined Wells Fargo/Wachovia."

While Wachovia's future appeared to be settled, the financial system was still sagging from the toxic assets bloating bank balance sheets.

On Monday, October 13, Columbus Day, Henry Paulson assembled the heads of nine major United States banks, including Bank of America and Wells, for a dramatic meeting. The gathering brought together recent foes such as Vikram Pandit and Dick Kovacevich, as well as new merger partners such as Ken Lewis and John Thain.

Paulson, flanked by Ben Bernanke, Bair, John Dugan, and Tim Geithner, had a simple message: Instead of buying up distressed assets, he was going to inject $125 billion directly into the nine banks. It was the closest thing to nationalization that the United States banking system had ever seen. The bank leaders could consult their boards but needed to sign one-page term sheets before they left. The goal was to stabilize the biggest banks so they could make the loans a faltering economy needed.

Kovacevich put up a fight, saying his company wasn't in trouble from exotic investments and didn't need the money. Lewis didn't think he needed the injection either but encouraged his colleagues to accept the investment. They would be "out of their mind" if they protested executive compensation strings attached to the money, he added.

By 6:30 P.M., the executives had signed their names. Bank of America would receive $15 billion and was in line for Merrill's $10 billion, once the deal received

Fed and shareholder approval and officially closed. Wells Fargo would receive $25 billion.

"Government owning a stake in any private U.S. company is objectionable to most Americans—me included," Paulson said in announcing the initiative. "Yet the alternative of leaving businesses and consumers without access to financing is totally unacceptable."

Weeks earlier, Wachovia likely would have been one of the big banks called to Paulson's meeting. But it was now set to merge with Wells Fargo. The Wells-Wachovia deal still needed shareholder permission, but it had already received speedy Fed approval on Sunday, October 12. When Bair met with the media on October 14, the day after the Treasury meeting, a reporter asked the FDIC chairman if Wachovia would have survived as a stand-alone bank if the plan had been enacted sooner. "It definitely would have made a difference," she said.

A day later, on Wednesday, October 15, the end of Wachovia's run as an independent company was brought home even more clearly to Charlotte. Wells CEO John Stumpf flew to the city to address a crowd of Wachovia employees packed into the atrium on its campus.

In 2002, Ken Thompson had appeared on the same stage to reveal the new logo for the company after the First Union–Wachovia merger. And just months earlier, Steel had made his first appearance before expectant employees. Chairman Lanty Smith had accompanied Steel for that appearance but wasn't onstage on this more sobering day.

The platform was decorated with blue and green balloons representing Wachovia and red and yellow ones representing owner-in-waiting Wells Fargo. Backstage, Steel and general bank chief Ben Jenkins checked their emotions before walking out with Stumpf.

Before introducing his Wells counterpart, Steel received a rousing ovation from the employees who had seen their company nearly torn apart before being handed to Wells. It was a reception once unthinkable for a CEO selling a Charlotte bank. The Wachovia CEO said he had mixed feelings about the company's sale but that the Wells deal was the best possible outcome in light of the financial industry's travails. Steel told the employees it wasn't fair for them to be "too uncomfortable" with the deal, considering how Wachovia itself was the product of "a hundred mergers."

Stumpf, a silver-haired Wells veteran with a politician's delivery, gave a self-deprecating account of his roots growing up on a Minnesota farm before touching on the topic on everyone's mind. He told the audience his job was "to help all of you stay with the company" but added that he could offer, "obviously, no commitments, no promises." Wells planned on cutting $5 billion in total expenses but hadn't provided any details on layoffs. As in its 1998 Norwest deal, Wells would take about three years to integrate the companies.

Later at a news conference, Steel told reporters it would have been unwise for Wachovia to try to go it alone, noting the conditions in the industry and the bank's particularly troublesome mortgage assets. Steel said the shift from keeping the company independent to finding a partner arose from a combination of factors—the collapse of Lehman, the Merrill takeover, government intervention at AIG, the failure of Washington Mutual.

"Confidence is a very subtle thing," Steel added in an interview with the *Observer*. "For us to take the risk of people becoming less confident in Wachovia, we had to find other alternatives."

Asked if Wachovia's fate would have been different if the government had taken equity stakes in banks sooner, Steel said it was a case of "woulda, coulda, shoulda," adding he would leave such questions to historians. Asked if the bank's fortunes could have been buoyed by the proposed $5 billion Warren Buffett investment, Steel said Wachovia would have needed an infusion of $15 billion to $20 billion, not incremental injections from various sources.

The next week, Wachovia revealed just how bad its third quarter had been. The bank posted a loss of nearly $24 billion in the period as it took a host of charges ahead of the merger, including an $18 billion-plus accounting write-down to reflect the company's lower market value and the terms of the Wells purchase. It was the sixth-worst quarterly loss ever for a company that had been in the S&P 500 index. The red-ink gusher was also the biggest for a financial services company, eclipsing the $9.8 billion losses each by Citigroup, Inc., and Merrill Lynch & Company in the fourth quarter of 2007.

Wachovia set aside $6.6 billion to cover loan losses during the quarter, about two-thirds of it for Pick-A-Payment mortgages. The bank now expected cumulative losses of 22 percent in the $118.7 billion Pick-A-Payment portfolio. That was nearly double a July estimate of 12 percent cumulative losses.

The blow to the bank's deposit base also came into focus. From the end of June to the end of September, Wachovia's overall deposits fell 6 percent to $418.8 billion, a loss of about $29 billion, the bank said. Commercial deposits fell by nearly one-fourth to $83.4 billion.

After releasing the report, Wachovia did not hold its traditional conference call with analysts. Instead, Steel and his lieutenants spoke on a prerecorded message, emulating a Wells tradition.

In a research note, a longtime critic of the bank's board and some of its acquisitions, analyst Dick Bove, now with Ladenburg Thalmann & Company, lamented the demise of a company that became an East Coast giant under CEOs such as John Medlin and Ed Crutchfield. During the tenure of Steel's predecessor, Ken Thompson, the bank became known for its stellar customer service, Bove noted, but ultimately Wachovia was "forced into a merger" because of its "penchant to buy questionable properties at high prices." "I never dreamed that Wachovia would come to such an ignominious end," Bove wrote. "Today three men who are not old Wachovians, reported in a recorded message, the passing of the company to buyer Wells Fargo, while explaining how Wachovia built one of the largest losses recorded by any bank in history."

Amid Wachovia's struggles, competitors eyed a chance to wrest away long-time customers. In his bank's third-quarter earnings conference call, BB&T CEO John Allison said his bank would benefit from the sale of Wachovia, its largest rival. BB&T had attracted $1.2 billion in deposits from Wachovia, he said. "Wachovia has violated a trust with its shareholders and clients that will be hard to repair," said Allison, who was retiring at the end of 2008 after 19 years with BB&T.

A month later, in November, investors learned more about the fragile condition of Wachovia's other potential merger partner. The government unveiled a plan to stabilize Citi that included investing an extra $20 billion in the firm and protecting it from losses on $306 billion of sketchy loans and mortgage-backed securities. The asset guarantee plan was similar to the one Citi had proposed when it tried to buy Wachovia.

Among Wachovia executives, employees, and investors, it raised an obvious question: Why hadn't the government bailed out Wachovia in a similar fashion? Regulators would later say privately that Citi was in too much trouble and that no other institution was available to save it. Inside Citi, some executives would point to the loss of the Wachovia deal as a major blow to confidence in the company, contributing to its need for extra aid.

In the lead-up to the December 23 shareholder vote on Wachovia's sale to Wells Fargo, more details dribbled out about the deal.

Filings by the bank showed that 10 Wachovia executives were eligible for up to $98.1 million in severance after Wells Fargo bought the bank. Steel wasn't one of them because he had joined Wachovia without an employment contract. Others would forgo the payments because they were staying on with the combined company. David Carroll, for example, was set to become the head of wealth management, the only Wachovia executive to join John Stumpf's 12-member top management team. Carroll would later reach a special retention agreement that awarded him an $8 million bonus if he stayed at the combined company for one year.

In line for the biggest payouts were general bank head Ben Jenkins ($13.3 million) and investment banking head Steve Cummings ($14.3 million), according to securities filings. In the end, four others were also eligible for undisclosed payouts—Sherburne, human resources executive Shannon McFayden, and two executives hired after Steel arrived, CFO David Zwiener and chief risk officer Ken Phelan.

A filing also revealed how much money Goldman Sachs had made advising Wachovia during its travails: $77 million in fees since October 2006. That included assistance with stock offerings and other "financial advisory services" since December 2007, including analysis of Wachovia's loan portfolio. Wachovia was also set to pay Goldman another $25 million for its fairness opinion once the Wells Fargo sale was completed. Its other adviser, Perella Weinberg Partners, was to receive another $25 million.

With Wachovia about to be sold, blame for the company's demise focused largely on the poorly timed Golden West deal.

The acquisition made Wachovia a larger mortgage player just as the housing market was crumbling, giving it a sizable portfolio of nontraditional loans in especially troubled markets in California. Washington Mutual's abrupt failure later cast a particularly harsh light on Wachovia, raising more questions about the losses embedded in its portfolio. The bank's option ARMs were a worry for the suitors who sought to buy the bank in the fall of 2008, although Wells later became more concerned about Wachovia's commercial loans.

It is impossible to say what would have happened to Wachovia and Golden West had they not merged. Wachovia might have survived, or it could have suffered from other issues in the financial crisis. Golden West would have faced the stresses of the housing market, but its executives had long touted the company's ability to weather tough times better than rivals could.

Wells Fargo said it planned to phase out the option ARM portfolio once it bought Wachovia. By the end of 2008, efforts to work with struggling borrowers had showed promise, but Wells now projected losses to reach $36 billion, or 29 percent of the portfolio. That was nearly four times Wachovia's initial estimate of about 7.5 percent in April 2008. "As we've always said," Wells Fargo CEO John Stumpf told analysts, "we do not like the option ARM product."

The Charlotte bank clearly had other problems as well. From the beginning of the credit crunch in 2007 through the end of 2008, Wachovia recorded around $13 billion in "market disruption" losses related to collateralized debt obligations, buyout deals, commercial mortgages, and other soured investments. For all of 2008, it posted a total loss of nearly $45 billion, including an $11 billion loss in the year's fourth quarter. The red ink was among the 10 biggest annual losses for all companies over a 30-year period, according to Capital IQ, a Standard & Poor's business.

Wachovia also faced problems with risk management and financial controls, issues later highlighted by a $160 million settlement with prosecutors and regulators related to its business with Mexican money exchange houses. The bank in March 2010 entered into a deferred prosecution agreement to resolve charges that it "willfully failed to establish an anti-money-laundering program" from May 2003 to June 2008, according to the United States attorney in Miami. Wachovia failed to effectively monitor more than $420 billion in transactions for potential money laundering, according to court documents. After the agreement, the bank noted that it cooperated with authorities and that charges would be dropped if it complied with the agreement's terms.

By the end of 2008, the Golden West deal spurred a number of legal probes and lawsuits. The United States attorney in San Francisco said the Justice Department and the SEC had launched a preliminary investigation into Golden West's lending practices and whether or not Wachovia misled borrowers and investors. Shareholders also filed suits alleging Wachovia failed to disclose its problems. One shareholder lawsuit alleged Wachovia "incentivized its employees to sell a higher volume of Pick-A-Pay loans by paying them extra commissions to do so, even though Wachovia's employees 'didn't understand the product.' " In a later securities filing, Wells Fargo said it was cooperating with government authorities and that motions to dismiss had been filed in the shareholder suits.

In the wake of the Wells Fargo sale, Ken Thompson, an architect of the Golden West deal, remained silent, as did most top executives and board members. Retired director Robert Brown, in an interview with the *Observer*, blamed the unprecedented collapse in the housing market that followed the deal. "If you look back on it, who could have predicted that?" Brown said.

On their Web site, the Sandlers say their Golden West stake was worth about $2 billion before the Wachovia sale. Before the deal closed, they contributed $1.3 billion to a charitable foundation, and they say the rest of the proceeds are also earmarked for philanthropy. After Wachovia's near-collapse and sale, the Sandlers found themselves defending their reputations, as even *Saturday Night Live* painted them as villains in the financial crisis. The TV show later apologized.

In a 2008 interview with the *Observer*, Herb Sandler said Golden West was unfairly blamed for Wachovia's myriad problems and that he suspected the bank had overestimated potential losses in the portfolio. He attributed the rising delinquencies to plunging housing prices and Golden West's concentration in California markets—not the nature of its product. "I plead guilty to being a residential lender," he said. "This has nothing to do with the quality of the lending."

He acknowledged Golden West may not have flagged problems in the Inland Empire and Central Valley regions of California soon enough. In the past, the lender had identified overheated markets such as Las Vegas and pulled back. "Maybe, you could say, 'Gee, we shouldn't have made loans in certain parts of California,' " Sandler said. "We used to pride ourselves in getting out. We probably were not as quick in Inland Empire and Valley areas."

After buying Golden West, Wachovia executives frequently cited the thrift's performance during a 1990s California recession that saw housing prices decline by 20 percent. But the recent housing collapse was much worse, helping spur what some would call "the Great Recession." Home prices nationally plunged 32 percent from the peak in the second quarter of 2006 to the trough in the first quarter of 2009, according to S&P/Case-Shiller Home Price Indices. During just 2008, Merced, California, in the state's Central Valley region saw housing prices fall almost 50 percent, the biggest plunge of any metro area tracked by the Federal Housing Finance Agency.

As the December shareholder vote approached, the sale price still rankled many investors. Wells was giving Wachovia shareholders about a fifth of a Wells share for each of their Wachovia shares. Equivalent to about $7 per share when the deal was announced, the figure vacillated each trading day.

The last-gasp hope to derail the deal came in the form of a shareholder suit filed by a New York investor named Irving Ehrenhaus. The investor's lawyers argued that granting nearly 40 percent of the vote to Wells Fargo was "draconian and unlawful." Wachovia's lawyers argued the agreement was necessary to assure the market that the deal could close and noted the merger deal had stabilized Wachovia. After a hearing in November, North Carolina Business Court judge Albert Diaz ruled in early December that the bank had acted in good faith and that granting the shares to Wells Fargo was permissible. The deal was all but sealed.

As Wachovia neared the end of its final year as an independent institution, employees found out in December that they would receive much smaller bonuses for 2008. The bank said it would pay an average of 20 percent of incentive targets, a blow to workers and the Charlotte economy. Steel made the call, deciding the bank had been unsuccessful and that compensation should be doled out accordingly. In the investment bank, where bonuses comprised a big part of annual pay, many bankers were upset by the decision. The bank, however, avoided the political backlash aimed at other firms that made big payouts at the end of a historically awful year.

On December 23, employees and shareholders passed through metal detectors before quietly filing into a ballroom at the Hilton Charlotte Center City hotel, adjacent to Wachovia's headquarters. Only five of 17 Wachovia directors attended, including chairman Lanty Smith and CEO Bob Steel. Smith had suffered a stroke in October that doctors attributed to bank-related stress and had missed chairing his last board meeting in November.

Before the vote, Steel, standing in front of a backdrop of dark blue curtains, gave a brief eulogy for a North Carolina bank with roots to 1879 that had been molded by more than 100 mergers. He admitted mixed emotions about the sale but said it was "an exciting outcome in what has become a challenging environment." Steel was set to leave his CEO post after the deal closed, although he would join the Wells board, along with Wachovia directors Mackey McDonald, Donald James, and John Baker II.

Smith introduced Steel but didn't offer his thoughts on the transaction. The other three directors in attendance were McDonald, Peter Browning, and Ruth Shaw. All three had North Carolina ties. "It's a sad day today," Browning said before the meeting. He declined to comment on the board's past actions but said, "It was important to be down here."

Despite the sizable crowd, only a handful of shareholders spoke. Their comments were less bitter than in April, when investors had called for the firing of CEO Ken Thompson. Charlotte shareholder activist John Moore returned to criticize the board for approving costly acquisitions over the years that he said enriched management while hurting employees and shareholders. "At this time, the CEO who presided over this debacle has been dismissed," Moore said. "However, the board of directors gave unanimous approval of every action until the time of his dismissal."

In the end, the merger was approved by about 76 percent of the votes entitled to be cast, including those from Wachovia's outstanding common stock and the preferred shares issued to Wells. Wachovia said a majority of the common stock holders backed the deal. After a dramatic year that saw Wachovia oust its CEO, border on bankruptcy, and forge deals with Citigroup and then Wells Fargo, the meeting was a somber, anticlimactic affair. The deal would close December 31, officially ending Wachovia's run as an independent company.

"It was a funeral," said shareholder Charlie Williams, 73, who owned stock passed down from his parents. "Frankly, I wish Wachovia had never heard of First Union or Golden West, for that matter."

Chapter 16

"What a Disaster!"

As was typical in a Bank of America merger, the bank quickly started work on the Merrill Lynch deal in September, following a basic playbook for reassigning employees, analyzing computer systems, and combining brands even before the merger officially closed. The Charlotte bank installed about 200 employees in Merrill's headquarters, among them human resources executive Andrea Smith and chief accounting officer Neil Cotty, who became the firm's acting chief financial officer. "Transition teams" paired up executives from divisions at both companies. The groups then began mapping out how to combine staff, operations, policies, and procedures.

One of the first priorities was keeping top executives and bankers, including Merrill CEO John Thain, from jumping ship. When the deal was being negotiated, Thain indicated to Ken Lewis that he was interested in staying on. The two continued to talk about his role in a meeting in Charlotte after the announcement. They didn't come to a formal agreement, but it was clear Thain would have a chance to succeed Lewis someday. Among the executives on his management team, he was the only one with CEO experience. Thain also felt he owed it to Merrill employees to continue with the company.

On October 2, the bank announced that Thain would become president of global banking, securities, and wealth management once the merger was completed. That meant he would be in charge of Merrill's former investment banking and brokerage operations, plus similar Bank of America units. The two banks' units would eventually be melded together.

The Charlotte bank also outlined an ongoing role for Brian Moynihan, Bank of America's head of corporate and investment banking, who would cede his post to Thain. The former Fleet executive was seen as a rising star in the company, so finding a new role for him was significant. Once the deal was completed, Moynihan would lead private-equity and global operations, in addition to being charged with analyzing the bank's overall business model.

While the companies made progress on their merger, both continued to struggle with roiling financial markets and a rapidly deteriorating economy.

On October 6, after the stock market closed, Bank of America rolled out its third-quarter financial results earlier than scheduled. The bank reported a nearly 70 percent decline in profits from a year earlier, to $1.18 billion. It also disclosed that it planned to raise $10 billion through a stock offering and to halve its quarterly dividend to 32 cents per share. The goal was to build capital needed to absorb loan losses.

In a conference call, analyst Nancy Bush of NAB Research asked Lewis about rising losses in the bank's small business lending portfolio. "Nancy, I don't want to mince words," Lewis said. "I'm very happy that this was relatively small, but it's a damn disaster."

"You get points for candor, Ken," Bush responded.

While the third quarter was ugly for Bank of America, results were even worse at Merrill.

On October 16, the firm disclosed a net loss of $5.2 billion in the period, worse than a $2.2 billion loss a year earlier. In a conference call with analysts, Thain said the Bank of America deal made even more sense in a difficult economic environment. "The diversity of our businesses and earnings power, the strength of our balance sheet, the access to financing and to liquidity all, I think, make the combination very powerful, and I'm optimistic in spite of a difficult economic environment for the next year or two that we will be very successful," he said.

The transition was going smoothly. He was "happy to be part of the team going forward," Thain said.

Despite dismal financial results, Bank of America was still faring better than rivals that had either failed, been sold, or dramatically altered their business models. The Charlotte bank appeared to have come out on top—and its triumph was getting some national attention.

In mid-October, the same week John Stumpf met Wachovia employees in Charlotte, *60 Minutes* correspondent Lesley Stahl came to Charlotte to interview Ken Lewis and Hugh McColl about how their once-small Southern bank had taken on Wall Street and won.

At the start of the interview in Lewis's office, Stahl asked about Henry Paulson's dramatic step that week to inject $125 billion into Bank of America and eight other big banks. Lewis confirmed that he had no choice in taking the money but said he supported Treasury's effort to thaw lending markets. "I think he was right on," he told Stahl.

In the meeting with Paulson, Lewis said, he told his banking peers they couldn't get hung up on compensation restrictions that came with the capital injection. "This was so much more important," he said. "All of us can take a little less money."

Financial services executives were "overpaid," he added. "We need to cut back compensation in this industry," he said.

Pressed by Stahl, Lewis wouldn't call the intervention "socialism" but said "it will be different." The "golden era" of financial services was over, he said, a line he had been using in speeches in recent weeks. He expected to pay back the government's investment in three to five years. Then the business would get back "more toward capitalism," he said.

In the piece, which aired Sunday, October 19, Stahl marveled at some of the big numbers attached to Bank of America. "No," she said in surprise when Lewis noted that the bank did business with one in every two American households. "Oh, my God," she said when Lewis told her the bank would cut $7 billion in annual expenses in the Merrill Lynch acquisition.

Stahl also played up Bank of America's Southern roots, noting its headquarters was 600 miles south of Wall Street. "The biggest bank in America is headquartered in *Charlotte*?" she intoned for effect, noting some people didn't even know whether the city was in North Carolina or South Carolina.

"I always say Charlotte, North Carolina, so they don't have to ask the question," Lewis responded.

In one scene, Lewis and Stahl strolled around Uptown Charlotte as the CEO pointed out the bank's forest of buildings. "Not surprisingly, B of A seems to own Charlotte," Stahl said.

In her interview with McColl, she asked the former CEO if his goal had been to beat New York. Turning on the bravado, McColl said, "I was more interested in America." The bank never liked being small, he added. "There's nothing attractive about being small."

While outlining the bank's successes, Stahl referred to its miserable third-quarter earnings report and rising losses from credit cards. Did Lewis think his job was secure? she asked. Caught by surprise, Lewis laughed and said he must think so, since it wasn't a question he thought about.

As the segment came to an end, Stahl pushed Lewis to declare victory over his Northern rivals.

Stahl: "Did you defeat Wall Street?"

Lewis: "No, to some degree, we're part of it. So I don't know that we defeated it."

Stahl: "Well, if you're number one . . ."

Lewis: "Right."

Stahl: ". . . and if the idea was to compete with New York or Wall Street, you won."

Lewis: "We have . . . Yes, we have won in that sense."

The *60 Minutes* stopwatch began ticking.

But just weeks later, Bank of America executives became increasingly on edge about Merrill Lynch's fourth-quarter 2008 performance. The deal hadn't closed yet, but the bank was getting regular reports from Merrill, and the numbers looked worse all the time. In particular, as financial markets remained in tumult, Merrill expected to take bigger and bigger write-downs on the toxic assets on its balance sheet. While the assets could recover value at a later date, they would in the meantime deplete the capital cushion Bank of America was about to inherit from Merrill.

"Read and weep," Bank of America executive Neil Cotty wrote in an e-mail to CFO Joe Price on November 5. He was forwarding a message from a Merrill employee about the company's October returns, which showed falling revenue and other red flags.

By November 12, the losses climbed to $5 billion, and the quarter wasn't even halfway over. Executives were growing anxious about whether or not to share the dire news with shareholders, who would be asked to approve the purchase in a little more than three weeks. Over the next nine days, Bank of America general counsel Tim Mayopoulos examined Merrill's performance in previous quarters, as well as disclosures Merrill and Bank of America had made to shareholders in the proxy statement for the merger. He also discussed the issue with two of the bank's outside lawyers at Wachtell Lipton.

On November 20, Mayopoulos held a conference call with CFO Joe Price, other bank executives, and Wachtell Lipton lawyers. The conclusion: No disclosure was needed. The thinking was that Bank of America hadn't disclosed any projections for the fourth quarter, so it had no estimates to update. And it wouldn't be surprising to most if Merrill posted a loss. Starting with the fourth quarter of 2007, it had *averaged* a quarterly loss of $5 billion.

As losses continued to mount, the communications got more pessimistic. On November 24, Nancy Meloth wrote that fellow Merrill executive Tom Montag, who was set to run trading operations for the combined company, wanted to cut jobs and other costs to cope with falling revenue. A few hours later, Cotty e-mailed Price and Bank of America human resources executive Andrea Smith, "This is not good."

Over at Merrill, executives were seeing the same rising loss estimates. Some privately wondered if Bank of America might try to renegotiate a lower price before the shareholder vote, but that call never came. If the deal fell apart, they knew it would likely be a death sentence for Merrill.

On November 26, the deal cleared one of its final regulatory hurdles when the Federal Reserve Board voted 5–0 to approve the merger proposal. The 14-

page order was less than half the length of the order approving the Countrywide deal back in June. Bank of America and its subsidiaries were "well capitalized and would remain so on consummation of the proposal," the order stated.

As the December 5 shareholder vote approached, Bank of America executives called on Mayopoulos for more legal advice. On December 1, the general counsel met with Price and strategy executive Greg Curl to review the material adverse change, or MAC, clause in the merger agreement. This was the provision the bank could try to use to escape the deal before the merger closed. The executives didn't indicate they were considering a MAC, Mayopoulos later told a congressional committee. In November, however, an investor had inquired whether or not Bank of America could renegotiate the deal by invoking the MAC clause.

Mayopoulos told Price and Curl that a key factor would be Merrill's performance relative to other companies in the industry, including Bank of America. He noted that Bank of America's and Merrill's stock prices had fallen by similar amounts since the deal was announced, and that the Charlotte bank had its share of problems, including lower-than-expected third-quarter earnings and a dividend cut. Mayopoulos's conclusion: There was no basis for a MAC.

On December 3, two days before the shareholder meeting, Merrill's loss estimate grew again. The losses had hit $7 billion, then grown to about $9 billion with a $2 billion "plug." That extra cushion would become known inside the company as a "wild-ass guess" or the "Cotty plug," after its advocate, the Bank of America finance executive.

Whether or not Mayopoulos knew about the $9 billion estimate on December 3 would later be disputed. New York attorney general Andrew Cuomo would contend that Price didn't inform the bank's general counsel of the $2 billion plug. But Price, according to an SEC document, said he provided Mayopoulos with the $9 billion figure. Mayopoulos recalled being given only the $7 billion estimate. At the time, Mayopoulos advised against disclosure. He later told Congress that if the $9 billion figure was based on a guess, he believed his legal advice would have been that disclosure was not necessary. Ken Lewis testified that he was informed of the number on December 3 in a meeting with Price, Cotty, and Merrill CEO John Thain.

Not every Bank of America executive was on board with the decision not to disclose. With losses projected at around $9 billion, Bank of America treasurer Jeff Brown told Price he felt the bank should go public with the numbers because the "losses were meaningful enough." Brown later told investigators that he warned Price they could face jail time: "I stated to Mr. Price that I didn't want to be talking through a glass wall over a telephone."

One way out of the purchase could have been to reveal the rising losses and urge shareholders to vote against it. But that would have been an embarrassing turnaround for the bank that could hurt its credibility in future deals. It also would have meant letting go of a chance to buy an iconic Wall Street institution that instantly turned the bank into a major player in investment banking and wealth management.

On December 4, Jennifer Burns, an official in the Charlotte branch of the Richmond Fed, sent an e-mail to colleagues saying that management at Bank of America and Merrill was confident the merger would get approved. If not, Merrill Lynch would have access to various government programs and likely warrant extra support "to preclude significant systemic disruption." The Federal Reserve Bank of New York would be standing by, she added.

The next day, Merrill shareholders backed the sale at a 45-minute meeting at the firm's headquarters. A small number of shareholders blamed the investment bank's demise on the board of directors and former chief executive Stan O'Neal.

Three hours later, at an auditorium across the street from Bank of America's headquarters, Lewis faced a smattering of shareholders who critiqued the deal and his pay.

"History tells us this: Commercial banking and investment banking do not mix," said John Moore, the Charlotte shareholder activist. "Exotic derivatives and structured security investment vehicles must never again be allowed anywhere near the mortgage on your daughter's house or your grandfather's certificates of deposit."

But at the end of the 90-minute meeting, more than two-thirds of Bank of America's shareholders sided with the deal. Executives did not discuss loss estimates at the gathering. The proxy and merger agreement sent to shareholders in advance of the meeting included a provision that said Merrill employees would not be paid compensation other than salaries or amounts specified by certain agreements, although there was mention of unspecified exceptions.

"When this transaction closes, Bank of America will have the premier financial services franchise anchored by the cornerstone relationship products and services of deposits, credit and debit cards, mortgages and wealth management," Lewis said in a news release issued after the vote. The bank said the acquisition was expected to close at year's end, "pending the satisfaction of customary approvals and closing conditions."

"Whhew!" a Federal Reserve official in New York wrote in a 2:31 P.M. e-mail.

Although Merrill had nearly collapsed in 2008, the firm was still intent on paying bonuses to employees. On Wall Street, bankers received sizable salaries, but they really didn't get "paid" until their bonus check arrived. If bankers felt slighted by their payouts, they were likely to jump ship, seeking more generous employers.

Merrill typically calculated bonuses in January, after full-year results were known. But when the merger was negotiated in September, Thain's understanding was that Merrill would pay its bonuses before the deal closed. On November 11, he recommended the payouts be made in December, and his board's compensation committee agreed. The cash part of the bonuses would be paid December 31, while stock awards would be granted in early January, after the deal closed. Thain informed Steele Alphin, Bank of America's chief administrative officer and Lewis's friend.

As for Thain's own payout, Alphin warned the Merrill CEO he should not expect the same kind of compensation at Bank of America as was customary at Merrill. He also told Thain it wouldn't go over well with the Bank of America board if he got paid more than Lewis in 2008.

On December 8, Bank of America and Merrill got their first taste of bad publicity over bonuses. The *Wall Street Journal*, citing unnamed people familiar with the matter, reported that Merrill's compensation committee was resisting a request by Thain for a $10 million year-end bonus. While Thain had received praise for salvaging the company, such a big payout would stoke growing public anger over excessive pay on Wall Street. That day, Merrill's compensation committee decided not to pay bonuses to Thain and four other top Merrill executives. The five hadn't received bonuses in 2007 and hadn't secured 2008 payouts during the merger negotiations with Bank of America.

For the rest of Merrill's employees, the compensation committee approved a total bonus pool of $3.6 billion, lower than the $5.8 billion cap agreed to in September. Before the number was set, Alphin urged Merrill to reduce the pool and change its composition. Instead of making the payout in 60 percent cash and 40 percent stock, the bank preferred a 70 percent cash, 30 percent stock split. Merrill complied, and Bank of America confirmed its understanding of the change in a December 11 letter sent to the firm's general counsel.

Two days after the bonus flap stirred by the *Journal*, Alphin sent an e-mail to Bank of America human resources executive Andrea Smith and Merrill executive Tom Montag that appeared to dispute the contention that Thain wanted a $10 million bonus. Instead, Thain had looked "simply to be paid fairly," according to the e-mail. Thain had already accepted that if Lewis received no bonus for 2008, he also wouldn't get one, Alphin wrote. If Lewis did take home a bonus, Thain's would be significantly less.

"John's reputation has not been damaged with our directors or management team which now includes him," Alphin wrote. "We move forward."

Lewis later testified in a deposition that Alphin told him Thain expected a bonus of around $40 million for pulling off the Merrill Lynch sale. But a spokesman for Thain, Jesse Derris, said that was "completely untrue." Thain's expectation was always that he would receive a bonus lower than what Lewis got, Derris said.

. . .

With less than a month left until the deal's closing, Merrill's losses kept getting worse. "What a disaster!" Merrill corporate controller Gary Carlin, referring to another set of estimates, wrote in an e-mail to Cotty.

On December 9, Price presented the projected $9 billion loss to the board of directors at a regularly scheduled meeting at Bank of America's headquarters. Another issue discussed at the board meeting was a coming shakeup of Lewis's management team. Brian Moynihan was set to leave the bank after turning down a request to head its Delaware-based credit card unit. Lewis wanted him to replace Bruce Hammonds, the retiring former MBNA CEO, but Moynihan didn't want to move his family from Boston. When his offer was rebuffed, Lewis, who had moved numerous times for the bank, gave a curt response: "Then I guess you're going to leave the bank?"

Bank of America even prepared a news release about Moynihan's departure, to be issued December 12. It had a quote from Moynihan: "I have enjoyed my time at Bank of America, but it is time to pursue new challenges." And one from Lewis: "Brian has been an outstanding executive who has taken on and done well with every challenge we have thrown at him. We know he will do well at whatever he chooses to do."

The planned departure didn't go over well. Some of the directors who knew Moynihan from his days at Fleet pushed back. They didn't want to see him go. Later in the day, the directors received an e-mail from Lewis: Moynihan was staying at Bank of America and becoming general counsel.

Early the next morning, December 10, Bank of America director William Barnet, head of a real-estate firm and mayor of Spartanburg, South Carolina, kicked off an e-mail exchange with fellow director Chad Gifford, the former Fleet CEO.

"Glad (I hope) Brian got saved . . . Last of the Fleet guys and good person and team player . . . Not sure what it does to Tim M," Barnet wrote, referring to Mayopoulos. "Numbers were numbing . . . too fast and overwhelming. . . . ML equally amazing. [N]o mention, except in passing, of holiday greetings. . . . Much pressure . . . felt KL feeling it," he added, referring to the ugly earnings outlook outlined at the board meeting.

"A bit scary willing to let Brian go . . . notwithstanding [F]leet he's a key character in understanding all that's on plate," Gifford responded later in the day. "But seems [K]en heard us a bit and at least we had an executive discussion with many seemingly agreeing."

Barnet, a former Fleet director, messaged back that the "board was getting it." But he feared "we let this get too far down the path. . . . Will be a very tough year and 'plan' seems unrealistic from today's perspective."

Concluded Gifford, "It's the way we approved acquisitions that tick[s] me off the most!!!"

A little before noon on December 10, while in a meeting about the merging of the Merrill and Bank of America legal departments, Mayopoulos's assistant told him that his boss, chief risk officer Amy Brinkley, wanted to see him. Back at Mayopoulos's office, Brinkley told him that Lewis had decided to replace him as general counsel. Moynihan was taking over his role immediately. A human resources representative came into the office, gave Mayopoulos his severance papers, and took his corporate ID, company credit card, BlackBerry, and office keys. The HR representative escorted him to the executive parking garage. The stunned Mayopoulos drove home. He lived in the same neighborhood as Lewis.

Later that day, the bank announced Mayopoulos's departure and Moynihan's appointment as general counsel. "Tim Mayopoulos served our company with distinction and we wish him great success in his future endeavors," Lewis said in the news release.

Mayopoulos wasn't the only employee on his way out. The next day, Bank of America said it planned to slash 30,000 to 35,000 jobs over the next three years, citing the merger and the weak economy. It was the biggest layoff in the company's history, part of its effort to excise $7 billion in combined costs. The bank started at the top, axing more than a dozen upper-echelon executives in the first week and sending ripples of fear through the rank and file. In most of the bank's mergers, employees back in Charlotte had emerged relatively unscathed from the layoff rounds that always followed, while workers at the banks being bought suffered the brunt of the cuts. This time, it felt like Charlotte was taking a deep hit.

The bad news out of Merrill didn't stop. After receiving another dismal set of projections, Price tracked down Lewis in New York on December 14 to tell him the firm's estimated loss had now hit about $12 billion. By the next day, Wachtell Lipton lawyers were examining the MAC clause in the merger agreement. Merrill had purposely negotiated the clause to leave little wiggle room for Bank of America to try to escape the deal. Under the provision, for example, a MAC didn't cover changes in "general business, economic or market conditions."

In their quick read of the situation, the lawyers found that Bank of America needed to show Merrill's troubles would damage the firm's earnings power over the long haul, not just the short term. The bank would also need to demonstrate that the losses were much worse than competitors'. Later in the week, Goldman Sachs would report a $2.1 billion fourth-quarter loss and Morgan Stanley a $2.4 billion hit.

On the morning of December 17, Lewis dialed up Treasury secretary Paulson in Washington. Bank of America was strongly considering a MAC, Lewis told him.

"We should probably talk," Paulson said. "Can you be here by 6:00?"

Chapter 17

"Fill the Hole"

T he main headquarters for the board of governors of the Federal Reserve System, officially the Marriner S. Eccles Federal Reserve Board Building, is one of the more imposing structures in Washington. The austere, sharp-edged white marble Art Deco building squats on Constitution Avenue with a broad view of the National Mall. A lone eagle sculpture tops the column-framed front door, the symmetrical base of the building almost an extension of the raptor's wings. The wide front lawn isolates the building from the street, almost a symbolic separation of the Fed from the political environs surrounding it.

To this intimidating setting, Ken Lewis brought CFO Joe Price and freshly appointed general counsel Brian Moynihan. Moynihan hadn't practiced law for years, in contrast to Tim Mayopoulos, a veteran general counsel schooled in the rough-and-tumble ways of Wall Street.

Henry Paulson, Federal Reserve chairman Ben Bernanke, and the Fed's general counsel, Scott Alvarez, hosted the bankers in the anteroom, a high-ceilinged venue off the boardroom where the Federal Open Market Committee made interest rate decisions. Portraits of seven former Federal Reserve chairmen ringed the room, stopping at Paul Volcker. A dining-room-sized table sat in the middle of the room, a speaker phone positioned in the middle.

Both the bankers and the regulators had prepped for the meeting. The Bank of America executives, after consulting with their outside lawyers, planned to make a case for triggering a MAC but expected stiff resistance. The regulators were intent on listening but not making a decision that evening.

Lewis kicked off the meeting by describing his bank's troubles. Rising loan delinquencies meant the bank had to set aside more money to cover losses. For the first time in 17 years, it expected to report a quarterly loss, the red ink likely exceeding $1 billion. Meanwhile, things were even worse at Merrill, its losses accelerating rapidly to $12.5 billion. The bank believed some of Merrill's earnings power had been destroyed and was inclined to call a MAC, Lewis said.

After Price ran through some more numbers, Bernanke spoke up: Wasn't it a bigger risk to trigger the MAC than to acquire the company? Calling a MAC would surely lead to a lawsuit with Merrill. It was a tough call, Lewis said. He was worried about the bank's capital ratios and stock price. His plan was to talk to his board, then John Thain by the end of the week. He still liked the "strategic potential" of the deal over time, he acknowledged.

Bernanke warned that pulling out would pose risk to both Bank of America and Merrill. The best thing was for the bank to go forward and then come back next year if it needed help from the government, he said.

The regulators had heard through back channels that Bank of America might be interested in a "Citi guarantee," an arrangement similar to the one reached in November that protected Citigroup from losses on its worst assets. On cue, Lewis brought up the idea of a Citi-like structure that would cap the bank's losses on the most troublesome holdings. The regulators pointed out that Citi was different because it had been in more imminent danger.

As the meeting wound down, Paulson and Bernanke signaled that Treasury and the Fed were committed to stopping the collapse of a "systemically important institution." The regulators asked Bank of America to give them more time to look at the numbers. In return, officials would provide more details about the Citi bailout structure. Lewis said he would wait, and both sides left without any commitments.

Soon afterward, Bank of America began handing over data about Merrill's and its own operations. Officials in Washington, New York, Richmond, and Charlotte started dissecting the reports. It wasn't a pretty picture for Merrill—or for Bank of America. "BAC trying to lay it all on ML weakness, but not the case, so pound of flesh from [Bank of America], after the merger, in exchange for support seems like likely recommendation," Tim Clark, a senior Fed official in Washington, wrote in a December 18 e-mail.

Bank of America's lawyers burrowed into the case for calling a MAC. In a memo prepared for Lewis, Wachtell Lipton lawyers indicated a Merrill lawsuit was likely if Bank of America exercised the MAC—and Merrill could win. The lawyers also cautioned the bank that its deal was governed by Delaware law, where they said courts had never allowed a buyer to use a MAC to back out of a deal. In a worst-case scenario, the bank could lose a legal challenge and be forced to purchase a weakened Merrill. To the bank's advantage, losses at Merrill were worse than at Morgan Stanley and Goldman Sachs.

On December 19, the bank's lawyers held a conference call with their government counterparts about the MAC. Tom Baxter, the New York Fed's top attorney, noted there had never been a successful use of a MAC. A Wachtell Lipton lawyer responded that each case was based on the facts, and that this one could be the first related to the size and duration of losses. But inside the Fed, officials weren't buying the bank's arguments. The call helped cement the belief that Bank of America didn't have justification for calling a MAC. Instead, some suspected the bank, arguably in a tough spot as Merrill's losses ballooned, was simply sniffing around for government aid.

At 3:30 P.M. that day, Paulson and Bernanke planned to talk with Lewis again, this time by phone. In preparation, the Fed's Tim Clark sent a message summarizing the findings so far, including the conclusion that Bank of America on a stand-alone basis was thinly capitalized. "Ken Lewis' claim that they were surprised by the rapid growth of the losses seems somewhat suspect," he wrote. "At a minimum it calls into question the adequacy of the due diligence BAC has been doing in preparation for the takeover."

In the call, Paulson reiterated that exercising a MAC was bad for the financial system and both Bank of America and Merrill. Renegotiating with Merrill was also "perilous" and would likely drag on, he said. Lewis again pushed for protection on losses as well as additional money from the Troubled Asset Relief Program. Officials needed to work quickly to get the bank's numbers and understand them, Paulson said. Both Paulson and Bernanke discussed aspects of the Citi rescue package, noting the bank took the first losses. Lewis asked why the government wanted the acquisition to proceed and got a pointed response: In addition to being bad for the financial system, the collapse of the deal would cast doubt on Bank of America's due diligence and management. They agreed to talk again.

By Saturday, December 20, the Fed's resistance to the MAC solidified. In an e-mail, Federal Reserve Bank of Richmond president Jeff Lacker told colleagues that Bernanke thought the escape clause threat wasn't "credible." Furthermore, if Bank of America tried to get out of the deal and later needed assistance, management was gone, Lacker said, although he had forgotten to tell Bernanke that Lewis was "near retirement."

Government officials, however, appeared ready to provide assistance to Bank of America. Although the Fed and Treasury had let Lehman Brothers collapse, the government since mid-September had shelled out aid to AIG, offered assistance for a potential Citi-Wachovia deal, injected capital into big banks, and provided extra aid to Citi. Bernanke hoped a Citi-like deal could be worked out with Bank of America, Lacker added in his e-mail.

As they probed the data, examiners became increasingly skeptical of the bank's ability to meet its financial projections. Bank of America's 2009 forecast showed net income for the year of $13.4 billion, which included the need to set aside $23.5 billion as a cushion against loan losses. That provision was $2.3 billion lower than what the bank had expected to take in 2008.

Fed officials in Richmond, already peeved over the bank's capital levels after the Countrywide deal, began discussing penalizing its management for getting into this situation. In an exchange with Lacker, Richmond Fed official Mac

Alfriend suggested the Fed do "what we did with Wachovia"—that is, require the bank to analyze its corporate governance and risk management practices.

Alfriend later passed along "preliminary thoughts on getting a pound of flesh out of Lewis" to Fed official Deborah Bailey. "Personally, I think management should be downgraded, no more acquisitions, raise some 'real capital,' frequent meetings with the Board, etc.," Bailey replied. "It will definitely [have] a price to pay."

Alfriend also e-mailed Lacker to say Bank of America CFO Price and risk officer Amy Brinkley still felt "comfortable" about getting out of the deal, saying they needed to protect their shareholders. "I did not get into the damage this will do to their relationship with regulators," Alfriend wrote.

At Bank of America, Moynihan, Price, and Wachtell Lipton lawyers geared up for Lewis's next talk with Paulson. According to Lewis's talking points, the bank's executives still thought it had a MAC but remained interested in a Citi-like rescue package. "Acquiring Merrill under these circumstances could do tremendous damage to BAC," the script read. "However, we understand your concerns about Merrill and are committed to working together to find a way to move forward with the acquisition without destabilizing our franchise."

Meanwhile, Merrill CEO Thain had no idea that Lewis was deep into discussions with the government and that his company-saving deal could potentially unravel. Bank of America executives hadn't shared their misgivings. Thain was headed to Colorado for a ski vacation, although he would be available for work if needed. On his way to Vail, he got a call from Paulson, who quickly got a sense that Thain wasn't aware of the brewing problem. Not wanting to disclose the government talks, Paulson asked him how the merger was going, and Thain said fine. The call didn't last long, leaving Thain wondering why the Treasury secretary had called.

On Sunday, December 21, Bernanke sent an e-mail to fellow Fed governors and other top officials in preparation for the next conversation with Lewis. "I think the threat to use the MAC is a bargaining chip, and we do not see it as a very likely scenario at all," he wrote. "Nevertheless, we need some analysis of that scenario so that we can explain to [Bank of America] with some confidence why we think it would be a foolish move and why the regulators will not condone it."

That Sunday, Lewis called Paulson, who also was in Colorado on a ski vacation. The Bank of America CEO laid out the bank's position again: The company believed it had a MAC but was willing to hold off in return for a bigger TARP investment and loss protection on $150 billion in assets.

A veteran deal maker from his days at Goldman, Paulson knew how to play hardball. "We're very supportive of Bank of America and we want to help but the government does not feel it's in your best interest for you to call a MAC," he said.

"We feel so strongly we would remove the board and management if you called it."

Lewis backed off. "Hank, let's de-escalate this for a while," he said. "Let me talk to our board."

Later on Sunday, Lewis talked with Bernanke, who took a more conciliatory tone. The Fed chairman was committed to a transaction that worked for the bank. The aid would come after the January 1 closing of the deal but before the bank's planned earnings announcement on January 20, inauguration day. President-elect Barack Obama's new administration, including incoming Treasury secretary Tim Geithner and economic adviser Larry Summers, was on board. Bernanke even praised the bank for stepping up when Countrywide was in trouble earlier in the year. The Fed would be flexible to ensure that the need for aid looked like a Merrill issue.

After five tense days, Bank of America appeared resigned to move forward with the deal—with the government's help.

"Lewis has withdrawn his threat to invoke a MAC to get out of the deal with ML," Bernanke wrote in an e-mail to Fed governors Elizabeth Duke and Randall Kraszner after the conversation. "With the MAC off the table, we have some time to work out what is needed."

Lewis convened his board the next day, Monday, December 22. Treasury and the Fed were unified in the view that a failure to complete the deal would result in risk to the financial system and to the company, he told directors. He also repeated Paulson's threat to remove management and the board, as well as the regulators' promise to provide aid. The rescue package wouldn't be ready by the January 1 closing date, but the company could rely on the word of Treasury and the Fed. Lewis recommended the bank go ahead with the deal. The directors asked him to get more details about the proposed aid and to try to obtain a commitment in writing. According to the minutes, the board also made the point that it wasn't influenced by the threat of removal.

That evening, Lewis e-mailed the board after a conversation with Paulson: "He said there was no way the Federal Reserve and the Treasury could send us a letter of any substance without public disclosure which, of course, we do not want."

In addition to asking for a written commitment for aid, Lewis expressed concerns on December 22 to Bernanke about being sued by shareholders for *not* exercising the MAC. The Fed chairman told Lewis he couldn't use a "government-made-me-do-it defense." But Bernanke acknowledged the Fed's analysis had shown that backing out would be damaging to the financial system and Bank of America.

Bernanke passed Lewis's concern along to Scott Alvarez, the Fed general counsel. Alvarez told Bernanke he didn't want the Fed to become a centerpiece of any litigation, which could also lead to the revelation of problematic documents for Lewis. "Some of our analysis suggests that Lewis should have been aware of the problems at [Merrill Lynch] earlier (perhaps as early as mid-November) and not [been] caught by surprise," the general counsel wrote. "That could cause other problems for him around the disclosures [Bank of America] made for the shareholder vote."

Alvarez added in an e-mail to Bernanke, "A different question that doesn't seem to be the one Lewis is focused on is related to disclosure. Management may be exposed if it doesn't properly disclose information that is material to investors."

At the Richmond Fed, officials discussed Lewis's request for a written commitment. After talking with the Fed chairman, Lacker wrote, "[Bernanke's] sense is that [Ken Lewis] is just generally anxious about the merger, not trying to shake anyone down."

Jennifer Burns, a Fed official in Charlotte, agreed: "We paint a bad picture of them—they are really difficult and often unlikable—but I think they have seen what has happened with other firms that have made bad acquisitions and they are worried. Me too!"

Alfriend was more skeptical: "I think he is worried about shareholder lawsuits; knows they did not do a good job of due diligence and the issues facing the company are finally hitting home and he is worried about his own job after cutting loose lots of good people."

As the parties hashed out the aid package, Kevin Warsh would be on point for the government. CFO Joe Price would lead the talks for the bank.

"We've heard it loud and clear that the agencies feel calling a MAC would be systemically unsafe and unsound to the system as well as Bank of America," Price wrote in an introductory e-mail to Warsh, adding, "Hope you are having as much fun as I am."

Kicking off the effort, Warsh wanted to look at various proposals and the possible market responses, especially the potential perception that the problem wasn't just a Merrill issue. One of the ideas was to match private capital raised by the bank, instead of having the government provide all the support. He also urged the bank to develop its own proposals. "They need to take more ownership of [the] situation," he complained in one e-mail. In one discussion of the aid package, he told a Fed official he was "worried too much about nationalizing the whole thing."

At Bank of America, executives hadn't totally abandoned the idea of using the MAC as they pressed forward with the negotiations. On Saturday, December 27, Moynihan told associate general counsel Teresa Brenner in an e-mail, "The basic concept is that the 'fill the hole' preferred or common [capital] has to be on terms which are extremely favorable in order for us to give up our rights to the [MAC] clause exercise."

In a December 29 call with Warsh, Price reminded the Fed governor that the company had a fiduciary duty to respond to the Merrill losses and had experience with calling a MAC in 2007 as part of the later-derailed acquisition of education lender Sallie Mae.

After the conversation, Warsh expressed frustration with the bank's executives in an e-mail to Bernanke, saying they didn't "instill a ton of confidence that they got a comprehensive handle on the situation." He thought the bank also felt entitled to favorable terms because it agreed to move forward with the deal. "I reminded them that they are the ones who would look equally bad in [the] eyes of [the] market and regulators if they chose to terminate [the] transaction," Warsh wrote. "They would hope to announce [a] comprehensive package with our support on Jan[.] 20 (happy inauguration day, mr. president)."

On December 30, Lewis went to his board again. He gave an update on the talks and the Fed's growing concern about the economy and Bank of America's health. The bank didn't have written commitments for aid but had oral promises of support from Paulson and Bernanke. Its executives would continue to iron out the assistance package. The MAC now appeared to be officially off the table.

On New Year's Eve, Lewis talked one more time with Bernanke before the deal closed the next day. He jotted down notes during the conversation. Bernanke, Lewis wrote, "wanted this to be seen as helping out with Merrill and issuing a vote of confidence in [Bank of America]." He added that Bernanke said the Fed "will not leave you in the lurch." In addition, the Fed viewed the bank "as a strong company that has acted very appropriately throughout very difficult circumstances." The Fed chair wished him a happy New Year.

After the chat, Bernanke e-mailed Warsh and Fed vice chairman Don Kohn. Lewis "seemed a little embarrassed—[it was] clear that an important reason for the call was to be able to say to his board that he had made the call," Bernanke wrote. "I reassured him without being specific, and he fully understands why more specificity isn't possible." As Warsh predicted, Lewis had complained about the bank's Richmond supervisors, who the CEO said were considering a management downgrade because Bank of America hadn't reduced its dividend fast enough. Now, the bank was planning a significant cut, Bernanke noted. "I said he should keep us informed and that the Board and Richmond would work together on this," he added.

The deal closed January 1. A Charlotte institution that had once been a secondary player in its own state was now the nation's biggest bank by assets and a giant on Wall Street. A news release issued that day held no hint of the tense negotiations simmering outside public view. "We are now uniquely positioned to win market share and expand our leadership position in markets around the world," Lewis said.

Chapter 18

"Ward of the State"

After New Year's, Bank of America and its regulators had only a couple of weeks to pull together a rescue package before the bank made its scheduled earnings announcement on January 20, 2009, the historic inauguration day for incoming president Barack Obama.

Fed officials, joined by officials from the OCC and the FDIC, made plans to scour Bank of America's and Merrill Lynch's assets. While Bank of America was cooperating, executives feared their merger partner might discover what was going on. Chief risk officer Amy Brinkley told Charlotte Fed official Jennifer Burns that the bank had trouble with leaks coming out of Merrill Lynch and wanted the officials to go into the firm "under a different guise." Ken Lewis was still figuring out how to tell John Thain, Burns added in an e-mail to colleagues.

From the beginning of the review, tension boiled among bank officials and regulators. On January 2, Fed officials griped that Bank of America wasn't providing the type of "granular" information that they needed fast enough. A week later, the bank began complaining about the types of assets on which the government was willing to provide loss protection. The bank also didn't like the Fed's plan to bring in outside money managers to check out its holdings. It was worried about leaks again.

Jeff Lacker, the Richmond Fed president, talked with Kevin Warsh, who backed the Richmond Fed's request to use the money managers. Burns gave the verdict to CFO Joe Price, who said he planned to talk to Ben Bernanke and Henry Paulson about the bank's growing trepidation regarding the aid package. "They feel that things have drifted too significantly away from the representations that were made to them in order to compel them not to pull the MAC clause," Burns wrote in an e-mail to colleagues. "Joe said that had they pulled the MAC they would have been able to renegotiate the transaction and extract some value from [Merrill Lynch's] shareholders."

In a January 8 e-mail to Price, Brinkley, and other officials, Bank of America treasurer Jeff Brown said the Fed and the OCC in a meeting that day had expressed concerns about the bank's liquidity, capital, asset equality, and earnings. In particular, they wanted to make sure the bank had the necessary short-term financing to meet its obligations. Officials didn't want a repeat of the type of liquidity woes that had waylaid Wachovia. Brown said he would do what was necessary but had pushed back when officials said there was a high probability the market would "attack" Bank of America after learning its need for government assistance. "I did get pointed in my response and remind them that (1) they forced us into this position and (2) they had provided every assurance of a positive market response to any action from their chairman to our chairman," Brown wrote.

During the week the bank's earnings were released, the regulators wanted to have officials sitting on the bank's trading desks in New York and Charlotte to monitor its liquidity. Brown had no choice but said he would complain if they became a hindrance. It was clear regulators were worried the bank would lose access to funding once the news came out about the government aid.

Among regulators, tensions also flared again. Warsh and Fed vice chairman Don Kohn briefed comptroller of the currency John Dugan and FDIC chairman Sheila Bair on the plan. As Warsh expected, Dugan was fine with it but Bair hated it. Bair would rather Bank of America "limp along" until it got more TARP funding, Warsh wrote in a January 8 e-mail. "She claims no responsibility for ML or non-bank subs," he added.

In a January 9 meeting, regulators got an update on the Bank of America talks and fretted about the potential fallout for the bank and the financial system. Bernanke worried about a potential run on Bank of America deposits. Dugan said he was concerned that Bank of America would "look like Citi" and that market worries could spread to other banks. Paulson complained that it would have been better to pull together an industry-wide solution instead of a package just for Bank of America, although that would require weeks. "Bank of America is the turd in the punchbowl," he remarked.

Regulators were now eyeing a two-part package for Bank of America: An injection of extra TARP funds and loss protection on certain assets. It was important to have the FDIC involved, Paulson added. Warsh wrapped up the meeting. The Fed staff had to grow comfortable with Bank of America's assets, get a term sheet to the bank, and try to meet an earlier deadline of Friday, January 16.

Bank of America's board also held a meeting on January 9. For the first time, Thain was in on the call. He had learned of the talks on January 5, nearly three weeks after discussions with the government began. He was shocked that Bank of

America had tried to use the MAC clause and that he hadn't been told. Already, two of his top lieutenants, Greg Fleming and wealth management head Bob McCann, had left the company. Lewis told the board the departures weren't a "big deal."

The earnings results for Bank of America's 2008 fourth quarter looked grim: A $2.4 billion loss, counting dividend payments for TARP. The dialogue was ongoing with the government. Some 60 officials were on the scene reviewing the bank's books. It looked like the bank might get another $15 billion from TARP and protection on about $120 billion in assets—about three-fourths from Merrill, one-fourth from Bank of America.

By Friday, January 10, Bank of America relented to the Richmond Fed's demand to bring in a money manager to assess its books. PIMCO, the California-based asset management giant, would handle the task. But officials were still having trouble getting the data they needed. Bank of America had delivered PDF files that were read-only, meaning analysts couldn't cut and paste the data into other files. Fed official Trish Nunley asked Jennifer Burns in Charlotte to call Lewis "and ask him to stop jerking us around."

Meanwhile, Lacker, known for contrarian opinions inside the Fed, pushed the board of governors to draw others into the approval process for the Bank of America rescue package. During a lengthy call on Friday, Lacker told Scott Alvarez, the board of governors' general counsel, that he was getting comfortable with the structure of the aid. But the Richmond Fed president thought the Federal Open Market Committee—the group of governors and rotating Federal Reserve Bank presidents that made interest-rate decisions—should be consulted.

Lacker thought the FOMC's January 16 meeting would be a good time. Alvarez told him Bernanke was increasing consultation with the FOMC but that the fluid nature of the deal had made it difficult to clue the committee in until now. Lacker, who wasn't on the FOMC at the time, wanted the body to have a formal role in the decision-making process and argued that the issue was "at the core of monetary policy," Alvarez wrote in an e-mail to Bernanke the next day. Lacker, who also wanted to consult his Richmond Fed board, seemed to settle for at least getting the FOMC's advice, Alvarez wrote.

"Thanks," Bernanke wrote in his response. "If we are nimble we can manage this."

The OCC, the FDIC, and multiple levels of the Federal Reserve were involved in the Bank of America discussions, but apparently the SEC hadn't been told about a deal that would certainly rattle markets and spur questions among shareholders about Merrill's massive losses. Over the weekend, Bank of America complained that an SEC official had heard about the situation and was asking questions. In an e-mail on Sunday, January 11, Alvarez advised another Fed official to give the SEC a broad outline of what was going on, so as to let the agency know that "we think this is a matter of systemic importance and that BAC is very sensitive about this."

After getting Bank of America's go-ahead on Friday, PIMCO and the Richmond Fed dug into the bank's books. Officials spent most of the weekend in the office and on conference calls. When PIMCO needed more data, the Fed got it from Bank of America. On Sunday afternoon, PIMCO came back with the results, identifying about $118 billion in assets that merited the government's insurance-like protection, under various stress test scenarios. That number would become the basis of the government aid.

Over the next few days, the bank and regulators negotiated the final details, bickering over issues such as when and how the bank could sell off money-losing assets. Bair continued to rail against the proposal, telling Bernanke in an e-mail on Wednesday, January 14, of the "strong discomfort with this deal at the FDIC." The basic structure of the so-called ring-fence around the troubled assets was that Bank of America would take the first $10 billion in losses. After that, the FDIC, Treasury, and the Fed would absorb 90 percent of losses, while the bank took 10 percent.

By Wednesday, Bank of America's return to the government aid trough began leaking out, sending shivers through financial markets. An institution thought to be reasonably stable appeared to be heading down the same path as Citi. The bank's stock fell 4 percent to $10.20. Just a couple of weeks into the year, its stock had lost about one-fourth of its value.

At the Fed, Alvarez sent an e-mail to Bernanke advising that it was still worthwhile to include the FDIC in the package, although it might signal that Bank of America, instead of just Merrill, had tainted assets. "On balance, I think it's better to have a full tent on this one," Alvarez wrote.

On Thursday, more news jolted Charlotte. A US Airways flight headed to the city belly-flopped into the Hudson River after taking off from New York's LaGuardia Airport. Employees from Bank of America and Wachovia were on the flight, a well-traveled link between two banking centers. Incredibly, all of the passengers and crew survived. The "Miracle on the Hudson" became a surprising ray of hope for New York and Charlotte.

Around noon, a Fed official sent a term sheet to Price and Brian Moynihan. It was the best offer available, he said. That day, as investors awaited the details of the government aid package, the bank's shares plunged another 18 percent to $8.32, reaching a level not seen since 1991.

That evening, Bank of America board members dialed into a conference call to get an update.

While they listened, directors Chad Gifford and Thomas May exchanged e-mail barbs sparked by a curious e-mail Gifford had received. Al de Molina, the former Bank of America CFO now leading GMAC Financial Services, had sent him an e-mail with the subject line, "Are you available."

"Interesting," Gifford remarked to May.

On the call, the directors learned the bank would slash its quarterly dividend to a penny a share as a requirement of the aid package.

"Unfortunately, it's screw the shareholders!!" Gifford ripped off.

"No trail," May responded, reminding Gifford to watch his e-mail traffic.

"Only stated in the context of a horrible economy!!! Will [a]ffect everyone," Gifford wrote back.

Back in Washington, the bank's arrangement with the government required systemic risk recommendations from the FDIC and the Fed. For the second time in four months, a Charlotte bank needed such an action. At the Fed, staff rounded up votes, in person and by phone, from the five governors, who approved the determination and the term sheet by a unanimous vote. The FDIC board gave its assent at a meeting that began at 10:03 P.M. Afterward, according to meeting minutes, board members and staff "briefly discussed their concern that the need for the [Bank of America] transaction may have negative consequences for the stability of Citigroup," noting that it was suffering from its "own unique problems" and had already received government aid.

On Friday morning, the bank laid out its fourth-quarter financial results four days earlier than scheduled. For the first time in 17 years, it reported a quarterly loss: $2.4 billion, counting dividends paid to the government for its TARP money. And Merrill had lost a stunning $15.3 billion for the quarter. A Bank of America dividend that had grown for 30 years, reaching a quarterly 64 cents per share, was now just a penny per share.

In the earnings conference call, Lewis calmly detailed the damage but also pointed out that the bank had made a profit for the year—$2.6 billion, a better result than many of its rivals. He also detailed an aid package that boosted the bank's TARP loans to $45 billion, counting the $25 billion invested in Bank of America and Merrill back in October. Treasury and the FDIC were also providing protection against "unusually large losses" on the pool of $118 billion in assets, including those backed by residential and commercial real estate and other types of investments. In addition, the Federal Reserve stood ready to provide a loan to cover "residual risk" if needed.

In a conference call with analysts, Nancy Bush of NAB Research asked Lewis what had gone wrong with the Merrill due diligence. Lewis said the problem wasn't identifying the assets but rather the sudden deterioration in their value in mid- to late December. "Frankly, I would think almost anybody in the capital markets business would have forecasted a lower loss rate than what we saw," he insisted. Bush also asked how quickly the bank expected to escape its new status as a "ward of the state." "Clearly, as soon as possible," Lewis said, although he acknowledged that was dependent on the economy.

Analyst Mike Mayo of Deutsche Bank raised another key issue: Why hadn't the bank backed out of the deal or renegotiated? Lewis called it a legitimate question. The bank had looked at its legal right to back out, he admitted, but Treasury and the Federal Reserve were "firmly of the view" that canceling or delaying the deal would carry serious consequences for the bank and the financial system. Renegotiating wasn't a good option because it would have required another shareholder vote and months of delay. If the deal closed on time, he said, the government promised the aid the bank needed to make the purchase work.

"So in view of all those considerations, and in view that strategically Merrill Lynch remains a solid franchise, we thought it was in the best interest of our company and our stockholders and the country to move forward with the original terms and timing," Lewis said. Bank of America was not only serving its shareholders but doing its patriotic duty, a theme Lewis would espouse again in coming months.

Investors continued to reel from the news. Bank of America's shares nosedived almost 14 percent to $7.18 that Friday. The shares had dropped 45 percent for the week. Some investors questioned whether or not Bank of America should have disclosed more about Merrill's situation before the deal closed. A raft of shareholder lawsuits appeared unavoidable. Lewis had recently been the savvy acquirer, capitalizing on other banks' missteps. Earlier in the financial crisis, *American Banker* had named him its "Banker of the Year" for 2008. Now, his own company was shaken, along with his job security.

"Is this Ken Lewis' Golden West?" Vernon Hill, chairman of investment firm Hill-Townsend Capital in Maryland and a former bank CEO, wondered after the stunning announcement. "Obviously, the market's current answer to that is 'yes.'"

Inside the Fed, officials weighed how the aid package was handled, as well as its future ramifications.

"Going forward I am concerned if we too quickly move to a ring fence strategy," Boston Fed president Eric Rosengren wrote in an e-mail to Bernanke Friday afternoon. "Particularly if we believe that existing management is a significant source of their problem and that they do not have a good grasp of the extent of the problems and appropriate strategies to resolve them." He raised the example of the Royal Bank of Scotland. The government had replaced its senior management and now owned 58 percent of the company. "Such a strategy obviously has pitfalls, but I would not want to discard this option prematurely," he wrote.

Another Fed official, reacting to a Goldman Sachs analyst's gloomy report on Bank of America's and Merrill Lynch's results, provided a grimmer assessment. "Nationalization here we come," Patricia Mosser wrote.

Over the weekend, Bank of America director Chad Gifford received an e-mail from a friend and former Fleet colleague, Gary Spiess, asking about the situation: "This looks like a big miss on the diligence numbers and a big mess. Does not reflect well. I have been a defender. . . . But are we seeing a little hubris here? I hope no future for Thain at least!!"

Gifford replied that he couldn't say much but admitted his friend's comments weren't "far from the mark," adding that it "will be interesting but surely not fun."

After a long holiday weekend for Martin Luther King, Jr., Day, Bank of America shares on Tuesday, January 20, fell a punishing 29 percent, the biggest one-day percentage drop since at least the mid-1980s. While most of the country took in the Obama inauguration, analysts digested the bank's earnings and reduced profit estimates. Its shares, which closed Tuesday at $5.10, had now lost nearly 85 percent of their value since the deal was announced.

On the evening of January 21, Gifford felt compelled to e-mail his wife and children about the precipitous drop, a major blow to their holdings. "I know you've watched and worried as the stock has sunk to depths nobody could have considered possible—and this exacerbated by the reduction to a penny of the dividend," he typed. "As you can imagine this is a 'bit' on my mind and [I] have been spending a ridiculous amount of time on the phone with other directors/management et al."

Gifford attributed the problems to three major issues: Struggling consumers, write-offs in Bank of America's investment banking operations, and Merrill Lynch. "This was a bad decision and when we realized same the US government pressured us to stick with it," he tapped. "That's when they agreed to give us more capital and guarantee some of their bad assets. . . . But the [S]treet worries that there is more crap and wonders why we got ourselves into this quagmire."

The next day, Bank of America's reputation took another blow. The *Financial Times* reported that Merrill had paid out $3 billion to $4 billion in bonuses before the deal closed in December. "Merrill Lynch was an independent company until January 1, 2009," the bank told the paper. "John Thain decided to pay year-end incentives in December as opposed to their normal date in January. Bank of America was informed of his decision." The statement appeared to lay the blame on Thain, although the bank had agreed to bonus payments in the merger agreement and had advised on the composition of the bonuses.

On Thursday, January 22, in a reality-TV fashion only Donald Trump could love, CNBC reported that Lewis was flying to New York that morning to fire Thain. When he arrived, Lewis went to Thain's office in Merrill's headquarters, where the former CEO had learned of his coming demise from the TV report. A week earlier, Lewis had told analysts he was happy Thain was on the Bank of America team. A day earlier, Thain had bought nearly $500,000 of Bank of America stock.

"Things aren't going to work out," Lewis told Thain. "You are going to take the blame for the fourth-quarter losses, and you can never succeed me, and we're going to replace you."

Thain explained what Lewis already knew: The losses were based on the valuation of assets that fluctuated quarter to quarter. "They will reverse themselves," Thain said.

Lewis didn't respond.

"Well, I guess we know where the leak came from," Thain remarked in a parting shot.

Lewis turned to leave. "We don't leak things," he said.

That day, more damaging reports about Thain hit the press. About a year earlier, he had spent $1.2 million redecorating his Merrill office, using the same decorator the Obamas were employing to spruce up the White House. The additions to his office, made in a year when Merrill was laying off workers, included an $87,000 area rug, a $68,000 credenza, and $35,000 for a "commode on legs," CNBC reported.

Previously, Bank of America's best-known executive ouster had come in 1998 when David Coulter stepped down shortly after the BankAmerica deal. Coulter announced his resignation after 20 days on the job. Thain lasted 22. The bank moved quickly to fill the void, selecting Moynihan to take over most of Thain's duties. He had served as general counsel a little more than a month.

While a blow to Lewis and his bank, the sudden departure also hurt Thain's reputation as a Mr. Fix-It. The square-jawed former Goldman Sachs banker helped revive the New York Stock Exchange before being tapped to restore Merrill in late 2007. He had looked smart when he agreed to sell to Bank of America in September, while rival Lehman collapsed. He had even emerged as a possible successor to Lewis.

Thain's camp believed Bank of America set him up for a fall, leaking the damaging information to soften the blow of his ouster. A Bank of America source denied that was the case.

After his dismissal, Thain hired a New York public relations firm, Sunshine, Sachs & Associates, to help craft his response. On Sunday night, he sent an e-mail to former colleagues and others tackling the allegations. He noted that Merrill's bonus pool had ultimately been 41 percent lower than in 2007 and less than the amount allowed under the merger agreement. The size of the pool, its composition, and the timing of the payments had been "determined together with Bank of America" and approved by the Merrill board.

Second, while the fourth-quarter losses were "very large and unfortunate," they were almost entirely due to market movements, Thain wrote. Merrill had been completely transparent with its acquirer. Bank of America's Neil Cotty even served as Merrill's acting CFO.

Finally, he addressed the office renovation, which he noted also covered two conference rooms and a reception area. Although the expenses were incurred more than a year earlier in a different environment, they were a mistake, he acknowledged. He would reimburse the company.

"I believe that the decision to sell to Bank of America was the right one for our company and our clients," he wrote. "While the execution has been difficult, I still believe in the strategic rationale of the transaction, and I wish you the best for the future of the combined companies."

The tumult in the executive suite struck as merger-related layoffs continued to roar through the company, intensifying in capital markets businesses where Bank of America and Merrill overlapped. After the December cuts in the upper ranks, the layoffs penetrated deeper into the company.

The bank acknowledged that layoffs had begun but was mum on details. The quiet nature of the cuts eroded morale and left many workers nervous about their posts. "They are chopping people left and right," one laid-off worker said.

As Lewis faced public fire for the Merrill deal, he didn't get a lot of sympathy inside the company. "People are angry at Ken," said one former executive. "Ken had the whole world telling him not to do [Merrill], and he did it anyway."

Lewis was a company lifer who had led the bank through some of its best years. But he was also known as a demanding executive who presided over tens of thousands of job cuts. Some employees and former executives felt the company had become more "mean spirited" under Lewis. "It's a different place than when Hugh McColl ran it," one former executive said.

In a September 2007 interview with the *Observer*, Lewis had said he didn't think he was a tough boss to work for, noting the long tenure of some of his deputies, but he acknowledged he was demanding. "I have to be," he said. "That is one of the aspects of my job. That doesn't mean you still can't win with friends."

At 61, about four years from retirement age, Lewis had no obvious successor in place. The gap in the bank's succession planning became more glaring now that his hold on the job seemed tenuous. With a regularly scheduled board meeting approaching at the end of January, speculation mounted that Lewis could be on the way out or about to lose his chairmanship, the tack Wachovia had initially taken with Ken Thompson.

Adding to the pressure on the bank, New York attorney general Andrew Cuomo was issuing subpoenas seeking testimony from Bank of America chief administrative officer Steele Alphin and Thain as part of an investigation of the Merrill bonuses. Cuomo, widely seen as a potential New York gubernatorial candidate, was following in the footsteps of predecessor Eliot Spitzer, who had gained national attention for taking on Wall Street. Targeting Alphin was particularly intriguing because he was widely seen as Lewis's de facto number two, a close friend and *consigliere* who counseled the CEO on personnel and other moves.

While the spotlight was hottest on Lewis, the bank's directors started to take flak from investors and corporate governance experts.

The 16-member board, which included Lewis, had approved the Merrill Lynch acquisition after less than two days of negotiations and had urged shareholders to vote for the deal. The directors had also stayed silent on Merrill's losses until after the deal closed.

"I am highly disappointed with this board," said Charles Elson, director of the Weinberg Center for Corporate Governance at the University of Delaware and a Bank of America shareholder. "Their role is to protect shareholders."

The board's job included supervising the company's operations, monitoring the CEO, approving executive compensation, and planning for CEO succession. It fell short in assessing risk and providing disclosure to shareholders about the bank's activities, said Jack Zwingli, chief executive of Audit Integrity, a research firm that analyzed corporate risk management practices. The firm gave Bank of America's accounting and governance its worst ranking of "very aggressive," indicating, in its opinion, a high risk for underperformance and lawsuits. "It's not surprising to see these recent disclosures that they were taking on too much risk," Zwingli said.

Many of the board members had known Lewis for a long time and had confidence in him. Of the 16 directors, six had been on the board since 2001 or earlier. That year, *Fortune* magazine had labeled the Bank of America board one of America's worst, saying it was packed with Hugh McColl's "Carolinas cronies." The composition had changed since then, thanks to the new directors who joined following Lewis's MBNA and Fleet acquisitions. Three Merrill directors were slated to join the board soon but hadn't yet been named. While silent about the bank's troubles, the directors did make a statement with their wallets. Eight directors, including Lewis, bought a total of more than 500,000 shares the week of Thain's departure in a move seen as a show of confidence in the company.

The January board meeting proved anticlimactic. "The board . . . during the regular meeting expressed support for Ken Lewis and the management team, noting their expertise in managing through challenging environments and in assimilating mergers," lead director Temple Sloan, Jr., said in a terse statement issued through a bank spokesman.

Lewis's job was safe, at least for now.

Chapter 19

"You Created the Mess"

While Ken Lewis's job remained secure, the shareholders of Charlotte's two big banks felt anything but safe. At the end of January, their portfolios were withering. Wachovia's takeover and Bank of America's recent pummeling had demolished a staggering amount of wealth.

Bank of America's total market value was now around $42 billion, down from about $183 billion at the end of 2007. Since the Merrill deal was announced in September, Bank of America shares were down 80 percent. In 2007, the bank had paid out $10.7 billion in dividends. Now, it was set to pay out around $250 million in 2009.

In 2008, Wachovia shares had fallen nearly 85 percent. Investors now owned stock in Wells Fargo, but each of their Wachovia shares had been exchanged for one-fifth of a Wells share.

Charlotte was at the epicenter of the damage as shareholders large and small watched their wealth shrivel.

Bank of America's biggest individual shareholders were C. D. and Meredith Spangler, the Charlotte couple who owned 32 million shares within their family and other entities. Spangler had gained his first shares in the bank in 1982 when he had sold the Bank of North Carolina to NCNB. Meredith was still on the bank's board. Their stake was worth $210 million at the end of January, down from $850 million in September. The Spanglers could expect a dividend in 2009 of around $1.3 million, down from $76.8 million in 2007.

Another prominent shareholder was Hugh McColl. At the end of 2001, according to a proxy filing, he had nearly 2.8 million shares, including options to buy company stock and restricted shares payable over 10 years. Bank of America shares split in 2004, which could have doubled that number. It wasn't clear how many shares he had retained.

The carnage was particularly sickening to employees, who watched their holdings vanish and also worried about their jobs. They also expected skimpy bonuses for 2008 performance, even as they learned that many counterparts at Merrill had already taken home sizable payouts.

Things didn't get better in February.

Financial stocks continued to flounder as speculation about the possible nationalization of major banks ramped up. Main Street anger over bailed-out banks that lavished big bonuses on executives and traders also boiled over. Looking to defuse the situation, Bank of America and other banks pledged to report periodically how much money they were lending to consumers and businesses—the primary reason they were given the original TARP installments.

Banks also began cutting back on marketing, employee appreciation events, and other spending deemed wasteful. The Wachovia Championship in Charlotte became the Quail Hollow Championship, named after the course. Wells closed Wachovia's Charlotte-based aviation department, while Bank of America sold three of its planes and Merrill Lynch's helicopter.

On February 6, Lewis hit the CNBC airwaves, giving an interview to Maria Bartiromo, the brunette anchor nicknamed "the Money Honey." It was a chance for the Bank of America CEO to boost confidence in his besieged bank. Earlier in the week, Lewis had bought 200,000 more shares for $1 million, and the bank ran ads promoting its commitment to the environment, philanthropy, and lending to low-income neighborhoods.

Asked about the prospect of nationalization, Lewis fired back, calling such talk "a bunch of malicious rumors." "It's just absurd," he said. In all his talks with government officials, he said, "I've never had anybody even hint at it."

Lewis said his bank wouldn't need any more government money and that it would work to pay off its loans "as soon as humanly possible." He also insisted the government didn't force him to purchase Merrill. He said that he and his executives eventually came to agree with the government's position: "They said, 'We strongly advise you that it is not in your best interest or the country's best interest to walk away from this.' " The answer shed little light on how seriously the bank had explored triggering the MAC—and how tense the negotiations with the government had really been.

Asked if government officials threatened his job, Lewis replied, "I promise you that that was not a factor."

In a sense, the interview was a prep session for Lewis's appearance on Capitol Hill the following week. The House Financial Services Committee summoned the eight bank CEOs bequeathed the first round of TARP money to see how they were spending taxpayer funds. John Thain, whose firm had received one of the first injections, didn't have to make the trip. After CEOs of big automakers were ridiculed in November for taking corporate jets to Washington, the bank CEOs ditched their fancy planes for this visit. Lewis took the train. John Stumpf of Wells Fargo flew commercial.

It wasn't the first time Lewis faced off with the committee's chairman, Massachusetts Democrat Barney Frank. The pair had tussled in 2004 over Fleet job cuts but appeared to make up after the bank agreed to bolster its presence in the state. Frank had praised the bank for buying Countrywide and had distinguished its troubles from Citi's. Citigroup "is in serious trouble," Frank told the *Observer*. "Bank of America is getting more TARP money because the Bush administration desperately wanted them to buy Merrill Lynch."

Among the eight panelists were Bank of New York Mellon CEO Bob Kelly, the former Wachovia CFO, and two CEOs who had considered buying Wachovia, John Mack of Morgan Stanley and Lloyd Blankfein of Goldman Sachs. The two bank chiefs who had dueled head to head for Wachovia, Stumpf and Vikram Pandit, sat next to each other.

Lined up shoulder to shoulder in dark suits, reminiscent of tobacco executives in years past, the banking leaders tried to assure lawmakers they were lending the taxpayer money they had received last fall. But they faced skepticism that they were doing enough to help struggling consumers and businesses. While the tone was mostly polite, committee members repeatedly highlighted the banking chiefs' salaries and bonuses and roasted them for their role in the nation's financial meltdown.

"You created the mess we're in," said Representative Michael Capuano, a Massachusetts Democrat. "Now you say, 'Sorry, trust us and by the way we really didn't want the money.' "

The CEOs were largely contrite about their pay and their stewardship of taxpayer money. Surrounded by news photographers in an overflow crowd of banking lobbyists, consumer advocates, and high-profile attendees such as Jesse Jackson, they outlined their efforts to make loans in difficult economic conditions and acknowledged the need for more regulation.

Among the peace offerings, Citigroup CEO Pandit said he would work for $1 in salary and no bonus until his bank returned to profitability. Lewis and Stumpf indicated they would be willing to delay some foreclosures until after new Treasury secretary Tim Geithner detailed a plan to help keep struggling borrowers in their homes. Going down the line, the CEOs also said they were eager to pay back the funds invested under TARP and that they didn't expect to go to the government well again.

All eight CEOs were asked to list their pay for 2008. Salaries ranged from $1.5 million for Lewis to $600,000 for Blankfein. None received a bonus.

Answering a question about the Merrill bonus controversy, Lewis downplayed his and the company's roles in dishing out the pay in December:

My personal involvement was very limited, but let me give you my general understanding of what happened. First of all, I do know that we urged the Merrill Lynch executives who were involved in this compensation issue to reduce the bonuses substantially, particularly at the top. I will remind you, though, that they were a public company until the first of this year. They had a separate board, separate compensation committee, and we had no authority to tell them what to do, we could just urge them what to do. So we did urge. There was some feedback, in that, to your point, at the very top there were some contracts that were of tens of millions of dollars to several individuals that were legal contracts that Merrill had made to those individuals. And it is my understanding those skewed these amounts pretty substantially. I can only contrast that to Bank of America's policies. First of all, as I mentioned, nobody on my management team received any incentives. Nobody on my management team has a contract or a golden parachute or severance. And then finally, we pay our bonuses on February the 15th of the following year. So major changes will be made, but we could not make them until we owned the company.

While mostly serious, the seven-hour session brought jokes about the CEOs' discomfort on the hot seat and the likelihood of *Saturday Night Live* spoofs. Frank mused the bankers might break into a rendition of "I Will Survive." One consolation was that all of their stocks rose during the day.

The hearing didn't defuse the harsh anti-banker rhetoric coming out of Washington. In his inaugural State of the Union Address later that month, President Obama assured a joint session of Congress—and the American people—that he would push banks to step up their lending and hold Wall Street accountable for its past and future misdeeds.

"We will act with the full force of the federal government to ensure that the major banks that Americans depend on have enough confidence and enough money to lend even in more difficult times," Obama said. "And when we learn that a major bank has serious problems, we will hold accountable those responsible, force the necessary adjustments, provide the support to clean up their balance sheets, and assure the continuity of a strong, viable institution that can serve our people and our economy."

Tapping a strong populist sentiment against overpaid bankers, he insisted bailed-out banks would not be able to continue their free-spending ways. Obama included a barb that appeared to be directed at Thain's redecorated office. "I intend to hold these banks fully accountable for the assistance they receive, and this time, they will have to clearly demonstrate how taxpayer dollars result in more lending for the American taxpayer," he said. "This time, CEOs won't be able to use taxpayer money to pad their paychecks or buy fancy drapes or disappear on a private jet. Those days are over."

. . .

Despite the turmoil in the banking industry and over the Merrill deal in particular, Bank of America forged ahead with integrating the two companies. Combining capabilities and wringing out $7 billion in annual expenses were essential
to making the deal work.

Merrill's roughly 16,000 financial advisers were already selling Bank of America products such as credit cards and mortgages. The downsizing of the combined investment banking operation was nearly complete by late February. And
Brian Moynihan, the Bank of America executive presiding over much of Merrill's
former operations, was traveling the globe talking up the merger with employees
and customers.

"Every piece makes more sense now than it ever did," Moynihan said in an
interview in his office in Bank of America's One Bryant Park tower in New York,
a building topped by a spire that could be seen from Merrill's headquarters. "And
you're starting to see it work."

In his new role, Moynihan was in charge of the investment bankers who
helped large corporations raise capital and forge merger deals, as well as the combined brokerage force, the Columbia asset management business, commercial
banking, and the U.S. Trust private bank. Tom Montag, the former Merrill and
Goldman executive, ran the global markets business, which included stock and
debt trading. Overall, the two executives oversaw about 90,000 employees, nearly
one-third of the bank's total combined work force.

In choosing Moynihan to replace Thain, Lewis picked an executive who had
run wealth management and investment banking businesses for Bank of America
and Fleet but whose résumé didn't include stays at signature Wall Street firms.
In a visit to Merrill brokers in Charlotte, Moynihan raised eyebrows by using the
term "customer" instead of the broker lingo of "client."

At Bank of America, Moynihan had become a "fixer" who handled tough
tasks for Lewis. He was a fast-talking, straight-ahead executive who engendered
loyalty among many of his colleagues. But to others, he came off as less impressive, especially when his rapid-fire speech bordered on mumbling. Tackling the
Merrill integration could be a signature accomplishment—or a career killer.

Moynihan still lived in the Boston area but spent his workweek in New York,
Charlotte, and other cities. His office on the 19th floor in the One Bryant Park
tower had majestic views but little decoration. His desk featured a nameplate with
the title "Director of Donuts"—a family joke from his days of picking up Sunday
breakfast.

One of his toughest tasks was presiding over deep layoffs—now in their final
stages—in the combined corporate and investment bank. He said the "fairly significant" cuts were difficult but necessary to conform to a slower business climate.
"We have downsized to the realities of 2009," he said.

On a Bank of America executive floor now filling up with former Merrill leaders, he downplayed talk of a culture clash among the Merrill and Bank of America work forces, although many at Bank of America still chafed at the big bonuses Merrill counterparts had been paid. "Winning with friends. Doing the right thing. All the things we talk about at Bank of America are very important to [Merrill]," he said. "My job is to let that come to the surface."

He had his work cut out for him. Just that week, the bank disclosed in a securities filing that Merrill's fourth-quarter loss had grown by about $500 million to $15.8 billion. Moynihan said the loss increased during the final audit and wasn't a sign of more trouble. For the year, Merrill lost $27.6 billion.

While capital markets showed signs of life early in 2009, investors remained uncertain about where the financial sector as a whole was headed. As he chatted, Moynihan checked a flat-screen monitor mounted on his office wall. Ben Bernanke was testifying before Congress about the banking industry's woes. Stock prices wriggled on his every word.

Into March, bank stocks continued to take a pounding as nationalization worries frayed investor confidence. Even Republican senator Lindsey Graham of South Carolina said a government takeover of the bank industry was an option worth considering. Bernanke and the White House attempted to douse the idea, but the flame was hard to smother. The theory was that bank balance sheets were so riddled with toxic assets that the institutions were technically already insolvent, so why pump more government aid into them? The big losers, of course, would be stockholders, whose holdings would be wiped out.

On March 5, Wells Fargo shares bottomed at $8.12 at the close of trading. Bank of America shares finished the next day at an astounding $3.14.

With former New York Fed president Tim Geithner now ensconced as Treasury secretary, the Obama administration began rolling out its plans for resuscitating the banking industry. In addition to proposing tighter regulation designed to prevent future crises, regulators planned to "stress-test" the 19 biggest banks to see if they had enough capital to withstand a deeper recession.

"Supervisors will work with institutions to estimate the range of possible future losses and the resources to absorb such losses over a two-year period," said a joint statement from four federal bank regulators—the Federal Reserve, the FDIC, the OCC, and the Office of Thrift Supervision.

At the end of the program, banks deemed to be short on capital would be given six months to raise more from private investors or to ask for government help. Although the stress tests threatened to reveal more problems in the financial industry, markets appeared to warm to the idea of a thorough examination of the nation's biggest banks.

By the end of March, with his bank's shares inching back up, Lewis started to exude optimism about the company's prospects. Bank of America could pay back its $45 billion in government capital by late in the year or early next year, depending on the economy, he told the *Observer* in an interview. He also expected his bank to be profitable in 2009 "absent some unexpected meltdown" and to pass the government's stress test. He wanted it to make $30 billion in a year before he exited.

Bank of America could turn over the money now if it weren't maintaining higher-than-normal capital cushions because of the "fragile" state of the financial system, he said. He also noted that the money was not a "gift." The bank has already made $402 million in dividend payments to taxpayers.

As for the recent upturn in bank stocks, Lewis said investors were wondering if the market had hit bottom. Bank of America shares had climbed 99 percent since March 6. "I'm as disturbed as anybody about the decline in the stock, since virtually all my net worth is tied up in it," he said.

Despite the controversy embroiling the Merrill acquisition, Lewis said he didn't regret forging the deal. "I have to look out over a longer horizon than, say, the last three or four months," he said. "If I look out over an intermediate time-frame such as the next three to five years or a longer timeframe of five to 10 years I think Merrill will prove to be one of the best acquisitions we've ever made."

Taking an extra dollop of TARP money, however, was a mistake, he said. The bank could have accepted $5 billion to $10 billion in January instead of $20 billion and kept its capital ratios in reasonable shape, Lewis said.

"It put us too far away from the mainstream, and it did lump us together with Citigroup," he said. "We did it in an abundance of caution because you just don't know how bad things could get, but that was a mistake and that caused us to be painted with a broad brush in ways that we don't deserve."

Lewis also addressed whether or not he was concerned about keeping his job amid the bank's recent struggles. "I have not given it one single moment of thought," he said. "I have been at this company almost 40 years, and what I want to do is see us get through this, and then start to realize our full potential and make $30 billion after tax, which is what we should make in a good time."

The next big test for Lewis was the bank's annual shareholder meeting on April 29. He would surely face sharp questions from shareholders, and he and his fellow directors needed to gather enough votes to be reelected to the board. A proposal called for splitting Lewis's CEO and chairman titles, a common cause of shareholder activists.

Typically, CEOs and directors skated through these elections. But a recent rule change adopted by the bank requiring board members to receive a majority of votes cast had made the contests more competitive. The union opponents who often railed against CEOs were pushing for Lewis's ouster. But another prominent voice also emerged: The Finger family of Houston. After receiving an initial investment from NCNB in 1986, Jerry Finger had sold his bank to NationsBank in 1996. Now, he and his son, Jonathan, were angered by the Merrill deal. The 1.1 million Bank of America shares they owned were a small percentage of the company's total, but the Fingers gained attention with securities filings detailing their complaints. "We are seeking to change the culture of corporate governance at the company, so that the board of directors oversees management more firmly and fulfills its duty to shareholders," they said in a presentation filed with the SEC.

Adding to the pressure, proxy governance firms that advised large shareholders on how to vote began recommending voting against Lewis, lead director Temple Sloan, and other board members. They also backed splitting the CEO and chairman posts.

Lewis helped his cause in April when the bank disclosed it had earned $2.8 billion in the first quarter of the year, helped by one-time gains. But he also faced another rash of bad publicity when New York attorney general Cuomo weighed in with the preliminary findings of his bonus investigation.

"While the investigation initially focused on huge fourth-quarter bonus payouts, we have uncovered facts that raise questions about the transparency of the [Troubled Asset Relief Program], as well as about corporate governance and disclosure practices at Bank of America," Cuomo wrote in a letter to Congress. The letter said that Lewis, who had also given a deposition, testified he was told not to disclose the bank's effort to abandon the Merrill deal. Henry Paulson and Bernanke responded with statements saying they left disclosure decisions to the bank.

In his deposition, Lewis had described Paulson's threat to oust management if executives didn't go through with the deal, highlighting the pressure the government placed on the bank. Paulson told Cuomo's office he made the threat at the request of Fed chairman Bernanke, according to the attorney general's letter. But a Paulson spokesperson backtracked, saying Paulson's words were his own and Bernanke "did not instruct him to indicate any specific action the Fed might take."

Lewis was losing momentum heading into the annual meeting vote. Although pension funds in California, Illinois, and Connecticut disclosed they had voted against Lewis and other directors, the bank continued to press other big investors to vote its way. One large investor the company talked with was Temasek Holdings of Singapore, but the firm was evasive about its plans. Later, officials discovered Temasek had already sold its shares. Going into the meeting, Lewis told colleagues he was prepared to give up the chairmanship even if the bank prevailed by a close margin.

The meeting drew protestors outside its site at the North Carolina Blumenthal Performing Arts Center, but the auditorium packed with employees stayed relatively supportive. Famed corporate gadfly Evelyn Y. Davis even gave Lewis a hug. McColl and predecessor Tom Storrs attended but didn't make any remarks.

Before the meeting, McColl said he backed Lewis and indicated he would decline the chairmanship if offered it.

The bank normally announced election results before the annual meeting was over, but Lewis told the audience the tally would be delayed. Officials decided to do a recount because the vote was so close. The bank didn't want to announce results, then have to flip-flop. Most of the votes were counted electronically off site, but ballots cast in person were tallied in the theater's McColl Room.

At 5:30 P.M., the bank revealed the results in a news release. Lewis had lost his chairmanship but kept his board seat. Lead director Temple Sloan had been elected with the lowest vote margin, followed by Lewis and director Jackie Ward.

In a meeting later that day, the bank's board tapped longtime director Walter Massey, a retired Morehead College president, as the new chairman, a choice backed by Lewis. The directors expressed their full support of Lewis, who remained CEO. Nearly one year after Wachovia's board stripped Ken Thompson of his chairmanship, shareholders had done the same to Lewis.

Another blow came the same day, although it wasn't made public. Regulators told the board they planned to lodge a memorandum of understanding, or MOU, against Bank of America. This was a serious supervisory action ordering the bank to improve its corporate governance and risk management practices. More than 80 years earlier, the CEO of American Trust had enthusiastically recruited a Federal Reserve branch to Charlotte, helping fuel the city's rise as a banking center. Now, the bank's examiners were carving out a pound of flesh from the institution that had grown into Bank of America.

Lewis and others inside the bank felt blindsided. Bank of America had agreed to move forward with the Merrill deal after getting assurances from Bernanke that it was still seen as a strong company. Now, regulators were hitting it with a major penalty. Inside the bank, much of the animosity was targeted at the Richmond Fed. While the New York Fed had worked to rescue capsizing firms like Bear Stearns and Citi, the Richmond Fed was piling on one of its own, Bank of America officials felt.

Chapter 20

Hubquarters

Eastover is one of Charlotte's most scenic—and elite—neighborhoods, housing many of the city's top business leaders beneath a leafy canopy only minutes from Uptown skyscrapers. With the Wachovia–Wells Fargo merger not yet closed, Bob Steel one Sunday afternoon bumped into Duke Energy chief Jim Rogers as the CEOs were walking their dogs. While their pets mingled, Rogers sparked a conversation about the 48-story Uptown tower Wachovia was building. It was well known that Wells wasn't eager to take over all of its vacant space.

Duke's drab, blocky headquarters building was across the street from the sleek new tower packed with environmentally friendly features. In fact, the utility was already planning to take 10 floors in the skyscraper. A couple of years earlier, Rogers had thought he was getting the top story, but Ken Thompson called him up with bad news: Wachovia had decided to hold onto it and make the building its new headquarters. A bit irritated, Rogers told his real-estate people to negotiate for the right of first refusal in case the top perch ever opened up.

Rogers had been dismayed by the downfall of his friend Ken Thompson and his bank, but now he couldn't pass up an opening. If the two companies could work something out, Duke Energy might be able to get a good deal on prime space while Wells saved on merger-related expenses. "You know, we have a right of first refusal," Rogers reminded Steel of the top-floor provision. "This is a perfect time for us to step in and go to work on stepping into Wachovia's shoes."

Steel laughed. But a few days later, he called Rogers and brought over a Wells Fargo real-estate executive. In February 2009, Wells announced that the Wachovia Corporate Center would become the Duke Energy Center when it opened in 2010.

The tower launched under Thompson—a symbol of Wachovia's growth and commitment to its hometown—would not open under the Charlotte bank's name, or that of its acquirer. Wells Fargo would lend its brand to the surrounding cultural campus and fill some space in the tower, but it would have a smaller presence than originally planned. Trading floors designed for the corporate and investment banking unit remained dark.

The building's name wasn't the only change.

After the official completion of the Wells Fargo takeover on December 31, 2008, for an ultimate price of $12.7 billion, a wave of former top Wachovia executives quietly disappeared from the company at the beginning of the new year.

Steel, who would stay on the Wells board, was the most notable departure. He returned home to Connecticut and took on the chairmanship of the Aspen Institute. He left without any severance, took stock holdings diminished in value, and eventually sold his Eastover home at a loss. Other executives to leave were general bank head Ben Jenkins, general counsel Jane Sherburne, investment banking chief Steve Cummings, human resources executive Shannon McFayden, CFO David Zwiener, and chief risk officer Ken Phelan.

Of Wachovia's top 16 officials before the merger closed, 10 departed. Of those who stayed, most were bumped down the corporate ladder. Wells was clearly in charge.

One of the big worries in Charlotte was Wells Fargo's previous lack of appetite for investment banking, a source of high-paying jobs in the city. But after probing the business, the bank decided to preserve the unit while shedding some of the riskier structured products and proprietary trading businesses. Two former Wachovia executives, Jonathan Weiss and Rob Engel, stayed in charge, although their bosses were Wells executives. "There are parts of investment banking that I do not like," John Stumpf said in a January 2009 interview with the *Observer*. "There are parts of investment banking that I do like where it serves customers, where we have a customer relationship."

Stumpf indicated that job cuts would start in 2009 but pledged to preserve as many positions as possible. The bank planned to cut $5 billion in costs in the combination. "I'm not going to kid anybody here," he said. "There will be some job loss, and minimizing that is going to be the challenge for everybody in this company."

The cuts emerged gradually, some employees learning their fate early on while others remained in limbo. In May, Wells Fargo told state officials it had issued layoff notices to 548 employees in Uptown Charlotte. It was one of the biggest job-cut notices filed in recent Mecklenburg County history. The bank said the layoffs would occur in a wide variety of business and staff units. A significant portion would be in the investment banking division.

The filing gave a glimpse of the job impact of the deal, although it likely didn't cover all the losses the city would experience in the merger. Employees would continue to trickle out of the company as the merger progressed and job duties changed. Some would struggle to adapt to a Wells business model that was highly decentralized.

By summer, Charlotte was shaping up as a center for Wells Fargo's East Coast operations, wealth management, and investment banking, in keeping with promises the San Francisco bank had made back in the fall. But most of the combined company's top leadership remained on the West Coast. Wachovia once had 15 of its 16 top executives—including the CEO, the executives who reported directly to him, and other top leaders—based in its Charlotte headquarters. Now, the city had just one executive, David Carroll, who answered to Wells Fargo CEO Stumpf. At least 15 others had jobs two rungs down from the CEO or with responsibility for East Coast businesses.

Overall, the merger stuck to the measured pace Wells pledged at the beginning, giving workers a longer-than-normal stay in their jobs but also prolonging their uncertainty. In mid-2009, many areas including bank branches were not yet integrated, but other businesses including the brokerage, investment banking, and mortgage units were beginning to meld and operate under the Wells Fargo name. The Wachovia brand was slowly fading away.

Blue-and-green Wachovia signs, however, remained plastered to bank branches around the city and all over the East Coast, almost as if a tradition-rich Southern institution was stubbornly clinging to the past—or was in a state of denial. Wells was rebranding branches, which it called "stores," in phases across the country. It would start with Wachovia branches in Colorado in late 2009, followed by other states where the banks had overlapping locations. The East Coast conversion would come last, Carolinas branches likely keeping the Wachovia name until 2011.

Wells planned to close some branches in states where both banks had locations. In California, this move would be particularly bittersweet. After assessing the branches, Wells said it would close 122 locations in the state, some from Wells and some from Wachovia. The number was almost identical to the 123 branches Wachovia had picked up in California in the Golden West acquisition, in essence wiping out one of the prime reasons the Charlotte bank did the deal in the first place.

Even as it cut jobs and slapped new names on Wachovia units, Wells continued to stress its dedication to Charlotte, Stumpf calling it one of the bank's 10 "hubquarters" in his annual letter to shareholders. The bank planned to make the same charitable donations—about $8 million—in Charlotte in 2009 as in 2008. One area of concern was the bank's plan for the sprawling complex Wachovia called its Customer Information Center, or CIC, in the University City area of Charlotte. Boasting about 10,000 employees, it was home to the call center, technology, operations, human resources, and other functions often targeted in merger-related cutbacks. But the bank insisted it was a "core facility" that would continue to be an "excellent investment."

"As a strong, stable and growing company, Wells Fargo is and will continue to be an important and vital part of the Charlotte community," spokeswoman Mary Eshet said.

In June 2009, Wells CEO Stumpf visited the city, bringing an upbeat message to a Charlotte Chamber event held on the 41st floor of Wachovia's former headquarters building. One floor higher was the former boardroom that held portraits of Cliff Cameron and Ed Crutchfield but not successors Thompson or Steel.

The night before his appearance, Stumpf dined with Hugh McColl. It was a chance for the two leaders to get to know each other and discuss the city that McColl had played a major role in building and that Stumpf would help shape for years to come. "We talked about what can we do and what he's doing to make this city an even better city than it is today," Stumpf said after the speech. "We both recognize this is a very special place. I think the long-term prospects are very, very bright."

In the midst of all this transition at Wachovia, one key figure, Ken Thompson, continued to live in Charlotte but out of the public eye. Reviled by many shareholders, he remained respected by a broad pool of friends and former colleagues, although most believed he made a bad decision in buying Golden West at the time he did.

In the spring of 2009, Thompson joined a private-equity firm called Aquiline Capital Partners, an investor in financial services firms. It was a second act for a CEO who had been pushed out of office a little less than a year earlier. In the job, he split time between Charlotte and New York. It was a source of surprise—and perhaps bemusement—for commuters to spot him flying commercial after years of being swept around the country via corporate jet.

A week after shareholders stripped Ken Lewis of his Bank of America chairmanship, the government revealed the results of its long-awaited stress tests of big banks.

Bank of America, the nation's biggest bank, needed the largest addition to its capital buffer—$34 billion to help it navigate a potentially steeper downturn in the economy. Executives said they didn't need any more government money to meet the requirement. Instead, Bank of America would issue common stock, convert preferred shares held by private investors, sell off shares in China Construction Bank, shed assets such as its Columbia asset management business, and generate more profits.

The test helped highlight that Bank of America's troubles weren't all tied to Merrill. As regulators investigated Bank of America, they found burgeoning losses in areas such as credit cards and home-equity loans—the same businesses the bank had pledged to expand back at the beginning of 2007. The bank had also used up capital for acquisitions just before the economy began to falter. In hindsight, paying cash for LaSalle in 2007 was a drain on the bank's balance sheet, some former executives believed. In return, it had landed prized branches in Chicago but also locations in Michigan just as the auto industry imploded.

Regulators found that Wells Fargo needed an additional $13.7 billion in capital, which it planned to muster through a stock offering and earnings over time.

While acknowledging the need to meet regulators' demands, Bank of America said the government overestimated the bank's potential losses and underestimated its potential earnings power. The government estimated Bank of America, with assets of about $2.3 trillion, could sustain losses of $136.6 billion in 2009 and 2010 in a more severe downturn. It cautioned that number wasn't a projection but a what-if scenario.

"Frankly we think that scenario unlikely and looking like less and less of a possibility every day," Lewis said in a conference call with analysts after the stress test results were released. He added that he believed the economy had hit bottom.

In March, Lewis had said he expected his bank to pass the stress test without needing any more capital. Asked about those predictions, he said he had couched his remarks to say the bank would pass by its own measures. But at some point, the matter was in the "government's hands," he acknowledged.

He also noted that the bank didn't expect to need any government capital beyond the $45 billion it had already received through TARP. Instead, the actions it planned to take would simply change the composition of its capital. Regulators wanted banks to hold more common equity, considered the first defense against losses.

Banks had been discussing the final numbers with the government since receiving the preliminary results of their stress tests. Lewis indicated the banks didn't have a lot of maneuvering room: "In virtually every case I wouldn't call them negotiations." In a sign of its weariness of dealing with the government, the bank said it wanted to drop the $118 billion "ring-fence" agreement. Despite the weeks spent negotiating the rescue package back in December and January, the final agreement had not been signed, meaning Treasury never had to make a final systemic risk determination.

"Our game plan is designed to get the government out of our bank as soon as possible," Lewis said.

That same evening, Bank of America announced steps to improve its corporate governance, although it didn't disclose the MOU. In his first remarks since the annual meeting, Lewis called losing his chairmanship "a humbling experience." "I think we have been very responsive to a number of things shareholders had in mind," he said. "You reflect on it, you try to see the trend, the themes that were being expressed, and react to them."

Walter Massey, the bank's new chairman, said the company needed directors with greater financial expertise and indicated a board shakeup was in the works.

"After much consideration after the shareholders meeting, [we] feel we need some different and new expertise on the board, and we're going about that in an orderly way," he said.

The board's reconstruction began later that month, when Temple Sloan, the bank's former lead director, stepped down. By September, the board shrank to 15 as it shed nine members and gained six new ones. Among the additions were former Morgan Stanley executive Robert Scully, former Fed governor Susan Bies, and former FDIC chairman Don Powell.

Next to go was chief risk officer Amy Brinkley, a veteran who had served with Lewis since the bank was known as NCNB. The bank said Lewis was looking for a "different approach" to risk management. It named Greg Curl, the strategy executive who negotiated the Merrill deal, to the post.

Brinkley's departure wasn't surprising because she had presided over risk management during a period of massive losses and write-downs. But her exit also highlighted the rampant turnover in Lewis's management team in the latter years of his tenure. The bank had lost 52 of the 100 top executives who were at the company in 2005. The executives left for multiple reasons, including jobs at other financial institutions, Merrill-related layoffs, retirements, and ousters under Lewis.

Some former executives said the turnover was a sign of the low morale under Lewis during the financial crisis. They worried about the bank's ability to attract and retain talented leaders. Some key positions that had seen high turnover were CFO and treasurer. Since June 2005, the bank had employed three CFOs and three treasurers.

Many companies worried if they lost 5 percent of their top executives per year, Bradford Bell, an associate professor at Cornell University specializing in human resources issues, told the *Observer*. Other experts said annual turnover around 10 percent would be considered at the high end. Bank of America's turnover of top executives since 2005 equated to 13 percent per year.

Others, however, said the turnover was likely in line with other banks that were losing executives in the financial crisis. "The level of leadership turnover we've experienced is consistent with the history of the organization and a consolidating industry," Bank of America spokesman Scott Silvestri said.

Perhaps the most notable departure under Lewis had been Al de Molina, who left at the end of 2006. As CEO at GMAC Financial Services, he lured away a host of Bank of America executives. Of de Molina's top 17 lieutenants, eight had worked at the bank. De Molina's backers wondered if he might have spoken out against some of the later deals, had he remained with the bank.

Lewis had made the infusion of new talent a major focus when he started as CEO in 2001, hiring executives from General Electric and Honeywell International to help the company improve customer service and internal processes.

But many of those executives, including at least three in the top 100 in 2005, had since departed. As the year went on, more changes would be in store.

Since the beginning of the year, Bank of America had primarily fought a two-front war when it came to investigations of the Merrill Lynch deal, dueling with New York attorney general Andrew Cuomo and private shareholder lawsuits. But the bank's antagonists multiplied as the House Oversight and Government Reform Committee, the SEC, the United States Justice Department, and the North Carolina Attorney General's Office joined the fray.

Starting in June, the House committee, led by New York Democrat Edolphus Towns, began a series of hearings that provided a rare window into the usually secretive world of mergers, boardrooms, and government regulation. The committee also shook loose reams of regulatory e-mails and documents normally kept secret.

In a conflict that lasted throughout the hearings, Democrats suggested the bank had threatened to escape the Merrill deal in December in a bid to win more government aid. Republicans contended government officials forced the bank to proceed with the purchase, part of the public sector's dramatic intervention in the banking industry.

In his June 11 appearance before the committee, Lewis, put in the uncomfortable position of being asked to publicly criticize his regulators, danced around questions about whether or not he was forced to close the Merrill deal. Government pressure was part of the equation, but Merrill's long-term value and a fear of lawsuits if he backed out also played a role, Lewis told the committee.

"So you were pressured?" Towns asked.

"It's hard to find the exact right word to describe what I've just described," he replied.

Asked about the government's role in his company, Lewis said an oversight committee looked at the bank's lending under the Troubled Asset Relief Program. He also referred to a stress test requirement to review management and the board. "We have been doing that, but no day-to-day decisions [are] made by regulators," he said.

Representative Gerry Connolly, a Democrat from Virginia, pressed Lewis on his selection of Greg Curl as chief risk officer, wondering if that was a "wise decision" considering Curl's role in the Merrill deal. "Mr. Curl didn't miss the instruments which caused the loss," Lewis responded. "What happened is we did not anticipate the meltdown of such significant proportions in the fourth quarter. He'd identified everything properly. No one thought things would get as bad as it did in the fourth quarter."

When Ben Bernanke testified later in the month, he faced an unusual fusillade of criticism for a Fed chairman. Most of the blows were landed by Republicans.

That was surprising because Bernanke had been nominated for the job by President George W. Bush. It was sign of the complex emotions surrounding the government's bailout of the banking industry.

Asked about the pressure exerted on Lewis, Bernanke testified that he never said he would replace the board and management if Lewis decided to invoke the MAC, although he did say that triggering the MAC would have "greatly reduced or destroyed" Merrill's value. "I expressed those concerns, which is appropriate, but it was always [Lewis's] decision whether or not to go ahead and take that decision," Bernanke said.

Under questioning from lawmakers, Bernanke acknowledged he had "concerns and questions" about Bank of America's management after it tried to cancel the transaction. He also acknowledged the Fed had asked the bank to "look at top management and make changes to its board."

In July, the third key player in the drama, former Treasury secretary Henry Paulson, took the microphone at the witness table and strongly defended his actions in the midst of the financial crisis. "Had the crisis of 2008 been left to unfold without strong federal reaction and intervention, the world of 2009 would look very different from the world we live in today," Paulson said. "Many more Americans would be without their homes, their jobs, their businesses, their savings, and their way of life."

Referring to their contentious December 21, 2008, conversation, Paulson said he told Ken Lewis that it would show a "colossal lack of judgment" and jeopardize the financial system if the bank exercised the MAC. "I intended to deliver a strong message . . . that it would be unthinkable for Bank of America to take this destructive action for which there was no reasonable legal basis," he said in his written testimony.

Paulson said he told Lewis the Fed could unseat him if he abandoned the deal, but he didn't consider his remarks a threat. "I prefer to characterize it as me explaining the Fed's supervisory authority to him," Paulson said.

The former Treasury secretary said he didn't threaten Lewis on behalf of Bernanke, although he knew the Fed also opposed Bank of America's effort to exit the purchase. The government never got close to booting management, Paulson said, adding that Bank of America, after its own consideration, acted appropriately in moving ahead with the deal.

During the hearing, Representative Dennis Kucinich, an Ohio Democrat, leveled the sharpest criticism at Lewis, asking why no top United States banking leaders, including those at Bank of America, were ousted in the financial crisis. "The biggest, most powerful bankers have essentially received a free ride at taxpayers' expense," he said.

Paulson responded that he and the bank's regulators decided it was "appropriate to keep Mr. Lewis," saying that removal was a decision for the bank's board.

During his tenure, he pointed out, the government had forced out leaders at Freddie Mac, Fannie Mae, and AIG. But taking such action required having a ready replacement, he noted.

"These large, complex financial service companies are not easy to run," Paulson said. "It's not easy to find [CEOs] in a financial crisis."

Paulson also denied any role in Bank of America's handling of disclosures to shareholders.

"I did not—nor to my knowledge did anyone at the Federal Reserve or Treasury—tell Mr. Lewis not to disclose any information to the public markets, including Merrill Lynch losses, that Bank of America believed it was legally required to disclose," he said.

Chapter 21

"Thank God He's One of Us"

Until the banking crisis erupted, Ken Lewis had long been expected to stay on as CEO until he turned 65 in 2012. But in the summer of 2009, he privately acknowledged the possibility of a shorter stay in the corner office.

Facing a board that had been dramatically remade in just a few months, Lewis told the bank's directors he planned to stay on as CEO until at least the end of 2010. The succession plan at the time was that Greg Curl would be his replacement in the proverbial hit-by-a-bus scenario. Otherwise, the board could evaluate Brian Moynihan and other younger executives over the next year and a half.

On August 3, Lewis announced another management shakeup and provided new public clues about the bank's succession planning. Consumer banking head Liam McGee was leaving the company, to be replaced by Moynihan. Once viewed publicly as a potential Lewis successor, McGee had gradually seen his turf shrink as loan losses erupted in the bank's consumer portfolio. McGee quickly resurfaced in a top job, becoming CEO of insurer The Hartford Financial Services Group.

In a splashy addition to his management team, Lewis recruited former Citi executive Sallie Krawcheck to run the bank's wealth management division, which included the prized "thundering herd" of Merrill stockbrokers. Krawcheck had overseen brokers at Citi and then served as chief financial officer before reportedly falling out with Vikram Pandit. She brought star power and Carolinas ties to the post. Although a South Carolina native and UNC Chapel Hill graduate, she would be based in New York. In other changes, Tom Montag, the former Merrill executive, would run all of corporate and investment banking, an area that had been partly overseen by Moynihan. In addition, bank veteran David Darnell, who ran commercial banking, now reported directly to Lewis, raising his profile at the company.

The moves injected new blood into the competition to succeed Lewis. They also slightly tilted power away from the bank's hometown. Following the management changes, five of the bank's top 11 executives were based in Charlotte. Before the changes, it had been five of 10. In a statement, Lewis said the moves were made in response to a new economic and business climate. The changes positioned "a number of senior executives to compete to succeed me at the appropriate time," he said.

The Boston-based Moynihan, taking charge of the trademark consumer banking unit, now looked like the clear front runner to someday replace Lewis. Other candidates included mortgage executive Barbara Desoer, chief financial officer Joe Price, Montag, Krawcheck, and possibly Darnell.

The maneuvering came on the same day Bank of America appeared to clear up one of its legal difficulties. The bank agreed to a $33 million settlement with the SEC over allegations it misled shareholders about bonuses paid to Merrill employees under the side agreement in the merger. But United States district judge Jed Rakoff had other ideas. Skeptical of the settlement, he invited both the SEC and the bank to a hearing in New York to defend the agreement and file supporting briefs.

After reviewing the case, Rakoff on September 14 rejected the proposed settlement. In his order, the sharp-tongued judge attacked the pact as unreasonable and told the two parties to prepare for a trial. The agreement "was a contrivance designed to provide the SEC with the facade of enforcement and the management of Bank of America with a quick resolution of an embarrassing inquiry all at the expense of the sole alleged victims, the shareholders," Rakoff wrote. He also said the SEC didn't dig deeply enough into who was responsible for preparing the allegedly misleading proxy statement sent to shareholders before they voted on the deal.

The rebuke came amid reports that top bank executives could soon face charges from New York's attorney general over similar accusations. A Bank of America spokesman said the company believed there was no basis for charges and that it had acted appropriately.

For much of August, Lewis vacationed at his home in Colorado. When he returned after Labor Day, he sported a rare beard for a day around the office. The facial hair spurred amusement at headquarters but was a sign of the CEO's changing mind-set. During his time away, he had reflected on the job he had clung to so tightly since the Merrill controversy erupted in January. Fatigued by the mud being thrown at him, he had decided he was ready to retire. Lewis told Steele Alphin, his friend and chief administrative officer, about his thinking. But later in the day, he told him he would stick it out longer.

However, Lewis continued to think about leaving. He found himself meeting with lawyers more often, in case he faced any personal legal exposure. On a trip to Asia, his remarks at an investor conference focused on a Japanese proverb that preached persistence.

"One year ago today, Bank of America and Merrill Lynch announced our intention to merge," Lewis said at the September 15, 2009, conference. "It's been quite a year . . . to say the least. But here's my bottom line: Today, Bank of America Merrill Lynch is a leading financial institution in Japan, in America and around the world. We are helping drive economic recovery and growth for individuals and businesses and institutions. We have the broadest financial capabilities and the best team in the world, and we are going to succeed."

But by late September, Lewis made up his mind. It was time to go. He wasn't enjoying the job. He had become a lightning rod for the company. And he wasn't the type of Washington creature the bank needed to network and schmooze with politicians and regulators. At a meeting of banking chiefs at the White House in March, Lewis had remarked bluntly, "Mr. President, I am not going to suck up to Larry and Tim like the rest of these guys," referring to Treasury secretary Tim Geithner and Larry Summers, the head of the National Economic Council. As he faced mounting criticism for the Merrill deal, Lewis felt betrayed by regulators who had promised Bank of America would not be seen as another Citigroup. He kept notes in his office from conversations with top government officials who had pledged their support for the company.

Lewis told Walter Massey of his decision, and then he and Alphin flew to Boston to deliver the news to some of the board's directors there. Later in the week, Massey sent a note to the board calling a meeting that Friday to discuss Lewis's retirement. Chief marketing officer Anne Finucane, who oversaw corporate communications, saw the note and feared the news would leak. Massey moved up the meeting to Wednesday, September 30.

In New York for a previously scheduled visit, Lewis dialed into the conference call from the bank's One Bryant Park tower in Midtown, the project he had heralded only days after the September 11 attacks in his first year as CEO. Lewis told the board he planned to retire at year's end. The directors hadn't prepared for such an early exit but didn't try to talk him out of it. Before the meeting, Lewis had given a heads-up to those who reported directly to him. The bank also tipped off the various regulators and law enforcement officials scrutinizing the company.

Less than a year after Lesley Stahl got him to say he had trumped New York, the Bank of America CEO decided to step down while he was in the nation's financial capital. The decision meant the end of his four-decade career and raised questions about the company's ability to continue its tradition of hiring its leader from within. The move also spurred concerns about whether or not the bank would maintain its Charlotte headquarters, which had become more entrenched under Lewis.

A news release went out that evening, even as the CEO's planned departure began surfacing on CNBC and other media outlets. "Bank of America is well positioned to meet the continuing challenges of the economy and markets," Lewis said in a statement. "I am particularly heartened by the results that are emerging from the decisions and initiatives of the difficult past year-and-a-half."

In a memo sent to employees, Lewis said he was comfortable with his decision personally and as someone "greatly invested" in the bank. "Some will suggest that I am leaving under pressure or because of questions regarding the Merrill deal. I will simply say that this was my decision, and mine alone," he said.

The next day, October 1, many of the city's top leaders and a handful of Bank of America officials gathered in Charlotte for the ribbon cutting at the new Ritz-Carlton built by the bank. The plan at first had been for the location to carry the bank's name, but the moniker was quietly dropped in the months before the ceremony. The newspapers delivered on the hotel's first day carried the front-page news of Lewis's exit.

After the event, Charlotte developer Johnny Harris, whose grandfather was former North Carolina governor Cameron Morrison, talked about the effect the appointment of a new CEO would have on the local economy. "Long-term, nobody knows the answer to that," he said. "I didn't ever think we'd be talking about Bank of America or Wachovia the way we have the last year."

Lewis's announcement left the board in a tough spot. The directors hadn't expected him to leave so soon. And the dramatically overhauled board was still coalescing. The directors barely knew each other, much less the company and its executives. Still, corporate governance experts said the board's inability to name a successor right away was a major failing, considering succession planning was one of the top jobs of any corporate board.

Massey said the board would launch a search to consider inside and outside candidates. The bank's chairman would lead a six-member search committee that included three former Fleet directors. That raised worries in Charlotte that Moynihan could be picked and possibly uproot the headquarters.

Although Bank of America had bought Fleet, the New England bank's directors formed a strong block on the board. In the 2004 acquisition, Fleet had received seven board seats to Bank of America's 12. But five years later, through retirements and other departures, six former Fleet directors remained on the board, compared to five of the original directors from Bank of America.

Shortly after his announcement, Lewis met with the search committee and made his recommendations.

The best choice was Curl, who could guide the company for two years while the board came together, he said. That would give directors time to get to know other executives. Curl wasn't a particularly charismatic leader, but he had the smarts, experience, and Washington connections to navigate the storm buffeting the company. The second choice was Moynihan, although Lewis said his selection could spur other internal candidates to leave. The third option was to pick an outsider, which Lewis thought was the worst choice. The bank's model wasn't broken and didn't need to be overhauled, he told the committee. And top executives were likely to depart if the new boss came from outside. Moynihan and Curl quickly became known as the leading internal candidates.

Many investors, however, favored an outsider to give the bank a new spark. Two obvious possibilities were former Bank of America CFOs Jim Hance and Al de Molina.

Hance, Lewis's one-time rival for the CEO post, was now working at the Carlyle Group private-equity firm and serving on corporate boards. He was a polished networker well liked in the industry and familiar with the company. He still had an office in the Bank of America Corporate Center. But he was older than Lewis, making him a short-term solution. During the hunt, Hance met with the search committee in New York. He laid out a to-do list that included paying off TARP, reducing the company's risk appetite, and closely examining the overall business model. His candidacy didn't go beyond the interview stage.

Another faction backed de Molina. He had kept GMAC alive during the financial crisis and built up operations in Charlotte. Now that Bank of America was struggling, some of the moves he had advocated when at the bank looked prescient. Worried about increasing risk in the financial system, de Molina had enhanced the bank's portfolio of credit default swaps, a type of insurance designed to protect against losses in its commercial loan portfolio. The protection, however, came at a cost—$241 million in 2006—and de Molina faced questions from other bank executives about whether or not the expense was worth it. The bank began reducing the insurance while de Molina was CFO and continued winding it down after he left. The protection could have been a significant source of profits when financial markets deteriorated.

De Molina also had detractors inside the bank. He had burned some bridges by recruiting Bank of America executives to GMAC. Critics said he had favored stock buybacks that depleted the bank's capital, and he had built up the corporate and investment bank before it was wracked by the credit crunch. His backers argued that the bank's capital levels fell after he left, beginning with the LaSalle deal. They also noted that he had kept a lid on riskier collateralized debt obligation arrangements that later were costly for the bank.

Back in January, when he e-mailed director Chad Gifford, de Molina had planned to offer himself as a possible CFO candidate if the board were considering a CEO change. His thinking was that he could be a steadying force on Wall Street for a new CEO like Brian Moynihan or mortgage head Barbara Desoer. He never heard back from Gifford in January, and the bank didn't contact him during the search to replace Lewis that fall. In November, GMAC's board pushed de Molina out. Among his conflicts with the board, de Molina had taken a stand against a possible bankruptcy filing for GMAC's mortgage unit.

Bank of America reached out to other outside candidates during the hunt. The search committee approached Barclays president Bob Diamond, who demurred. Other candidates were Mike O'Neill, the former BankAmerica CFO, and William Demchak, a PNC Financial executive. "It's nice to be loved," Demchak later said coyly about Bank of America's advances. The bank also approached Bob Kelly, the Bank of New York Mellon CEO and former Wachovia CFO. But in early November, he sent an e-mail to his executive team saying he wasn't interested.

Bank of America's search for a new CEO was complicated by a number of factors.

First, offering big money to lure a candidate was virtually impossible at a time when Americans were increasingly fed up with high-priced compensation packages. Obama administration pay czar Ken Feinberg planned to review the pay of the incoming CEO. Even swapping out the stock holdings that candidates had accumulated at their current employers for Bank of America shares was a potential hurdle. Such an exchange would make it look like Bank of America was handing out a huge pay package.

Second, the job came with unresolved lawsuits and ongoing government scrutiny of the bank's operations. During the search, Massey updated Kevin Warsh, Jeff Lacker, comptroller John Dugan, and other officials. While the regulators left the actual search to the bank, it was clear that a candidate unacceptable to Washington was not going to pass muster.

As the CEO search lingered, the bank continued to tackle other issues clouding its future. On the executive compensation front, Lewis agreed to accept no pay for 2009, after negotiations with pay czar Feinberg. Breaking another logjam, the bank agreed to release additional e-mails and documents to New York attorney general Andrew Cuomo and other investigators, dropping previous objections that the material was protected by attorney-client privilege. The bank briefed officials in Congress, Cuomo's office, the SEC, and the United States Justice Department. In a letter to the House Oversight and Government Reform Committee chairman, the bank argued that it had followed the advice of its counsel, conformed to securities laws, and considered a MAC back in December to protect its shareholders.

"While there obviously will be differing perspectives on the various documents provided today, a fair reading of the information in its totality will demonstrate that Bank of America at all times acted in good faith with the best interests of its shareholders in mind, and did so in close consultation with some of the most preeminent and accomplished lawyers and firms in the world," the bank's lawyers wrote.

In mid-October, Lewis held his final earnings conference call with analysts.

The bank had posted a third-quarter loss of $2.2 billion, but he expressed optimism in the company's future. His voice even seemed to crack with emotion. "It's been a pleasure to lead Bank of America and interact with you," he said.

As the search continued, worry mounted in Charlotte about the possibility of losing the bank's headquarters, a potential second blow following Wachovia's sale. After being elected Charlotte's new mayor in November, Democrat Anthony Foxx received a congratulatory call from President Obama. He used the time to pitch the importance of keeping Bank of America in Charlotte. Representative Mel Watt, a Charlotte Democrat, also discussed the issue with House Financial Services Committee chairman Barney Frank, who assured him that he wasn't trying to lure the headquarters to Boston. Throughout the search, however, speculation persisted in Charlotte about the push Moynihan might be getting from directors, executives, and politicians with ties to Boston.

Moynihan received some unwanted attention in November when the House Oversight and Government Reform Committee asked him to testify, along with former general counsel Tim Mayopoulos and two directors, Chad Gifford and Thomas May. Sitting next to Mayopoulos, Moynihan faced questions about his own near-departure from the company and his brief stint as general counsel. Representative Elijah Cummings, a Maryland Democrat, painted Moynihan as a blindly loyal company man who didn't even try to find out why Mayopoulos had been abruptly fired. Moynihan said such dismissals were part of life at big companies. After the hearing, Edolphus Towns, the committee chairman, said he didn't find some of Moynihan's answers believable. "He didn't show the kind of leadership a company would seem to need," he said.

Democrats and Republicans still couldn't agree on whether to blame the bank or the government in the Merrill mess. But Representative Dennis Kucinich, the Ohio Democrat, indicated it was time to move on. Republican Jim Jordan of Ohio bemoaned the government's intervention in the financial sector altogether. "This whole escapade," he said, "highlights why we should never have traveled down this road."

Pressure mounted on Bank of America's board after the search stretched past a Thanksgiving deadline. Massey raised eyebrows for taking a long-planned cruise in the midst of the hunt. Speculation increased that Lewis might have to stay on longer than December 31. Inside the boardroom, factions developed, gumming up the process.

In what was expected to be his last public appearance as Bank of America CEO, Lewis on December 2 received two standing ovations at the Charlotte Chamber's annual economic forecast luncheon. Before the meeting, he chatted briefly with Lacker, his regulatory foil during the past year. Instead of being joined onstage by a Wachovia CEO, Lewis this time had as his banking counterpart Wells Fargo CEO John Stumpf.

Showing a reflective side rarely displayed publicly, Lewis said the bank's toughest times had actually come in the 1970s as it reeled from the southeastern real-estate collapse. He praised Tom Storrs, his NCNB predecessor, who guided the company through those troubles. "He's one of the great CEOs this city has ever known, this country has ever known," Lewis said of Storrs, who wasn't in attendance as in years past. "I appreciate it more now after the last two and a half years what he did for us."

During the event, Lewis kept a lid on a major secret. Later in the day, after the stock market closed, Bank of America announced an agreement to pay back its TARP money—all $45 billion of it—pending a stock offering. A huge albatross in the CEO search was lifted. Greg Curl had led the TARP negotiations, raising his profile in the bank's hunt for a new leader. He had spent weeks in Washington meeting whomever he could to broker a deal that some officials were reluctant to make. Some of the secret talks were held in offices in the Treasury Department's basement. Curl was so focused on the effort that he ignored a painful broken tooth until after the negotiations were completed.

The TARP payback came with a costly $4 billion accounting charge but freed the bank from expensive dividend payments and extra government scrutiny. Lewis wasn't going to come close to achieving his goal of making $30 billion in annual profits by the time he stepped away. In January 2010, Bank of America would disclose that it lost $2.2 billion, including TARP-related costs, for all of 2009. For the year, it had set aside an incredible $49 billion for current and future loan losses.

Still, Lewis fulfilled a key pledge to pay off government loans before exiting. "It was a priority to get this done," bank spokesman Bob Stickler said. "He feels like he kept the faith with taxpayers."

Two weeks after the TARP announcement, the CEO search zeroed in on Bob Kelly again. Sources said Kelly wanted a large pay package, but his spokesman insisted pay wasn't at the top of his list. Kelly was also pushing for dual headquarters in Charlotte and New York, sources said. In the end, it's unclear how close the bank got to hiring Kelly. The New York Mellon CEO publicly dropped out of the running on Monday, December 14. That same day, he and other bank leaders, including Lewis, went to the White House to meet with President Obama, who again chided the bankers on pay.

The search committee was now down to the two internal candidates: Curl, the 61-year-old veteran strategist, and Moynihan, the 50-year-old problem solver. Both were heavily involved in the Merrill purchase. Curl had gained points by negotiating the TARP payoff. But his candidacy took a hit when Cuomo's office began questioning the accuracy of testimony he had given around his role in Merrill-related disclosure issues. The bank said it was confident in the "consistency and truthfulness" of the testimony of its executives. But the message Cuomo appeared to send to the board was that picking Curl could lead to more attention from the New York attorney general.

On Wednesday, December 16, Bank of America directors convened around five in the afternoon in the bank's 60th-floor boardroom in Charlotte. Fourteen directors participated in person and one by phone. Moynihan appeared the likely choice, but some directors still weren't sure that was the right move. For part of the debate, the board went into executive session, meaning Lewis couldn't attend. He was pushing for Moynihan, worried that the bank could turn to an outsider. Around 7:30 P.M., the board finally made its decision, ending a two-and-a-half-month hunt for Lewis's successor. The directors called for Moynihan, who had been sequestered in a 58th-floor office. Ratified by a unanimous vote, the bank's newly anointed CEO entered the room to a round of applause.

Investors and analysts greeted the pick with mixed opinions. Most were simply relieved the bank had ended uncertainty about its leadership. Moynihan was a young leader who could helm the nation's biggest bank for many years. The Ohio native and rugby enthusiast was a lawyer by training but had gained experience in various parts of the business. On the downside, he brought ties to the troublesome Merrill deal. Although he was viewed with trepidation in Charlotte, he confirmed the headquarters would stay in the city and that his office would be in the bank's hometown. Later, he would rent an apartment in Charlotte. But he gave no indication he planned to move his family to the city.

On Thursday, December 17, the bank invited employees to an Uptown Charlotte theater for appearances by Lewis and Moynihan. On a cold morning, they trekked up Tryon Street to pack the 750-seat McGlohon Theatre at Spirit Square.

As Lewis was introduced, the crowd stood and applauded. He said he had been impressed with Moynihan since meeting him in 2003, when the bank was considering buying Fleet. "Many of you know him because he's been in so many different jobs," Lewis said, drawing laughter from the audience. "So hopefully, he'll stay in this job longer. . . . A CEO's legacy is the next CEO, so I want him to do real well."

Lewis acknowledged it had been a tough year but said there were reasons to believe the future was brighter. He called paying back TARP the "single biggest morale booster in the history of our company."

"You're happy, I'm happy, my mother's happy," he said, referring to complaints he had heard from his mother about the bank's receipt of government money.

Lewis said he was counting on Moynihan, calling him a smart and humble leader who cared about his customers. "Another unique characteristic about him is, he wanted the job," he joked. "That may end up in the category of, 'Be careful what you wish for.'" Lewis also called on employees to "circle the wagons and give him the support he needs." As Lewis presented Moynihan to a cheering crowd, he added, "Thank God he's one of us."

"Thank you, Ken," Moynihan responded, smiling. "My mother is happy, too."

The incoming CEO praised Lewis for his forward-looking strategy—buying Fleet to fill a gap in the Northeast, for instance, and merging with Merrill to better serve the bank's affluent customers. When he first met Lewis several years ago, he had been impressed with his succinct goal for Bank of America: To make it the most admired company in the world.

"We have to fulfill that mission to be the most admired company," Moynihan said. "We have an obligation to fulfill that mission for Ken."

During the session, Moynihan also summed up his view of a company built through decades of acquisitions. "We don't have to think about buying something," Moynihan said. "We don't have to think about something we don't have. We have everything. . . . It's just about execution."

The employee meeting was Lewis's last major appearance as Bank of America CEO. Unlike some departing CEOs, he left without a severance package or extra perks. Still, his financial future was secure. A later filing said he departed the company with at least $70 million in pension benefits, stock, and other compensation.

On Hugh McColl's last day as Bank of America's chief executive in 2001, the departing leader had tipped his cowboy hat to a throng of applauding employees. Perhaps fitting his more introverted personality, Lewis quietly exited after the Moynihan announcement. Staff cleaned out his office that weekend, even though Lewis officially had two more weeks as CEO.

Epilogue

Through decades of bold acquisitions, the banks that became Bank of America and Wachovia broke free of the bonds of North Carolina and the South to achieve the status of major national financial players—just in time to become icons of the nation's banking meltdown. For both Ken Thompson and Ken Lewis, their biggest deals were their most troublesome.

Buying Golden West at the peak of the housing bubble burdened Wachovia with billions in worrisome loans in troubled areas of California as the housing market collapsed. While the bank also had problems in investment banking and other areas, its option ARM portfolio became a glaring concern for investors as the financial crisis bubbled over in the fall of 2008.

As was the practice of his predecessor Hugh McColl, Ken Lewis preyed on a wounded foe when he pounced on long-coveted Merrill Lynch over the fateful weekend Lehman Brothers died. But in contrast to the First Republic deal that buoyed NCNB in Texas, he paid a premium price and didn't win government assistance *before* agreeing to the purchase. The Merrill deal, in the long run, may prove a financial success—providing investment banking and brokerage profits for Bank of America—but it damaged the bank's reputation, battered the stock price, cost thousands of jobs, and helped shake Lewis from his CEO post.

Hugh McColl agrees with the one-deal-too-many conceit—to a point.

"I think it's very clear that the Golden West thing destroyed Wachovia/First Union," he said in an October 2009 interview at his Charlotte art gallery. "That's very clear. It is not clear that Merrill Lynch will quote 'destroy Bank of America.' Bank of America has not been destroyed. It has been damaged, but it's not destroyed."

One factor observers often miss, he said, is that Bank of America, as the nation's biggest retail bank, is a mirror of the greater economy. "So with the Bank of

America the very thing that makes it strong and powerful are some of the things that are hurting it at the moment," he said. "The Merrill Lynch acquisition I do believe damaged the stock badly. And it has been a really miserable year since then. And it's not over, but it will be over sometime."

He said he didn't want to make a judgment on Lewis, his hand-picked successor. "Time will tell," he said. "I choose not to have a stated view about it."

For their part, the Sandlers continue to defend Golden West, which has seen a once-sterling reputation diminished since Wachovia's downfall.

They took particular offense after *60 Minutes* in February 2009 highlighted the story of a former Golden West employee, Paul Bishop, who in a May 2008 lawsuit alleged he was dismissed after threatening to warn Wachovia about problems at the company. Herb Sandler fired off two letters to the program in which he raised concerns about Bishop's background and stood up for Golden West's lending practices. The lender maintained high standards, and many of Wachovia's loan losses stemmed from mortgages made after the 2006 sale, he wrote. The Sandlers' website—www.goldenwestworld.com—calls Golden West "a unique and successful residential mortgage lender that operated from 1963 to 2006." The site lists factors that set the company apart from other lenders, including keeping loans in its portfolio and offering products "fundamentally different and safer for consumers than Option ARMs securitized and sold by mortgage bankers."

In April 2010, Wells Fargo said that Wachovia's Pick-A-Payment portfolio was performing better than the 29 percent life-of-loan losses projected at the time of the merger, although the bank didn't provide a new estimate. In an investor presentation, Wells noted that older Pick-A-Payment loans were faring better than newer ones.

As Bank of America and Wachovia struggled in the financial crisis, they were caught up in a global economic disaster that was partly the result of forces beyond their control—and partly of their own making.

The ingredients of the financial crisis are well known by now: Loose credit standards, low interest rates, weak regulators, overzealous borrowers, bonus-driven bankers, yield-hungry investors, conflicted rating agencies, and a pervading assumption that housing prices would never go down again. The explosion of subprime loans made to borrowers who later couldn't make their payments has received particular blame for spurring the housing crisis. Neither Charlotte bank was a big player in originating subprime mortgages, but both participated in the Wall Street side of the mortgage catastrophe: The packaging of these loans into securities that facilitated the industry's growth. In the end, both banks' executives and risk managers failed to rein in their institutions before damage was done.

One of the consumer advocates who raised red flags about the role of Bank of America and Wachovia in the subprime market was Matthew Lee of New York–based watchdog group Inner City Press/Fair Finance Watch. He often voiced concerns during regulatory reviews of the banks' acquisitions. "I hate to say it's been validated," he said in 2007 of his warnings.

In another irony of the financial crisis, Bank of America and Wachovia found themselves in the government's uncomfortable grip after decades of breaking down regulatory barriers to unleash their expansion. After turning Charlotte into a major banking center, both banks had much of their fate decided in regulatory halls in Washington, as well as lawyers' offices in Midtown Manhattan.

In Charlotte, some have suspicions that government officials treated the North Carolina banks as pawns in a game to save bigger New York banks. While the regulators' motives may never be fully known, their actions indicate they were more focused on dousing one fire after another than on dramatically reordering the financial system. A major reason Charlotte suffered outsized damage in the crisis, of course, was because it had an outsized role in the banking industry. Banking centers from New York to Cleveland to Seattle all sustained blows during the meltdown.

At the Richmond Fed, Jeff Lacker, who sometimes tangled with the Charlotte banks he regulated, said his institution was just fulfilling its mission. "Our folks focus on doing the job the best we can," he said. "We've been able to build up expertise just like the big banks had to build up expertise down in Charlotte. I think we've done that. We were never trying to protect anybody or protect our role."

Interviews for this book and other publications suggest that Tim Geithner, the New York Fed president turned Treasury secretary, felt that marrying Wachovia with Citigroup was as important for the New York bank as the Charlotte bank. And when the deal fell through, he protested to Sheila Bair. Geithner, through a spokesman, declined to comment on his role in the Citi and Wachovia deals. In the end, however, Wachovia merged with a San Francisco bank without interference from government officials.

The expectations raised by the initial TARP proposal in September 2008—and its failure to quickly pass—shook confidence in Wachovia, FDIC chairman Sheila Bair believed, according to sources. If TARP had been in place earlier, it might have brought much-needed stability to the bank, she felt.

The FDIC chairman, however, does not absolve Wachovia of blame, noting the bank bought Golden West at the top of the market and continued selling option ARMs, according to sources. She doesn't believe the agency's handling of the WaMu failure, which protected all of the Seattle thrift's depositors, had a crippling ripple effect for Wachovia. The only indirect impact may have been that the sale to JPMorgan Chase highlighted troubles at West Coast mortgage lenders, which Wachovia had become with the Golden West purchase.

In April 2010, Senator Carl Levin, the Michigan Democrat chairing the Senate Permanent Subcommittee on Investigations, concluded that the Office of Thrift Supervision, which regulated WaMu, "never said 'no' to any of the high risk lending or shoddy lending practices that came to undermine WaMu's portfolio, its stock price, its depositor base, and its reputation." In her testimony to Levin's committee, Bair said the OTS restricted her agency's efforts to regulate WaMu. She also defended the decision to fail the thrift. "Critics may say it was overly harsh to close WaMu, but the reality is that mortgage losses were mounting, downgrades were occurring, and efforts to raise capital had been exhausted," she said. Former WaMu CEO Kerry Killinger, in his testimony, took responsibility for the firm's performance but called WaMu's seizure unfair. The company "was excluded from hundreds of meetings and telephone calls between Wall Street executives and policy leaders that ultimately determined the winners and losers in the financial crisis," he said. It's a sentiment that likely resonated with some in Charlotte.

According to an April 2010 report by the Government Accountability Office, regulators agreed to aid Wachovia's initial sale to Citigroup because they were worried about losses to foreign depositors, runs on mutual funds, and damage to other banks and the economy. The FDIC told the congressional watchdog agency that Wachovia's rapidly deteriorating condition was due "largely to its portfolio of payment-option adjustable-rate mortgage (ARM) products, commercial real-estate portfolio, and weakened liquidity position," the report stated.

The FDIC and the Fed determined Wachovia could be closed with no loss to the FDIC's deposit fund, but that would have caused "significant losses" to subordinated debt holders and possibly senior note holders. Regulators' concerns were amplified by the WaMu failure, which Treasury determined caused "large losses" for senior and subordinated debt holders but no losses for the deposit insurance fund, according to the report. In addition, officials worried a Wachovia failure could raise concerns about similar United States financial institutions, spur losses for mutual funds that held Wachovia's short-term commercial paper debt, and disrupt payment and settlement systems.

Although Wells later trumped the Citi deal, Treasury and FDIC officials told the GAO that one measure of the agreement's success was that Wachovia was able to remain open and meet its obligations on September 29, 2008. "As Wachovia did not fail, the extent to which a Wachovia failure would have had adverse effects on financial stability is not known," the report said.

In a 2009 interview with the *Observer*, Wachovia general counsel Jane Sherburne contended the resolution for Wachovia was better than it could have been. "It's been hard for individuals, but for the company and for shareholders and even employees we got a result that was vastly better than receivership and clearly much better than the agreement with Citi," she said.

As for Bank of America, politicians and investigators have painted the bank's effort to exit its Merrill Lynch purchase as either a case of the government's strong-arming the company or the bank's shaking down the government for aid. Government officials have argued they were acting in the best interest of the financial system and the United States economy, while the public remains largely unhappy about expensive bailouts. The bank contends its executives acted in good faith during a difficult time. In the first quarter of 2010, Bank of America returned to profitability, and officials signaled that loan losses may have peaked.

Perhaps regulators' biggest failing was not getting ahead of the crisis with a comprehensive solution, although an effort to do this—TARP—was initially delayed by machinations in Congress and has been viewed as mostly unpopular. The government's decision not to save Lehman Brothers came under particular fire after it helped spawn another wave of market turbulence in September 2008. Ben Bernanke in April 2010 testified that the Fed understood Lehman's collapse would shake the financial system, but that the regulator didn't have the tools to help the firm. "At that time, neither the Federal Reserve nor any other agency had the authority to provide capital or an unsecured guarantee, and thus no means of preventing Lehman's failure existed," Bernanke said. As part of financial reform efforts, regulators want more power to wind down large financial firms.

In addition to the forces in Washington, a cadre of New York lawyers and bankers was heavily involved in the events surrounding Bank of America and Wachovia. The firm with the most obvious ties to the situation was Goldman Sachs, including former executives Henry Paulson and Bob Steel. The New York investment bank ultimately didn't forge a combination with Wachovia and took a pass on investing in Merrill Lynch. Goldman, however, did benefit financially, billing Wachovia for more than $100 million in fees for advisory services starting in late 2006.

Although Goldman emerged from the financial crisis in better shape than most institutions, criticism of its pay and other practices have mounted. In April 2010, the SEC charged the company and one of its traders with civil fraud for allegations that the firm misled investors about subprime-backed securities it sold. The company has denied the allegations.

So who should be held responsible for the mess?

It's a pretty long list—bankers, boards, politicians, regulators, investors, and consumers all played a role.

Some of the key figures in the Charlotte drama have already lost their jobs, although many shareholders say that's not enough, considering the wealth many of the executives had already accumulated. Out in the wake of the crisis: Thompson, Steel, most of Wachovia's directors, John Thain, many of Bank of America's directors, and Lewis. Of the 11 Bank of America executives pictured in the company's 2008 annual report, six had left or were leaving as of March 2010, including Steele Alphin and Greg Curl.

In February 2010, Bank of America agreed to a $150 million settlement with the SEC over Merrill-related disclosure issues. The North Carolina attorney general joined in the agreement, which did not include charges against any individuals. As part of the settlement, which Judge Jed Rakoff later reluctantly affirmed, the bank agreed to hire an independent auditor to review its disclosure practices and to hold an annual nonbinding shareholder vote on executive compensation.

On the same day, New York attorney general Andrew Cuomo filed a civil securities fraud lawsuit against the bank, Lewis, and former CFO Joe Price, who became the company's head of consumer banking. The complaint accused Bank of America and the executives of intentionally withholding information from shareholders in order to win their approval of the deal in December 2008.

The bank, Lewis, and Price blasted Cuomo's decision, noting the SEC had determined that no executives should be charged and asserting they did not intentionally mislead investors. All three pledged to vigorously defend themselves. "Mr. Lewis has been unfairly vilified by the political search for accountability for the financial meltdown," Mary Jo White, a New York attorney representing Lewis, said in a statement. For Cuomo, who announced in May 2010 that he was running for governor of New York, the case may be a political boon if he is successful or a liability if the charges unravel.

After his very public ouster in January 2009, former Merrill CEO Thain slipped the spotlight that fell on Bank of America executives after the deal's problems emerged. He has since been named chief executive of CIT Group, Inc., a lender in need of his Mr. Fix-It reputation.

In January 2009, the SEC reportedly began investigating the comments former Wachovia CEO Bob Steel made in his *Mad Money* appearance in September 2008. "In an extremely challenging and volatile time, Mr. Steel always did his best to convey the position of Wachovia accurately," a spokesman for Steel said at the time. "Should any questions arise, he is very comfortable addressing them."

Although few shareholders would profess sympathy for the Charlotte banks' former CEOs, Thompson's and Lewis's falls have tragic elements.

Thompson revived First Union, forged a successful merger with Wachovia, and largely avoided expensive deals until Golden West. He was well liked by almost everyone he met and became the civic successor to Hugh McColl, using his company's muscle to build the city around him. His Golden West deal was widely seen as Wachovia's downfall, but the bank also faced risk management issues and suffered major losses in its corporate and investment banking unit unrelated to the California lender.

Critics have wondered if Thompson had a good-enough grasp of the complex company that Wachovia had become, and if he was too driven by competition with Bank of America. The First Union–Wachovia deal was such a success that perhaps he became overconfident or was forced to take big risks to continue the bank's growth, others said.

"I thought he was in way over his head and way over his ability to run the company," said former SouthTrust CEO Wallace Malone. "He didn't understand the mistakes he made. They needed some better management in that company or to hire a chief operating officer. He clearly wasn't capable of digesting that merger. That's my opinion after years in the business."

But after the crushing loss of Wachovia, Thompson still has supporters. "I will stand by Ken Thompson," said Greg Fleming, the former Merrill Lynch executive now at Morgan Stanley. "He made a big mistake with Golden West. But he did an excellent job for that bank. He paid a high price personally."

Lewis rose from modest roots to the top of one of the world's largest companies. He refined operations and produced huge profits during good times. But he also pushed the bank deeper into consumer lending areas that later bled losses and forged big deals that turned problematic. In addition, the bank experienced a talent drain. "The first five years of his tenure were really strong," one former executive said of Lewis. "Maybe he got bad advice or got overconfident. Beginning in 2007, he clearly took the company in a different direction."

Defenders say Lewis was a strong leader who left behind an industry powerhouse for his successor, despite the bank's Merrill-related troubles.

"Bank of America and Charlotte are blessed with having really strong, smart, aggressive leaders at the top—Tom Storrs, Hugh McColl and Ken Lewis," said former Bank of America CFO Marc Oken. "These are guys who saw the banking scene was going to change, impacted by changes in banking laws, competition and the scramble for customers. They looked ahead and saw what needed to be done to come out on top and be a survivor. Everyone realizes it's the greatest banking franchise in the world."

Painful what-ifs will haunt Charlotte's banks for years to come. What if they hadn't done some of their big deals? What if TARP had passed earlier? What if Lewis had renegotiated with Thain or resisted government entreaties to close the Merrill deal? What if First Union had lost its bid for Wachovia?

In the end, a city that built its reputation as a banking center over more than 80 years suffered a major blow because of the financial institutions that unraveled in its midst. Thousands of banking jobs disappeared, millions in wages vaporized, and billions in shareholder wealth tanked. The city's Teflon, can-do image sustained its first significant dents.

A good indicator of the damage suffered by shareholders is the decline in the banks' market capitalization—the total value of their outstanding shares. At the end of 2006, Wachovia had a market capitalization of about $108 billion. But by the end of September 2008, more than $100 billion of that was gone. At Bank of America, the company's market cap slumped to $130 billion at the end of 2009 from $238 billion at the end of 2006. By the end of March 2010, its market value climbed back to about $180 billion, helped by a rising stock price and the issuance of new shares.

The decline has hit small and large shareholders. The C. D. Spangler Foundation saw its assets fall by nearly two-thirds in 2008, to $133.2 million from $366.5 million, largely because of holdings in Bank of America and Wachovia stock. Charlotte businessman Cameron Harris has alleged in a lawsuit against Wachovia that he and his wife, Dee-Dee, held a "significant portion of their wealth" in Wachovia stock as the shares collapsed in 2008. Harris sold his namesake insurance firm to Wachovia in 2002. His grandfather was former North Carolina governor Cameron Morrison, the toastmaster for the Federal Reserve branch banquet in 1928.

Cliff Cameron, the former First Union CEO, has been to several lunches at which he and former First Union colleagues commiserated about their losses. All of them held onto their shares through Wachovia's downfall. "It's tough," he said. "It's sad it happened like it did."

The local job market has also taken a major hit. Finance and insurance jobs in the Charlotte metro area peaked at 65,000 in August 2006 but fell by 15 percent to 54,800 by the end of 2009, according to Labor Department data. In January 2010, the Charlotte-area unemployment rate hit 12.8 percent, its highest level in at least 20 years.

Economic development officials have landed new jobs for the city, thanks to firms in need of available financial workers. Ironically, two of their biggest scores have been expansions by an outsourcing company, Zenta, and Bruce Marks's NACA, which is staffing its foreclosure prevention effort. The city also has an array of other financial firms, from community banks to boutique investment banks to private-equity firms. Former Bank of America and Wachovia executives including Gene Taylor, Chris Marshall, and Walter Davis are organizing new banks that will aim to buy struggling institutions. One of the proposed banks is to be called Union National Bank, the same name as the First Union forerunner. But the lingering question for Charlotte is whether or not the city can replace the salaries of high-paying bank jobs. Officials are intent on diversifying the economy by targeting energy and other green jobs.

For now, Bank of America and Wells Fargo remain formidable corporate players in the city. Bank of America in early 2010 said it continued to employ about 15,000 in Charlotte, while Wachovia's ranks had slipped to about 19,000 from a peak of 21,000. New Bank of America CEO Brian Moynihan has reiterated that the bank's headquarters will remain in Charlotte, although many still wonder about forces pulling toward New York and Boston. Wells has also signaled its commitment to Charlotte, but power in the bank has clearly migrated to San Francisco.

The merger will hit home more deeply when Wells changes North Carolina branch signs, likely in late 2011. It is sure to be a bittersweet coda for a bank brand dating to 1879. In yet another irony, while the Wachovia name is going away, a reincarnated Money Store remains in business. Wachovia sold off the name after it no longer needed it.

The former Wachovia cultural campus in Charlotte initially took the Wells Fargo name but will become the Levine Center for the Arts after a major donation by the founder of discount retailer Family Dollar Stores, Incorporated. As the banks have struggled, Leon Levine and his wife, Sandra, have emerged as a major philanthropic force in the city.

During his first official workday as Bank of America CEO, Brian Moynihan on January 4, 2010, appeared before the same group of bankers in Raleigh that Ken Thompson had addressed back in 2006. He expressed contrition about the industry's role in the economic collapse, although he didn't specifically apologize for anything Bank of America had done. "We as an industry cannot avoid the simple fact that we caused a lot of damage, and we have to help make sure it doesn't happen again," he said. Moynihan also drew applause when he stressed the bank's Charlotte roots dating all the way back to 1874, the founding of Commercial National Bank. Bank of America "has thrived for 135 years as a North Carolina company, and it will continue to do so," Moynihan said.

In Moynihan's first 100 days, the bank announced plans to stop charging unpopular overdraft fees on debit card transactions. The new CEO outlined plans to improve risk management by encouraging "robust debate" among executives and employees. And he reminded his leadership team that a company the size of Bank of America can't grow much faster than the economy unless it's overreaching. Still, questions remain about the bank's business model.

In an April 2010 interview, Moynihan told the *Observer* that "in some of the consumer areas, we extended credit to people who found themselves overburdened by it. We don't do that anymore, and we won't do it in the future. We fixed that." He also argued against disassembling the nation's biggest bank: "We have this company and the capabilities we provide because that's what our customers want. If you break it into pieces we couldn't do what our customers need, and we couldn't be as competitive as we need to be over the next decades."

The controversy embroiling the financial services industry remains a complicated topic for Charlotte. While big bonuses for executives have been vilified in many quarters, these payouts form a significant chunk of the city's wages. In pushing to break up giant banks, lawmakers could hurt the city by downsizing its corporate citizens—or protecting them from future meltdowns.

Twenty-five years after the southeastern banking compact unleashed interstate banking for North Carolina institutions, Hugh McColl remains unapologetic about building a behemoth bank. At a Queens University of Charlotte event in February 2010 commemorating the 30th anniversary of the McColl School of Business, a student asked the retired CEO if he felt bad about creating a bank considered too big to fail.

"I feel no regret about building a large company that spread across the United States," McColl replied, arguing that big banks mean more competition, lower prices, and better service. But he said he "might have some regrets" about not building his bank larger—meaning the company should have socked away more capital in good times to help it weather downturns.

McColl remains optimistic about the city's future, although he envisions a diminished role for its giant banks.

"We've got to get over the fact that we used to have two rich uncles," McColl said. "We have to reinvent ourselves. We have done that before. This city has prospered through many hard times and continued to grow and we need to look at our assets rather than our liabilities at this stage. . . . We have a huge backlog of financial talent, and it will bring us businesses. Now, are they going to just walk in like they used to do? No. We're going to have to get off our butts and go solicit companies from other cities. We're going to have to go on offense. It's always my plan to attack."

ACKNOWLEDGMENTS

I owe a special thanks to a number of people for their encouragement and assistance in writing this book.

I was fortunate to have the support of the top editors at the *Charlotte Observer*, Rick Thames and Cheryl Carpenter, during a stressful time for the newspaper industry. Business editor Patrick Scott was a sounding board on the nebulous idea of a book about Charlotte's banks for a number of years and remained a key adviser, editor, and booster during its writing. I've been lucky to have such a skilled and supportive editor during my time in the business section.

My colleague on the banking beat, Christina Rexrode, deserves credit for her outstanding coverage of the banking crisis as well as for carrying a heavier load while I took on this project. The other members of our current business staff—Stella Hopkins, Kerry Hall Singe, Kirsten Valle, Jen Aronoff, and Ron Stodghill—also deserve praise for their work during the financial crisis and its ongoing fallout. I am indebted to researchers Maria David and Marion Paynter for their help tracking down everything from hard-to-find phone numbers to 1920s stories on microfilm. I also owe a big thanks to Bert Fox, Don Williamson, and Laura-Chase McGehee for doing extra duty in the photo department.

In writing this book, I was reminded of the tremendous storytelling by previous *Observer* banking reporters over the years. Their reporting was crucial to my understanding of the history of the two banks. One of my former colleagues on the bank beat, Binyamin Appelbaum, has been a supporter of this book over the years. He and his wife, Kytja Weir, get extra thanks for putting me up on a trip to Washington.

I owe a big thanks to former *Observer* editor Mitch Weiss, now with the Associated Press, for his advice, time, and infectious enthusiasm during the proposal stage. Marion Ellis, coauthor of *The Story of NationsBank*, also offered advice and support as I was getting started. I'd also like to thank Tom Hanchett of the Levine Museum of the New South and Lissa Broome at the University of North Carolina School of Law for their help.

I'm grateful to all the folks at John F. Blair for tackling this project and guiding me through the book world. Special thanks go to president Carolyn Sakowski and editor in chief Steve Kirk. I'd also like to thank attorney Elizabeth Spainhour for her advice.

A book of this kind can't be written without the people who lend their time and knowledge to reporters trying to figure out what's going on in the world. I owe a special thanks to those who have trusted me and others at the *Observer* in sharing stories of important public interest, even if it posed a risk to their careers.

Finally, I am thankful to family and friends who offered their encouragement as I labored on this project. My wife, Jen, and our boys, Jack and Will, get the biggest thanks of all.

NOTES

PROLOGUE

By showtime: "CNBC's Jim Cramer interviews Wachovia president & CEO Robert Steel," transcript on CNBC.com, Sept. 15, 2008.

CHAPTER 1   BANKTOWN BEGINNINGS

For decades: Thomas D. Hills, "The rise of Southern banking and the disparities among the states following the Southeastern Regional Banking Compact," *University of North Carolina Banking Institute* 11 (2007).

Unable to meet: Howard E. Covington, Jr., and Marion A. Ellis, *The Story of NationsBank: Changing the Face of American Banking* (Chapel Hill: University of North Carolina Press, 1993), 202–8; Ross Yockey, *McColl: The Man with America's Money* (Atlanta: Longstreet, 1999), 295–98.

North Carolina was the last: Lissa Lamkin Broome, "The First One Hundred Years of Banking in North Carolina," *North Carolina Banking Institute* 9 (2005); T. Harry Gatton, *Banking in North Carolina: A Narrative History* (Raleigh: North Carolina Bankers Association, 1987), 27–28, 39, 51–56.

North Carolina banks survived: "Wachovia: The First 100 Years," *Wachovia* (June 1979); *History of Banking and Wachovia* (Wachovia Corp., 1994), 24–31.

To the west: Thomas W. Hanchett, *Sorting Out the New South City: Race, Class, and Urban Development in Charlotte, 1875–1975* (Chapel Hill: University of North Carolina Press, 1998), 19–28.

In 1874: "Becoming Bank America: NCNB—Our Foundation," exhibit at Bank of America Heritage Center, Founders Hall, Charlotte, N.C.

In 1908, H. M. Victor: "Company history," Wachovia website; additional Union National history provided by Wachovia archivists, citing *The Employment Security Commission Quarterly* (Winter 1949), a 1952 history by Celestia Smith, and a 1988 article from the North Carolina Citizens for Business and Industry, Inc.

The Charlotte region: Jack Claiborne, *The Charlotte Observer: Its Time and Place, 1869–1986* (Chapel Hill: University of North Carolina Press, 1986), 170.

As early as 1915: Hanchett, *Sorting Out the New South City*, 198–200; Claiborne, *The Charlotte Observer*, 192.

Charlotte's reputation: Federal Reserve Bank of Richmond Charlotte branch exhibit commemorating the 75th anniversary of the branch, 1997.

At least five cities: Claiborne, *The Charlotte Observer*, 170.

Behind the more: "Move for Bank Led by Wood," *Charlotte Observer*, Feb. 26, 1927; H. E. C. Bryant, "Elation greets board verdict," *CO*, Feb. 26, 1927; "Carolina bank heads elated over victory," *CO*, Feb. 27, 1927; "Financial boom to follow branch," *CO*, Feb. 26, 1927.

On January 19, 1928: "Bankers plan ovation for Mellon and party today," *CO*, Jan. 19, 1928; "650 Bankers celebrate U.S. branch opening," *CO*, Jan. 20, 1928.

At American Trust: Covington and Ellis, *The Story of NationsBank*, 23–38.

On November 29, 1957: Larry Jinks, "Commercial National, American Trust Join," *CO*, Sept. 18, 1957.

The hometown merger: Kays Gary, "Total resources to be $110 million," *CO*, May 29, 1958.

As the merger rivalry: "Union National Bank begins move today," *CO*, Feb. 18, 1955; Roy Covington, "Union National Bank to open doors of its new home today," *CO*, Feb. 21, 1955; Doug Smith, "Wachovia to vacate building," *CO*, Aug. 7, 2003.

Meanwhile, Winston-Salem's: Yockey, *McColl*, 19.

Reese in particular: Covington and Ellis, *The Story of NationsBank*, 39–74; Yockey, *McColl*, 16.

Initially, Cameron: M. S. Van Hecke, "The coach retires," *CO*, Feb. 21, 1991; George Frye, "One-bank firms fight for life," *CO*, July 19, 1970; George Frye, "Bank law 'loophole' closed," *CO*, Dec. 27, 1970; Phillip L. Zweig, *Wriston: Walter Wriston, Citibank and the Rise and Fall of American Financial Supremacy* (New York: Crown Publishers, 1995), 237–39.

NCNB gained: Covington and Ellis, *The Story of NationsBank*, 107–24.

Interstate banking: Arnold G. Danielson, *Consolidation of Banking* (Bethesda, Md.: Danielson Capital, 2007), 19.

NCNB, now the nation's: Covington and Ellis, *The Story of NationsBank*, 150–77.

Although Walter Wriston's: Zweig, *Wriston*, 462.

NCNB struck: Covington and Ellis, *The Story of NationsBank*, 166–77.

The next step: Hills, *University of North Carolina Banking Institute*.

CHAPTER 2 RIVALRY PERSONIFIED

Born the son: Elizabeth Leland, "McColl, the misunderstood," *CO*, Apr. 30, 1989.

After getting: Yockey, *McColl*, 58–59.

When he became CEO: Amber Veverka, "Banker McColl to retire in April," *CO*, Jan. 21, 2001.

After an initial rejection: Bart Fraust, "Proposed merger would rank firm 2d in N. Carolina," *American Banker*, Mar. 5, 1985.

As the Lone Star State's: *Managing the Crisis: The FDIC and RTC Experience, 1980–1994* (Washington: Federal Deposit Insurance Corp., 1998), 605.

After winning: Covington and Ellis, *The Story of NationsBank*, 266–67.

The back-and-forth acquisitions: M. S. Van Hecke, "Big banks step up rivalry, one-upmanship or coincidence?" *CO*, Mar. 13, 1989.

In the fall of 1994: Yockey, *McColl*, 471–74; James Greiff, "NationsBank, First Union and Wachovia poised to grow when new interstate banking law takes effect," *CO*, Sept. 15, 1994; Dave Skidmore, "Interstate banking bill clears house, but faces delay in Senate," Associated Press (published in *CO*), Aug. 5, 1994.

Once the new law: Pamela L. Moore, "Expensive, but worth it," *CO*, July 22, 1997.

As 1997 came to a close: Pamela L. Moore, "No. 2 banking city: right here, folks," *CO*, Nov. 25, 1997.

One of the industry's: Pamela L. Moore, "Shareholders OK First Union's proposal to acquire First Fidelity," *CO*, Oct. 4, 1995.

McColl and Crutchfield also feuded: Melissa Wahl, "Barbed-tongue banking battlers," *CO*, Dec. 1, 1997.

In the March 4, 1998: "First Union and the Money Store sign merger agreement," First Union press release, Mar. 4, 1998.

Just a few months earlier: William D. Cohan, *House of Cards: A Tale of Hubris and Wretched Excess on Wall Street* (New York: Doubleday, 2009), 295–97; "First Union Capital Markets Corp., Bear, Stearns & Co. price securities offering backed by affordable mortgages," First Union press release, Oct. 20, 1997.

CHAPTER 3 THE NEXT GENERATION

Hugh McColl had rejected: Hills, *University of North Carolina Banking Institute.*

NationsBank CFO Jim Hance: Yockey, *McColl*, 538–76; Melissa Wahl, "13 days that led to nationwide bank," *CO*, Apr. 19, 1998.

On April 13: Melissa Wahl, "We will be America's bank," *CO*, Apr. 14, 1998.

Though Wall Street loved: Pamela L. Moore, "Banking in a backwater?" *CO*, Apr. 19, 1998; Pamela L. Moore, "Exit brings loss home in Calif. city," *CO*, Oct. 25, 1998.

NationsBank countered: Pamela L. Moore, "Bank merger hearing a forum on meeting local credit needs," *CO*, July 10, 1998.

After winning Federal Reserve: Amber Veverka, "That would be Bank of America, Charlotte, 29255," *CO*, Oct. 1, 1998.

While Bank of America's: Pamela L. Moore, "Merger shock's early ripples," *CO*, June 7, 1998.

On October 14: Sharon R. King, "Operating income plunges at BankAmerica," *New York Times*, Oct. 15, 1998; Pamela L. Moore, "Bank defends disclosure timing," *CO*, Oct. 17, 1998; Pamela L. Moore, "Shaw losses mount, but bank sells positions quickly," *CO*, Jan. 20, 1999; Pamela L. Moore, "Exit brings loss home in Calif. city," *CO*, Oct. 25, 1998.

Litigation related to: "SEC agreement," Bank of America press release, July 30, 2001; "Merger-Related lawsuits," Bank of America press release, Feb. 8, 2002.

The bank's third-quarter: Amber Veverka, "Cracks show in Money Store, higher-rate mortgage lenders facing tough times," *CO*, Nov. 3, 1998.

Overall, though: Richard Maschal, "84-story tower only on paper," *CO*, July 10, 2005.

As the year closed: Pamela L. Moore, "First Union lays groundwork for a big year," *CO*, Dec. 13, 1998.

On January 14, 1999: Amber Veverka, "Bank has good momentum," *CO*, Jan. 15, 1999; Pamela L. Moore, " '99 profit estimates too high, bank says," *CO*, Jan. 27, 1999.

The CoreStates takeover: Joseph N. DiStefano, "First Union acknowledges its sins of past, stresses future's promise," *CO*, Aug. 22, 1999.

The projected drop: Pamela L. Moore, "What's gone wrong at First Union?" *CO*, May 30, 1999.

Thompson described: Irwin Speizer, "George Kennedy Thompson: Reluctant rebel," *North Carolina Business* (Nov. 1, 2000).

Thompson won: Jerry Adams, "Roommates rise to the top," *Wake Forest MBA Business* (Winter 2004).

To tackle the Money Store: Carrick Mollenkamp, "Subprime asset," *Wall Street Journal*, July 25, 2000.

In June 2000: Amber Veverka, " 'Chipping away rough edges,' " *CO*, June 27, 2000.

With his cancer: Amber Veverka, "Ed Crutchfield: 'There's a time for the former CEO to move on,' " *CO*, Oct. 20, 2000.

His retirement agreement: Form DEF14A, First Union, Mar. 31, 2001, www.sec.gov.

In his remarks: "Senior leadership conference: Ed Crutchfield Tribute," First Union videotape, Oct. 17, 2000.

In January 2001: Amber Veverka, "Banker McColl to retire in April," *CO*, Jan. 21, 2001.

In his retirement: Form DEF14A, Bank of America, Mar. 19, 2001.

Kenneth Lewis was born: "Kenneth Lewis oral history," Computerworld Honors Program International Archives, May 3, 2004.

By the early 1990s: Pamela L. Moore, "Who'll succeed Hugh McColl?" *CO*, Sept. 21, 1997; Doug Smith, "NationsBank executive buys Charlotte landmark," *CO*, Nov. 6, 1993.

Especially in contrast: Paul Davis, "Lewis Emerges as Exemplar of Leadership in Time of Crisis," *American Banker*, Dec. 5, 2008.

At the meeting: Amber Veverka, "McColl sets the suit aside," *CO*, Apr. 26, 2001.

CHAPTER 4 THE NEW WACHOVIA

Since taking over: Audrey Y. Williams, "Wachovia's Bud Baker looks ahead while he builds on a solid tradition," *CO*, May 8, 2000.

By June of that year: Audrey Y. Williams, "Bank stocks take a slide," *CO*, Dec. 4, 2000.

SunTrust had long: Form PRRN14, SunTrust Banks, June 18, 2001.

Starting in September 2000: Form S-4/A, First Union, June 27, 2001.

SunTrust executives: Form PREC14, SunTrust Banks, May 14, 2001.

Ken Thompson found: Audrey Y. Williams, "Longtime suitor determined to win Wachovia Corp.," *CO*, June 24, 2001; Amber Veverka and Audrey Y. Williams, "Secret meetings, taut nerves," *CO*, Apr. 22, 2001.

On Monday, May 14: Audrey Y. Williams, "SunTrust enters bid to take over Wachovia," *CO*, May 15, 2001.

Within days: Amber Veverka, "Dueling CEOs battle for Carolinas minds," *CO*, May 18, 2001.

To combat personal: Amber Veverka, "CEO cuts his perk from bank deal," *CO*, May 19, 2001.

On May 22: Amber Veverka, "Wachovia turns down SunTrust bid," *CO*, May 23, 2001.

The Wachovia team: Amber Veverka and Jen Talhelm, "SunTrust loses 1, wins a
     2nd," *CO*, June 15, 2001.
Wachovia's annual: Amber Veverka and Rick Rothacker, "Team Wachovia wins,"
     CO, Aug. 4, 2001.
First Union's victory: Patrick Scott, "N.C. execs dominate new Wachovia board,"
     CO, Sept. 5, 2001.

CHAPTER 5 EXPANDING EMPIRES

As Lewis moved: Meg Richards, "Accused fund settles in illegal trading case," As-
     sociated Press (published in *CO*), Sept. 4, 2003; Sarah Jane Tribble, "BofA
     looks inward amid allegations," *CO*, Sept. 6, 2003.
The mutual fund scandal: Sarah Jane Tribble, "BofA to buy FleetBoston," *CO*,
     Oct. 28, 2003.
In another conservative: Form DEFM14A, SouthTrust, Sept. 27, 2004.
"We're pretty sure": Rick Rothacker, Andrew Shain, and Binyamin Appelbaum,
     "BofA leaps to top of credit card industry," *CO*, July 1, 2005.

CHAPTER 6 WACHOVIA HEADS WEST

In a December 2005: John C. Dugan, "Remarks before the Consumer Federation
     of America," speech at Washington Plaza Hotel, Washington, D.C., Dec. 1,
     2005.
Wachovia's plan: Form S-4, Wachovia, June 1, 2006.
In more than: Patricia Sellers, "Hubby, wife are golden duo," *Fortune* (Mar. 4,
     2002); Alec Rosenberg, "She's a role model for any CEO," *Oakland Tribune*,
     Nov. 14, 2004; Dan Fost, "Do they have a good marriage? You can take that
     to the bank," *San Francisco Chronicle*, June 4, 2006; Laura Mandaro, "Golden
     sticks to Knitting," *American Banker*, July 8, 2003.
Thompson was back: Ron Green, Jr., "5 Questions with Ken Thompson," *CO*,
     May 4, 2006.
Wachovia reviewed: Form 10-K, Golden West Financial Corp, Mar. 8, 2006.
In further talks: Form S-4, Wachovia, June 1, 2006.
He introduced the Sandlers: Form 425, Wachovia, May 9, 2006.
As the bank's shares: Form 425, Wachovia, May 16, 2006.
Soon after the announcement: John C. Dugan, testimony at House Committee on
     Financial Services hearing, Oct. 29, 2009.
At a special meeting: Binyamin Appelbaum, "Wachovia deal takes 1 more step,"
     CO, Sept. 1, 2006.

A couple weeks later: Mara Der Hovanesian, "How toxic is your mortgage?" *BusinessWeek* (Sept. 11, 2006).

Wachovia had no way: *Securities and Exchange Commission v. Angelo Mozilo, David Sambol and Eric Sieracki*, Civil Action No. 09-CV-03994 (C.D. Cal., June 4, 2009).

Chapter 7 Boom to Bust

During the integration: Jared Sandberg, "Corporate enthusiasm, from winning to wincing," *Wall Street Journal* (published in *CO*), Nov. 26, 2006.

Bank of America announced: Arthur Max, "Doozy of a deal," Associated Press (published in *CO*), Apr. 24, 2007.

Thompson had pledged: Binyamin Appelbaum, "Wachovia agrees to buy A. G. Edwards," *CO*, July 20, 2007.

Since the spring: Jeannine Aversa, "Fed chairman vows to curb mortgage abuses," Associated Press (published in *CO*), July 20, 2007.

Soon, the subprime: Greg Ip, "Bernanke, in First Crisis, rewrites Fed playbook," *Wall Street Journal*, Oct. 31, 2007.

Bank of America had: Binyamin Appelbaum, "BofA takes Countrywide stake," *CO*, Aug. 23, 2007.

O'Neal, however: Andrew Ross Sorkin, *Too Big to Fail* (New York: Viking, 2009), 314–16; William D. Cohan, "Merrill's $50 billion feud," *Fortune* (Apr. 15, 2010).

Bernanke was joined: Ip, "Bernanke, in first crisis."

Weeks later: David Wessel, *In Fed We Trust: Ben Bernanke's War on the Great Panic* (New York: Crown Publishing Group, 2009), 134–35.

Since mid-November: Form S-4, Bank of America, Feb. 13, 2008.

Chapter 8 "Moment of Truth"

"Based on recent action": "Wachovia Q4 2007 earnings call," Bloomberg transcript, Jan. 22, 2008.

Publicly, the bank: David Mildenberg, "Wachovia says home loans stay profitable as rates dip," *Bloomberg News*, Feb. 13, 2008.

"We do believe": David Mildenberg, "Wachovia expects higher losses on mortgage defaults," *Bloomberg News*, Feb. 28, 2008.

Wachovia struggled: Yalman Onaran, "Bailout shores up Bear Stearns," *Bloomberg News* (published in *CO*), Mar. 15, 2008.

CHAPTER 9 "I DIDN'T THROW IN THE TOWEL"

Over a 12-day: Charles Duhigg, "Papers show Wachovia knew of thefts," *New York Times*, Feb. 6, 2008.

Some analysts questioned: Stella M. Hopkins, "New chairman has broad background," *CO*, May 9, 2008.

Next came Steel's: Christina Rexrode, "Steel targets problems," *CO*, July 11, 2008.

Robert King Steel: Rick Rothacker, Stella M. Hopkins, and Christina Rexrode, "His challenge: Save Wachovia," *CO*, July 13, 2008.

In his United States: "Insider: Wachovia CEO invests in film about a racist murder in N.C.," *CO*, Nov. 20, 2008.

CHAPTER 10 FROM LEHMAN TO MERRILL

Optimism about: Joe Bel Bruno, "Lehman stock dives as investor talks fail," Associated Press (published in *CO*), Sept. 10, 2008.

Even as its prognosis: Christina Rexrode, "Steel lays out strategies," *CO*, Sept. 10, 2008.

Lewis turned down: Sorkin, *Too Big to Fail*, 204–6.

Treasury and Fed officials: Wessel, *In Fed We Trust*, 160–61, 178.

Later on Tuesday: Sorkin, *Too Big to Fail*, 248–63.

On the morning: Joe Bel Bruno, "Lehman selling asset to soothe Wall Street," Associated Press (published in *CO*), Sept. 11, 2008.

On Thursday, September 11: Sorkin, *Too Big to Fail*, 267–68; William D. Cohan, "Checkmate for a Wall Street wizard?" *Fortune* (Sept. 14, 2009).

Although the list: Henry M. Paulson, Jr., *On the Brink* (New York: Business Plus, 2010), 180.

Little more than: "Breaking the Bank," interview with Ken Lewis on *Frontline*, PBS.org, June 10, 2009; Sorkin, *Too Big to Fail*, 300.

On Friday: Paulson, *On the Brink*, 187.

That afternoon: "Breaking the Bank," interview with John Thain on *Frontline*, PBS.org, June 10, 2009.

In a call that afternoon: Sorkin, *Too Big to Fail*, 299-300; Paulson, *On the Brink*, 189.

Inside the New York Fed: Interview with John Thain on *Frontline*.

Bank of America's corporate: James Stewart, "Eight days," *The New Yorker* (Sept. 21, 2009); interview with Ken Lewis on *Frontline*; interview with John Thain on *Frontline*.

The Bank of America CEO: Form S-4, Bank of America, Oct. 2, 2008.

Later in the weekend: Susanne Craig, Jeffrey McCracken, Aaron Lucchetti, and Kate Kelly, "The Weekend That Wall Street Died," *Wall Street Journal*, Dec. 29, 2008.

Around eight: Stewart, "Eight Days."

While price was: Securities and Exchange Commission v. Bank of America Corp., Civil Action No. 09-CV-6829 (S.D.N.Y. Aug. 3, 2009).

During the board's deliberations: House Committee on Oversight and Government Reform hearing, Nov. 17, 2009.

CHAPTER 11 FOR SALE: WACHOVIA

On Tuesday, September 16: Form DEFM14A, Wachovia, Nov. 24, 2008; affidavit of Dona Davis Young, *Irving Ehrenhaus v. John D. Baker II, et. al.*, Civil Action No. 08-CVS-22632 (N.C. Business Court, Oct. 17, 2008).

As part of the company's: Jeff Horwitz, "Wachovia's End," *U.S. Banker* (Nov. 2009).

By Wednesday evening: Sorkin, *Too Big to Fail*, 434.

Wachovia board member Neubauer: Paulson, *On the Brink*, 272.

Inside the Fed: Paulson, *On the Brink*, 276.

CHAPTER 12 THE PASSING OF A GREAT INSTITUTION

On Thursday, September 25: Jay Newton-Small, "Who's to blame for the bailout deal's stumble?" Time.com, Sept. 26, 2008; David M. Herszenhorn, Carl Hulse, and Sheryl Gay Stolberg, "Talks implode during a day of chaos; Fate of bailout plan remains unresolved," Newyorktimes.com, Sept. 25, 2008.

On Thursday evening: Robin Sidel, David Enrich, and Dan Fitzpatrick, "WaMu is seized, sold off to J. P. Morgan, in largest failure in U.S. banking history," *Wall Street Journal*, Sept. 26, 2008.

WaMu's collapse: "JPMorgan Chase acquires the deposits, assets and certain liabilities of Washington Mutual's banking operations," JPMorgan Chase press release, Sept. 25, 2008.

That Thursday night: "Back to school with Vikram Pandit: CEO Speaks at Wharton and the Columbia Business School," Citigroup press release, Oct. 16, 2008.

At 4:27 A.M.: Form DEFM14A, Wachovia.

Despite these assurances: Rick Rothacker and Kerry Hall, "Wachovia faced a 'silent' bank run," *CO*, Oct. 2, 2008; declaration of Edward J. Kelly III, *Wachovia Corp. v. Citigroup, Inc.* Civil Action No. 08-CV-8503 (S.D.N.Y Oct. 4, 2008).

If deposits kept flowing: Form DEFM14A, Wachovia.

That evening: Affidavit of Dona Davis Young, *Irving Ehrenhaus v. John D. Baker II, et. al.*

The law firm: Form DEFM14A, Wachovia; affidavit of Robert K. Steel, *Wachovia v. Citigroup.*

Adding to the surreal: Clay Barbour and Christopher D. Kirkpatrick, "More fuel on the way today," *CO*, Sept. 26, 2008.

Chapter 13 Systemic Risk

Bob Steel and David Carroll: Hotel fact sheet, www.thecarlyle.com.

Kovacevich was one: Zweig, *Wriston*, 538, 839–40.

Wachovia had only: Affidavit of Robert K. Steel, *Wachovia v. Citigroup.*

The agreement-in-principle: Form DEFM14A, Wachovia.

Bair was stationed: Minutes of Federal Deposit Insurance Corp. Board of Directors meeting, Sept. 29, 2008, obtained through Freedom of Information Act request.

Treasury secretary Henry Paulson: Paulson, *On the Brink*, 316.

At 7:55 A.M.: E-mail obtained under FOIA by banking consultant Ken Thomas.

Chapter 14 "You're Not Going to Believe This"

Former Wachovia and First Union: Stella M. Hopkins, "Former bank chiefs lament the loss," *CO*, Sept. 30, 2008.

The city's anxiety: Peter St. Onge, "A city proud of the prestige and prosperity that its two brawling banks bestowed now worries what will happen when one goes away," *CO*, Sept. 30, 2008.

For investors: Jen Aronoff, "Shareholders lament their losses," *CO*, Sept. 30, 2008.

Adding to the turmoil: Lisa Zagaroli, "N.C. GOP votes to halt bailout," *CO*, Sept. 30, 2008.

Over the weekend: Paulson, *On the Brink*, 316.

After hearing these concerns: Form DEFM14A, Wachovia.

As the week progressed: Form DEFM14A, Wachovia.

Early in the morning: E-mail obtained through FOIA.

Boosting Wells Fargo's: Binyamin Appelbaum, "After change in tax law, Wells Fargo swoops in," *Washington Post*, Oct. 4, 2008.

Around 7:15 P.M.: Affidavit of Robert K. Steel, *Wachovia v. Citigroup.*

While Steel flew back: *Wachovia v. Citigroup.*

Wells had initially: Affidavit of Dona Davis Young, *Irving Ehrenhaus v. John D. Baker II, et. al.*

The directors didn't: Form DEFM14A, Wachovia.

Wells trumpeted: Form DEFM14A, Wachovia.

Some interpreted: Lisa Zagaroli, "Some Charlotte-area lawmakers warm to Wells Fargo offer," *CO*, Oct. 4, 2008.

Charlotte Chamber president: E-mail obtained through *CO* public records request.

In another turnaround: E-mail obtained under FOIA by banking consultant Ken Thomas.

CHAPTER 15 LIKE A FUNERAL

As the talks proceeded: Declaration of David Carroll, *Wachovia v. Citigroup*.

Paulson, flanked by Ben Bernanke: Records obtained by Judicial Watch, Inc., through FOIA.

Kovacevich put up: Mark Landler and Eric Dash, "Drama behind a $250 billion banking deal," *New York Times*, Oct. 14, 2008; "Under New Ownership: Bank Of America," *60 Minutes*, Oct. 19, 2008.

Weeks earlier: Christina Rexrode, "Bank rescue too late for one," *CO*, Oct. 15, 2008.

A day later: Christina Rexrode, "Wells CEO rallies workers in the Wachovia atrium," *CO*, Oct. 16, 2008.

Amid Wachovia's struggles: David Ranii, "Competitors seek profit from Wachovia's woes," *News & Observer* (Raleigh), Oct. 17, 2008.

A month later: Jeannine Aversa, "Government unveils plan to save Citigroup," Associated Press (published in *CO*), Nov. 24, 2008.

Filings by the bank: Form DEFM14A, Wachovia.

By the end of 2008: "In Re: Wachovia Preferred Securities and Bond/Notes Litigation," Civil Action No. 09-CV-6351 (S.D.N.Y., July 15, 2009).

The Sandlers' 10 percent stake: "S&L tycoons make big donation: The Sandlers of Golden West report $1.3 billion gift in stock to an unnamed charity," *Bloomberg News* (on *Los Angeles Times* website), July 10, 2006; Michael Liedtke, "Sandler defends Golden West in Wachovia debacle," Associated Press (published in *USA Today*), Oct. 5, 2008.

As Wachovia neared: Christina Rexrode, "Smaller bonuses for bank workers," *CO*, Dec. 13, 2008.

CHAPTER 16 "WHAT A DISASTER!"

Note: Chapters 16–18 extensively reference e-mails sent by Federal Reserve officials, Bank of America executives, Merrill Lynch executives, and lawyers working for Bank of America. These e-mails were obtained by the House Committee on Oversight and Government Reform as part of its investigation of the Merrill Lynch deal and were later made public. An e-mail sent by Bank of America executive Steele Alphin was obtained from another source.

As was typical: Testimony of John Thain, "In Re: Executive Compensation Investigation, Bank of America–Merrill Lynch," Office of the Attorney General, State of New York, Feb. 19, 2009; Susanne Craig, "Thain Fires Back at Bank of America," *Wall Street Journal*, Apr. 27, 2009.

In Mid-October: "Under New Ownership: Bank of America," *60 Minutes*.

On November 20: Statement of Timothy Mayopoulos, House Committee on Oversight and Government Reform hearing, Nov. 17, 2009.

As the December 5: Statement of Timothy Mayopoulos, House Committee on Oversight and Government Reform; Christina Rexrode, "How BofA almost lost Moynihan," *CO*, Feb. 18, 2010.

On December 3: Supplemental statement of facts, *Securities and Exchange Commission v. Bank of America Corp.*, Civil Action No. 09-CV-6829 (S.D.N.Y., Aug. 3, 2009), Civil Action No. 10-CV-0215 (S.D.N.Y., Jan. 12, 2010).

Whether or not Mayopoulos: *The People of the State of New York By Andrew M. Cuomo, Attorney General of the State of New York v. Bank of America Corp., et al.* (Supreme Court of the State of N.Y., Feb. 4, 2010); supplemental statement of facts, *Securities and Exchange Commission v. Bank of America Corp.*, Civil Action No. 09-CV-6829, Civil Action No. 10-CV-6829; deposition of Ken Lewis, *SEC v. Bank of America*, Civil Action No. 09-CV-6829, Oct. 30, 2009.

Not every Bank: *The People of the State of New York By Andrew M. Cuomo, Attorney General of the State of New York v. Bank of America Corp., et al.*

One way out: William D. Cohan, "The final days of Merrill Lynch," *The Atlantic* (Sept. 2009).

The next day: Christina Rexrode, "Stockholders say yes to BofA purchase of Merrill Lynch," *CO*, Dec. 6, 2008.

But at the end: Form S-4, Bank of America, Oct. 2, 2008.

Merrill typically calculated: *SEC v. Bank of America*, Civil Action No. 09-CV-6829; Testimony of John Thain, Office of the Attorney General, State of New York.

As for Thain's: Testimony of Steele Alphin, "In Re: Executive Compensation Investigation, Bank of America–Merrill Lynch," Office of the Attorney General, State of New York, Mar. 4, 2009.

On December 8: *SEC v. Bank of America*, Civil Action No. 09-CV-6829.

For the rest: Testimony of Steele Alphin, Office of the Attorney General, State of New York; Testimony of John Thain, Office of the Attorney General, State of New York.

Lewis later testified: Testimony of Kenneth Lewis, "In Re: Executive Compensation Investigation, Bank of America–Merrill Lynch," Office of the Attorney General, State of New York, Feb. 26, 2009.

On December 9: Statement of Timothy Mayopoulos, House Committee on Oversight and Government Reform. Christina Rexrode, "SEC probe puts light on BofA shuffle," *CO*, Feb. 23, 2010.

The planned departure: House Committee on Oversight and Government Reform hearing, Nov. 17, 2009.

A little before noon: Statement of Timothy Mayopoulos.

The bad news: Testimony of Kenneth Lewis, Office of the Attorney General, State of New York; "[Material Adverse Event] Analysis," prepared by Wachtell Lipton Rosen & Katz for Bank of America, obtained by House Committee on Oversight and Government Reform.

On the morning: Testimony of Kenneth Lewis, Office of the Attorney General, State of New York.

CHAPTER 17 "FILL THE HOLE"

Lewis kicked off: Testimony of Kenneth Lewis, Office of the Attorney General, State of New York; meeting notes taken by Federal Reserve general counsel Scott Alvarez and Bank of America chief financial officer Joe Price and released by the House Committee on Oversight and Government Reform; Paulson, *On the Brink*, 425–27.

Meanwhile, Merrill CEO Thain: Interview with John Thain on *Frontline*.

That Sunday: Paulson, *On the Brink*, 429; testimony of Kenneth Lewis, Office of the Attorney General, State of New York.

Later on Sunday: "Talking points for board call," obtained by House Committee on Oversight and Government Reform.

Lewis convened: Board minutes obtained by New York Attorney General's Office.

On December 30: Board minutes obtained by New York Attorney General's Office.

On New Year's Eve: Ken Lewis notes obtained by House Committee on Oversight and Government Reform.

CHAPTER 18 "WARD OF THE STATE"

In a January 9: Notes taken at Jan. 9, 2009, meeting of federal regulators and obtained by House Committee on Oversight and Government Reform.

Bank of America's board: Interview with John Thain on *Frontline*; board member notes obtained by the House Committee on Oversight and Government Reform.

Back in Washington: Minutes of Federal Deposit Insurance Corp. board of directors, Jan. 15, 2009, obtained through FOIA.

The next day: Greg Farrell and Julie McIntosh, "Merrill delivered bonuses before BofA deal," *Financial Times*, Jan. 22, 2009.

On Thursday, January 22: Interview with John Thain on *Frontline*; interview with Ken Lewis on *Frontline*.

That day: "Merrill Lynch CEO Thain spent $1.22 million on office," CNBC.com, Jan. 22, 2009.

CHAPTER 19   "YOU CREATED THE MESS"

While Ken Lewis's job: Kirsten Valle and Rick Rothacker, "Charlotte's battered bank wealth," *CO*, Feb. 1, 2009.

On February 6: Christina Rexrode, "Lewis: Talk of nationalizing 'absurd,' " *CO*, Feb. 7, 2009.

Lined up shoulder: Rick Rothacker, Lisa Zagaroli, and Christina Rexrode, "Congress grills CEOs over banking 'mess,' " *CO*, Feb. 12, 2009.

"My personal involvement": House Committee on Financial Services hearing, Feb. 11, 2009.

With former New York: Kevin G. Hall, "U.S. to back big banks," McClatchy Newspapers (published in *CO*), Feb. 26, 2009.

CHAPTER 20   HUBQUARTERS

Asked about the pressure: Jeannine Aversa, "Bernanke says he didn't bully BofA to buy Merrill," Associated Press (published in *CO*), June 26, 2009.

CHAPTER 21   "THANK GOD HE'S ONE OF US"

But by late September: Rob Blackwell and Robert Barba, "Washington people," *American Banker*, Mar. 30, 2009.

Bank of America reached: Thomas Olson, "PNC's heir apparent predicts anemic recovery," *Pittsburgh Tribune-Review*, Feb. 19, 2010.

As the search: Rick Rothacker, Christina Rexrode, and Steve Harrison, "Foxx tells Obama Charlotte needs BofA," *CO*, Nov. 6, 2009.

Moynihan received some: Bradley Keoun, David Mildenberg, and Ian Katz, "BofA CEO hunt to go into next year?" *Bloomberg News* (published in *CO*), Nov. 23, 2009.

The search committee: Louise Story, "Bank of America executive under scrutiny," *New York Times*, Dec. 7, 2009.

Investors and analysts: Christina Rexrode and Peter St. Onge, "Moynihan touted for his focus, energy," *CO*, Dec. 19, 2009.

On Thursday, December 17: Rick Rothacker and Kirsten Valle, "Moynihan: BofA will be 'most admired,' " *CO*, Dec. 18, 2009.

EPILOGUE

In April 2010, Senator Carl Levin: "Opening statement of Senator Carl Levin, D-Mich.," hearing of U.S. Senate Permanent Subcommittee on Investigations, Apr. 16, 2010; "Statement of the Federal Deposit Insurance Corp.," hearing of U.S. Senate Permanent Subcommittee on Investigations, Apr. 16, 2010; "Written statement of Kerry K. Killenger," hearing of U.S. Senate Permanent Subcommittee on Investigations, April 12, 2010.

According to an April: "Federal Deposit Insurance Act," U.S. Government Accountability Office, Apr. 2010.

In addition to the forces: Form DEFM14A, Wachovia.

The decline has hit: Form 990-PF, C. D. Spangler Foundation, Inc., 2008.

During his first: Brian Moynihan, "Remarks to N.C. Chamber and N.C. Bankers Association Economic Forecast Forum," Progress Energy Center for the Performing Arts, Raleigh, N.C., Jan. 4, 2010.

INDEX